Against *the* Wind

Against
the Wind

Memoirs of a German Immigrant
and an American ER Doctor

HORST AND SUE FREYHOFER

TRANSATLANTIC BOOKS

Bible quotes on pages 190, 278, 289, and 361 are from the King James Version.

Published by Transatlantic Books, Kansas City

GIRL FRIDAY
PRODUCTIONS
Edited and designed by Girl Friday Productions
www.girlfridayproductions.com

Cover design: Paul Barrett
Interior design: Rachel Marek
Editorial production: Reshma Kooner
Images were provided by the Freyhofer family.

ISBN (paperback): 979-8-218-71197-9
ISBN (ebook): 979-8-218-71198-6

Library of Congress Control Number: 2025917427

First edition

To our family and friends

Contents

HORST

SUE

HORST

Introduction

This is the biography of my wife, Sue, and me. It presents stories of our lives in our own words and includes stories of family and friends as well. We have written this book relying mainly on personal memory, which in many cases required some touch-ups and in some cases even imaginative reconstruction. But we have tried to stick to core facts as much as possible. And while we have attempted to portray everyone in a fair light, a few unflattering impressions were unavoidable. Judging people and events along reasonable lines where appropriate should not be avoided. No story worth its salt could be written otherwise.

This is primarily a biography, not a chronology. As much as possible, we have described individuals and their daily struggles, the motivations driving them, and their failures and successes, particularly those of Sue and me. To help understand the choices we made—both good and bad—we have provided as much context as we felt necessary. This in some places might seem overdrawn, perhaps even unrelated to the subject at hand, namely in the stories of individuals, but it is done for a purpose. Context shows the range of choices available to individuals at a given time and the limits placed on making them. And the more context is known, both in a wider and a narrower sense, the better the choices individuals make can be understood. If at times it seems we bombard the reader with too much far-reaching social, political, or economic information, bear with us. It will all make sense in the end.

Initially, this biography was written for the benefit of those who will come after us, mainly our children and grandchildren. They should find comfort in learning how their family managed to join two cultural traditions for their continuing benefit. I am a German immigrant and my wife is from Arkansas. This blending of cultures makes for interesting stories, as the reader will soon find out.

The most logical way to start sharing our common journey is by dealing with my own life before shifting to that of Sue and eventually to the stories of family members and friends. My life was that of a typical German child at the time, enduring the horrors of World War II and the turmoil of postwar existence. Eventually I searched for a better life in affluent America. This is also the story of the love of my life, Sue, and the roller coaster of a journey we experienced together, where many jolty turns kept our heads spinning until today. It is also the story of our children, grandchildren, parents, and siblings, as well as friends and those who have shared part of our remarkable epic with us. We have tried to include their tales along with our own larger story in the following pages in hopes you may find them enriching.

At our recent family reunion in Branson, Missouri, all those in attendance who had read the manuscript urged us to share it with a wider audience. Much of the information in it, they insisted, would help people to better understand their own world, particularly the horrors of war, ethnic strife, racism, and the various justifications often given for them. But mostly, we were told, readers would see our personal struggles in life as inspiring examples of how unwavering determination can overcome seemingly unsurmountable odds. With this in mind, we are now sharing our journey through life together with you and the wider readership.

Many names and places in this biography are cited mainly from memory and may not always be correct. Some names are not given in full to protect the privacy of individuals. No names have been changed, however.

May this book bring you much joy and personal enrichment.
Horst Freyhofer

HORST

ONE

My Beginning: 1938 and Historical Context

I was born the eldest of three children, all boys, at St. Joseph's Hospital in Düsseldorf, Germany, on February 14, 1938 (Valentine's Day). My father, Christian Freyhofer, was a low-level postal worker at the city's central train station (Hauptbahnhof). My mother, Helga Freyhofer, had been a sales clerk. They had a two-room apartment close to the train station in a typical four-story rental house of the type that lined most of the inner-city streets. My mother's parents lived across town in a similar apartment.

My grandfather was a painter, and my grandmother, who had been orphaned as a small child, had worked as a housemaid for a wealthy lawyer. My father, born on May 11, 1912, in Fürth, Bavaria, moved to Düsseldorf during the Great Depression in search of work. Like his three siblings, he was an "illegitimate child" of a factory worker. When I was growing up, he never talked much about his past; everything my brothers and I learned we found out much later.

I was fourteen when I first visited my father's family in Fürth and obtained very little knowledge of what I suspected were complicated

My parents' wedding. My grandmother is seated to the left of my
father. My grandfather is in the back, second from the left.

family relations. His mother, my grandmother, had died in 1930, and
a five-minute meeting with a tight-lipped stepfather of my father revealed nothing. But I learned that my father had started an apprenticeship as a typesetter in a small printing shop in Fürth. He never
finished because, during the Great Depression, the printing shop went
under. He then held various odd jobs and eventually made it to the
industrialized city of Düsseldorf. There, he held more odd jobs, including that of a drummer for a band that played at Tanzcafés. By the time
I was born in 1938, he worked as a baggage handler at the central train
station.

   In many respects, 1938 was a memorable year. The world was in
economic and political turmoil, with Germany at its center. The dev-
astation caused by World War I had left the country in shambles, from
which it seemed incapable of emerging intact. The world, particularly
Europe, was split along ideological lines: liberalism, socialism/com-
munism, and fascism. The end of World War I in 1918 did not end
hostilities between the war-torn countries. Quite the contrary.

Heavy industrialization since the mid-nineteenth century created masses of workers, who were, for the most part, overworked and underpaid. Most of these workers had organized around labor unions and political parties trying to make society more socially responsible through drastic reforms aimed at sharing the wealth. They called themselves socialists.

Many laborers and sympathizers went one step further and worked for the overthrow of the—as they saw it—exploitative, profit-oriented, liberal-capitalistic system, with the aim of taking total control of all of its aspects themselves and communalizing all private properties in the process. They called themselves communists.

People who were afraid of socialist and communist reforms and takeovers organized groups and created parties either to sustain existing liberal institutions or to search for an ideal society whose roots lay way back in the past of the "Volk" and was neither liberal nor socialist nor communist. They largely referred to themselves as fascists. Fascists mostly wanted to reinstate feudal conditions that existed before the emergence of mass industrialization. Fascists shared with socialists/communists a deep desire to eliminate most vestiges of liberal society from the world, such as the rule of law, individual freedom, and peaceful competition for economic gain.

Advocates of all three ideologies mostly agreed that coexistence was impossible and that impending mortal struggle was inevitable. To strengthen their respective positions, each group increasingly looked for support among the various segments of society whose interests they professed to advance: Liberals looked to the profit-seeking commercial class, socialists/communists looked to the exploited working class, and fascists looked to those who thought the struggle between the first two would destroy their traditional way of life.

These three ideologies were entrenched in all populations of the industrialized world and by around 1938 had maintained or assumed total or partial control in different countries. Liberalism dominated in Great Britain, France, and the US; communism in the Soviet Union; and fascism in Italy, Spain, Japan, and Germany. As a result, there were three groups of countries, each determined to subjugate and potentially destroy the other two. Germany played a key role in this conflict. People who for various reasons tried not to become caught up in these ideological struggles and upheld other positions (royalists, religious fundamentalists, internationalists, and the like) found themselves increasingly marginalized.

During the first part of the twentieth century, reasons for outbreaks of hostilities offered themselves on a regular basis. Not a year went by without either an economic collapse, a civil war, or a violent takeover somewhere in Europe. By 1938, more countries in Europe had dictatorships than democracies, and all had uncertain futures. In 1933, the German electorate had given the fascist Nazi Party a majority vote, allowing its leader, Adolf Hitler, to become head of state, or chancellor. The Nazis were elected on the promise of saving Germany from imminent collapse, a collapse that would be engineered by communist forces and liberal Jewish conspiracies to control the global financial market. They were also elected because they promised to restore the glory of the German Empire (Second Reich) that was dismantled, along with the Austro-Hungarian Empire, as a result of military defeat in 1918. Hitler, Austrian by upbringing, promised to reshape both Germany and Austria into one single empire, the Third Reich. In the process, the Nazis would mete out punishment to those responsible for this defeat, mainly communists and Jews. After the Nazis assumed power in Germany in 1933, they rounded up millions of people, put them in camps, and, after the renewed military conflict in 1939, killed them under cover of war.

Many more millions of people had already been killed in the Soviet Union under Stalin. By 1938, by threatening force, Hitler had managed to add Austria and the Czech Republic to Germany and was aiming at the "re-annexation" of Pomerania and West Prussia (the Danzig Corridor), which the victors of World War I had granted to the newly created state of Poland. The crossing into Poland by the German military in 1939 formally started World War II. The war ultimately pitted Germany and its allies, including Italy and Japan, against a whole host of countries, including France, Great Britain, the Soviet Union, and the US.

TWO

Surviving Air Raids and
Evacuation: 1941–1945

Like millions of children born at the time, I was a child of war and have the memories to prove it. By 1941, the air war that Germany had started over the British Isles in 1940 had shifted to Germany itself. In 1942, British and American planes dropped incendiary bombs, first on strategic targets and later on civilian populations.

My father had been drafted as an infantry soldier to participate in the 1940 campaign against France. In 1941, his unit was shipped east to participate in the offensive against the Soviet Union. My brother Erwin was born in August 1942, so our father must have been home on furlough around Christmas 1941. He was wounded in the battles to secure Stalingrad. When my father was fit to rejoin his unit, Stalingrad was lost, and those still alive in his unit were shipped to prison camps in Siberia. That would have been his fate had he not been wounded. My father eventually volunteered to join General Rommel's Afrika Korps in early 1943. In late 1943, he was taken prisoner by the British forces in Tunisia, who handed him over to the American forces. He eventually ended up in a number of POW camps in the US, mainly Camp

Aliceville, Alabama, and Camp Gordon Johnston, near Carabelle, Florida. It was from there that he was released at the end of the war.

I remember throughout this time sitting in basements and bomb shelters, mostly with my mother, baby brother, neighbors, and sometimes my grandparents. After our house was destroyed by bombs in late 1943, my mother, my brother Erwin, and I lived on a small farm in Thuringia. I still can hear the wailing cry of the sirens that sounded the alarm of imminent attacks.

Every block in the city was assigned a particular bomb shelter, some as far as a twenty-minute walk away. We had the choice of running to the shelter, which was more secure, or going to the basement, which was quicker. In the beginning, we tried to make it to the shelter as often as possible, but we did not always make it in time. On our way, we often would see searchlights of the German flak batteries scanning the sky for enemy planes. Advance planes would drop colorful flares, which we called Christmas Trees, to show the area marked for bombing. On clear nights we could even get a glimpse of the bomber formations themselves. The planes, often hundreds of them, came in close in seemingly endless streams. They were called Flying Fortresses, and they made a monotonous sound that chilled the bones. That sound has stayed with me and will continue to do so for the rest of my life.

The planes would not always drop their loads on our city, Düsseldorf; often they would fly over it to aim at more distant targets. We still had to sit in the shelter until the sirens sounded the much-welcomed, steady sound of all clear. I remember sleeping through most of the raids. According to my grandmother, I developed the skill of sleeping while walking.

Sometimes, when bombs struck close, there was pandemonium. Everyone tried to judge the distance of the impact by the sound of the explosion. Close impacts would elicit gasps, sometimes screams, and often loud prayers in the dimly lit shelters and basements. I do not remember there being toilet facilities, and as a result I often wet my pants. In fact, just like my brother, I wet my bed for many years to come, probably until I was eight or nine.

I do not remember adult men sitting in shelters. They usually had some function to perform like helping people find their way in a hurry or taking care of medical emergencies, especially during heavy

Typical view of a German town after World War II. This is Köln, close to Düsseldorf.

bombing. There were also the Blockwarts, people who made sure no one stayed in their apartment or wandered the streets. They made sure that the lights were out and doors were secured.

Sometimes when there had been close hits, everyone tried to get to their apartment in a rush afterward to inspect the damage. Children were often taken to more secure places, such as undamaged ground-level apartments. On several occasions, I remember hectic activity in the street, rescue squads trying to get people out of burning houses, leaning over bodies lying in the street, while others yelled loudly to get out of the way. We could hear the sounds of the fire trucks and Red Cross ambulances on their way.

One night, it was our turn. By 1942, strategic bombardments of German cities had increased to a point where destruction from the skies would sometimes continue around the clock, with US planes dropping their loads during daylight and British planes doing the same at night. Under the leadership of Air Chief Marshal Arthur Harris, the RAF Bomber Command had designed plans to create firestorms in German cities that would either burn or asphyxiate people to death. Attacks came in predictable patterns. First, explosive bombs were dropped, shattering doors and windows throughout entire neighborhoods. Then, incendiary bombs were dropped, creating long burning areas that would consume much, if not most, of the surrounding oxygen, while sometimes creating temperatures that would even melt stone and cause firestorms that would suck people out of their houses and slowly turn them into charcoal.

In May 1943, nearly 800 British heavy bombers descended on our city of just under 600,000 and turned it into a scene from Dante's *Inferno*. As described by Jörg Friedrich in his book *Der Brand*, it was the heaviest attack the city experienced. I must have been in it, either with my mother and baby brother or, as was often the case, with my grandparents. We survived another day, only to be hit again a few days later.

The night our four-story tenement house finally sustained a direct hit, the surrounding houses got hit as well, shaking the whole housing block to its foundation. A thunderous explosion collapsed the house right above our basement. The walls of the basement shook violently but held. Dust flew everywhere, and an eerie darkness was filled with screams and sobs. From what my mother recalled later on, we were lying there half conscious for a while until being dug out by a rescue squad. I recall that later we were sitting with other neighbors amid the debris that covered the streets, watching the burning houses. There were no fire trucks at first, and I later learned that they were unable to make it through the rubble. I also learned that my favorite person in the neighborhood, the candy man at the corner store, had not survived. Many others hadn't either.

The days and weeks following the attack remain a blur to me. They were full of temporary shelters, soup kitchens, hospitals, long walks, and stays at my grandparents' apartment on the other side of town until we boarded a train that took us to a farm in a small village, Ringleben, in the eastern state of Thuringia, where we stayed for a good two years, until the end of the war.

Aside from some vague memories of a dismal train ride, I don't remember exactly how we got to Ringleben, a village of less than 1,000 people about 225 miles east of Düsseldorf. We ended up living on a small farm owned by a middle-aged couple who ran it with two maids and, occasionally, a Polish prisoner of war. The couple had three sons; all of them were fighting on the Russian front and never returned.

My brother Erwin and I in Ringleben, Thuringia, 1944.

Everyone on the farm was overworked and glad that we had been placed on their farm to be of help.

Their two-story house stood among similar houses in the middle of the village along a cobblestone street. A small courtyard behind the house was enclosed by a few small buildings: a stall that housed some cows, pigs, and chickens, and next to it, a barn, a tool shed, and the outhouse. My mother, brother, and I had a small room in the loft of the main house. The room was hot during summer and cold during winter.

The farmhouse was located across from a Protestant church, the only church in town, and the elementary school. Because we were registered Catholics, I don't think we ever set foot in that church, although I do remember playing in its courtyard all the time. I also remember the beautiful organ music during Sunday mass and other occasions.

The farmer's name was Heuschkel. Mr. Heuschkel ran the farm with an iron hand. His wife was ill with tuberculosis and was limited to doing minimal kitchen work. The older maid did most of the housework, though she was helped by a younger maid who did other household chores such as feeding the animals, milking the cows, and operating the water pump in the courtyard (there was no indoor plumbing).

Mr. Heuschkel did most of the heavy farmwork, such as working the land—a few plots outside the village for subsistence farming—taking care of the animals, and maintaining equipment, and was mostly assisted by a Polish laborer, when he had one, or one of the maids. Sometimes my mother helped out; occasionally I did as well. I sometimes went along to help with tasks such as taking the cows to and from the grazing pastures, removing debris and stones from the fields, and preparing them for plowing and, later, assisted with the harvest. I was of general help with odd jobs as they occurred, unlike Erwin, who was a little more than a year old when we arrived in Ringleben. My mother took him with her almost everywhere she went, generally in a handheld basket, which I sometimes had to watch when she worked in the fields.

The Heuschkels kept us on a tight leash, especially when it came to feeding us. They seldom let us sit at the kitchen table to eat with them and gave us very skimpy food rations, often leftovers from their earlier meals. I remember being hungry a lot, despite living on a farm, and remember my anger when I once accidentally entered their food pantry and saw what seemed to me like mountains of cheese, sausages, and pies. I could not get the sight out of my mind.

My mother became quite skillful at stealing small food items and always signaled to us kids to eat them fast and never say a word about it to anyone. The Heuschkels must have known about this, and I learned that Mr. Heuschkel used to berate my mother for it.

I don't remember ever seeing the Polish worker around the kitchen table. He probably ate by himself in his servant's room in the barn.

I entered elementary school in April 1944. Our class had around twenty students. Soon afterward I was diagnosed by a school nurse with TB, which I had caught from Mrs. Heuschkel. There was another boy in the class who had it too, and we were isolated from the rest of the class, placed in the back of the room with several empty seats between us and the other kids. The other boy and I soon became friends, but he looked paler every day and started coughing a lot. Eventually, he stopped coming to class and died soon after at home. I, too, fell ill and had to stay in bed for a long time. I had open sores for months and could see the bones of my TB-infected legs. My mother later told me that I was not expected to live, but somehow I pulled through.

Later, I learned that there were many more TB cases in town, but little was done to help the afflicted. They were expected to die in the care of their family or somehow pull through as I did. There was no doctor in town, only a nurse. Many infected people went undiagnosed until help came too late. General ignorance about the symptoms, causes, and contagiousness of the illness and how to cure it made matters worse. I think that most villagers drank unpasteurized milk, fresh from the cow, which contained bacteria that caused the illness. In retrospect, it is remarkable that no one aside from Mrs. Heuschkel showed TB symptoms in the Heuschkel household.

I do not remember whether I went back to school after my recovery, but I don't think so. There was a sense of doom in the air as the war drew to a close, and in the end, people had to deal with more disasters than they were prepared to handle. Colds and bronchitis were common among us kids during winter and chickenpox and diarrhea a constant threat.

I vividly remember the Hitler Youth meetings in the school-yard and the smart way the older boys would present themselves to us younger kids. A boy became a Hitler Youth at the age of ten, and we younger kids couldn't wait to join. The disciplined marches of the older kids, accompanied by their songs, drums, and fanfare, displayed an irresistible sense of strength and optimism.

I was dismayed that I couldn't join immediately because of my age and asked my mother to see whether she could do something so I could join early. I was, of course, oblivious to my mother's foreboding sense of doom, reflecting her awareness of things going awry. For instance, one day our schoolyard was full of German military trucks that we marveled at. One of the soldiers asked us if we wanted to see the front line. A few of us said yes, and he took us along in the cab of his supply truck to a group of freshly dug trenches many miles away. All along he talked about his family, the wife he missed, and the kids he wanted to play with. We tried to help him unload what looked like metal boxes of ammunition. He let us go into a trench and showed us a machine gun pointed in the direction of the enemy, the "Amis." Later that evening, exhilarated, I told my worried mother where I had been for so long; she just stared at me in disbelief.

Days later we heard the rumbling of heavy guns, and at night we saw the flashes of their fire reflected in the sky. The Germans were holding the line against American troops advancing eastward. We were all starving for news and could not get any. There was usually only one radio in the house, the standard little black, boxy Volksempfänger, which blasted favorable and mostly nonspecific accounts of war activities.

The villagers were hoping for more concrete news from the town. Ringleben had a town crier, like many other small towns in the region, an apparent leftover from medieval times. He stopped at various public places, rang his loud bell, and read the news of the day from a short prepared statement. Sometimes villagers stood close by, and sometimes nobody seemed to be listening. The whole thing lasted less than five minutes and seemed to focus on town activities. Every so often there was a reference to the valiant fight of victorious German troops in faraway places. I think as the fight drew closer to home, the town crier's appearances became less frequent, and in the end, he only showed up to announce measures being taken to deal with increasing economic hardships and political chaos.

In the spring of 1945, German troops in Thuringia tried to halt the advances of the American forces on their drive east to link up with the Soviet forces that were sweeping through Germany from the east and moving west. The German forces were sandwiched in between. So was Ringleben. As the front lines drew near, we could see German troops in retreat. I remember a few German foot soldiers looking like they had not slept in weeks, sleeping in our barn for about half an hour before moving on, appearing like ghosts.

The advancing American forces did not enter our village immediately. We were told that the mayor had surrendered the town and had declared a curfew. A friend and I decided to sneak outside and see whether we could greet the Americans waiting to enter the town. No one saw us as we headed in the direction where shooting noises could be heard during the last few days. After walking for about a mile, we ran into the tanks and the tired GIs resting in the grass. They looked at us like we were strange apparitions from a different world, not knowing what to do with us. Eventually, one GI came down from his tank, fell to his knees, embraced us, motioned for us not to move, went back into the tank, and reappeared with all sorts of unbelievable food items. He made us sit on his lap as he opened a can of fish (probably sardines), something we had never seen. He placed the fish on slices of white bread that we also had never seen and watched us with apparent delight as we devoured them.

Other soldiers joined and offered more food, mostly chocolate bars, candy, and chewing gum, all of which were new to us. Several soldiers talked to us in an incomprehensible language. We had never heard non-German speakers before. Even the Poles in our area knew a bit of German. But far from being scared, I remember how fascinated we were by the strangeness of the environment. After a while, the soldiers collected more food items, put them in a bag, and motioned for us to return to the village. The soldier who had made us the fish sandwiches kissed our hair and abruptly turned away with tears running down his cheeks.

Back in town there was pandemonium. My mother and my friend's parents had noticed our absence and gone to search for us. Normally, children were watched by all of the villagers and no one found it strange that some were out of sight for many hours; they always came back. But these were different circumstances. Things calmed down when we showed them the food we'd brought back. No one had ever seen such items before. But things would soon change.

The town crier announced that the American troops would enter the following day, that all buildings had to display white sheets of surrender, and that no one was allowed in the streets. And indeed, the following day, jeeps, trucks, and tanks rolled down the main street while we watched the spectacle from inside.

The American forces set up headquarters in the city park. Soon they would move farther east, still in pursuit of German fighting units, but a small occupying contingent would remain. Later, townspeople would recall that a lone German motor vehicle with a swastika displayed entered the town, drove at high speed through occupied Ringleben, and stopped in front of city hall, right across from the city park. A German soldier ran into the building, reappeared with a black briefcase, and sped back out of town, all under the watchful eyes of bewildered American soldiers.

The only thing I remember about city hall at that time was that a dead horse lay in front of it for days, smelling so intensely that many people threw up.

Occupation disrupted many of Ringleben's institutions and routines, such as schools, kindergartens, transportation, communication, and cultural activities. But economic life in this agricultural community continued as before, albeit under harsher conditions. Fields had to be tended to; animals had to be fed; bread had to be baked. But everyone was weak and shorthanded. A scarcity of everything, particularly food, at the end of the war drove affected populations close to despair. Families had lost sons and daughters. For farmers, like our host family, the Heuschkels, this increased the workload considerably for those who survived. Mr. Heuschkel, who had lost his three sons in Russia, asked my mother if he could adopt me as the heir to the farm. Her answer was obvious. Otherwise, I wouldn't be sitting here today writing these memoirs.

Mr. Heuschkel's Polish worker, like all forced laborers under the Hitler regime, was liberated by the Allied forces, in his case by the

Americans. But like all such liberated laborers, he couldn't immediately go home. The Allies had programs to feed and house these workers wherever possible. What I remember is the distribution of "luxury items" to the liberated laborers in Ringleben. The GIs would ride around in open jeeps calling out "Polski, Polski." I saw groups of Poles on the main street sidewalks raising their hands, calling out "Here!" The GIs would drive up to them and give them shoeboxes full of scarce items, mainly cigarettes and chewing gum. Times had indeed changed for us children. The GIs in the jeeps ignored us.

There was another big change waiting for us. Ringleben is located in Thuringia, a state (Land) in the center of Germany. American forces advancing into Germany from the west and Soviet forces advancing from the east met at the River Elbe in April 1945. Germany surrendered some days later, a few days after Hitler committed suicide. In July, the leaders of the three allies mostly responsible for winning the war in Europe—Harry Truman for the US, Joseph Stalin for the Soviet Union, and Winston Churchill and the incoming prime minister, Clement Attlee, for Great Britain—met in Potsdam to discuss the fate of defeated Germany, as well as much of Europe.

Germany was divided into four occupational zones and two provinces. The zones were administered separately, each by one of the major Allied powers, a group to which France would soon be added. Thuringia, along with several other German Lands, was to be administered by the Soviet Union. (In 1948, those Lands together would constitute a separate, Soviet-controlled state, the German Democratic Republic, or East Germany. The Lands to the west would constitute a separate and mostly US-dominated state, the Federal Republic of Germany, or West Germany. The provinces, the German territories to the east of East Germany, were at first administered by Poland and later annexed outright.) According to the agreements put in place, the US would hand over control of Thuringia to the Soviet Union. US troops would withdraw and Soviet troops would move in. This caused great anxiety among the population. Stories of atrocities committed by Soviet troops toward German civilians (mass rapes, wanton shootings, random deportations, and more) circulated widely and were also part of Nazi propaganda. I had just turned seven (Erwin was two and a half), but I could clearly see the desperate looks on the faces of the women in town, including my mother, when they talked to each other. I understood that they were making plans to hide, possibly somewhere outside town.

One evening, my mother took me and Erwin and told us we couldn't remain with the Heuschkels. They wouldn't want us there when the Russians came. We had to find another place to stay. We knocked on various doors, but people either wouldn't open them or told us we couldn't stay. I remember roaming around town for a while and eventually sleeping in the churchyard. A day or two later my mother was told that town officials had made an agreement with the soon-to-enter Soviet troops that the occupation would proceed in an orderly way, without endangering anyone. Mr. Heuschkel accepted us back into his house. Just as when the Americans arrived, we were told to stay inside the house as the Soviet troops entered the town. This time, however, there were no white sheets on display. Once hostilities had ceased, they were no longer required. When the troops appeared, we were surprised to see only a few armored trucks followed by a long line of horse-drawn wagons.

The Russians took over the positions the Americans had abandoned. Curfew was lifted and we were back on the streets again. I remember a horse-drawn wagon going by and a Russian soldier tossing a pear at me. I must have looked hungry, and the pear was gone in less than a minute. But unlike the Americans, the Russians were not seen much in town. One day, a very friendly German in civilian clothes visited us and explained what the Russian occupation meant to the town. As best as I could tell, we were told that we had been liberated from the Nazi regime and that life would be much better under Soviet rule. All measures taken would be for our benefit if we followed orders.

I remember that during the following weeks, Russian military trucks stopped here and there in town and took people with them. We were told they were going to work. Some came back; some did not. And no one seemed to talk. I remember a truck full of German men stopping at a house to pick up someone, and a woman screaming relentlessly. That scream stayed with me for a long time. Sometimes women were taken too. The trucks seemed to know where to go to find them. One morning, my mother was taken. When she came back hours later, she told us that she had been put to work in the kitchen, mainly peeling potatoes. She was picked up a few more times, but she never showed any signs of abuse.

Erwin did not understand what was going on. Life at the farm continued as it had before, albeit more harshly on account of being short-handed. But I picked up on the nervous tension of the adults, many of whom had been known supporters of or active members in the Nazi regime and certainly must have dreaded being hauled off by the next Soviet truck. I don't know whether the Heuschkels had anything to fear. But nothing happened to them. The phase of searching for people did not last long. Most of the people that were picked up, mainly men, never returned.

THREE

Returning Home and the Years Following

It must have been around October 1945 when we received a letter from some government agency ordering my mother, Erwin, and me to return to our hometown of Düsseldorf. We quickly learned that everyone who had been evacuated from bombed-out areas to live on farms had received the letter. Soon we were given details of the trip. We would board a train in Ringleben, which would take us to a large holding camp in Friedland, Lower Saxony (Niedersachsen), about eighty miles west of Ringleben. There, we were told, we would receive further instructions about getting to Düsseldorf, another 170 miles farther west.

One early morning we trotted to the Ringleben train station and, along with many other returnees, were crammed into a boxcar like sardines. It was standing room only, and as far as I know, there were no toilet facilities. At various points, we had to switch to a boxcar sitting on another track. Once we were transported in an open boxcar at very cold temperatures. The train would sporadically stop and stand still for an indeterminate length of time. At one of those stops, a woman with two or three small children insisted on leaving the boxcar to relieve herself. No sooner had she left the train than it started moving again, and she was unable to get back on. Her screams were dreadful and stayed with me for years. So did the desperate sobbing of her children. I, too, almost lost my mother. During the last few miles to Friedland, we had to walk. I remember a seemingly endless line of gaunt, cold, and hungry people, mostly women and children who hadn't slept in days, stumbling more than walking in the pouring rain. Erwin, just a few months over three, walked next to me, but for long stretches he had to be carried by our mother to keep up the pace. In the process, I lost sight of them and yelled out for them, but to no avail. I stepped outside the slowly moving row of bodies and ran up and down the line while screaming "Mutti, Mutti!" for several minutes. My mother was also running up and down the line, with Erwin in her arms, on the other side of the row. Eventually, we heard each other and reunited. Some other families were not so lucky.

When we got to Friedland, we had to register at the huge camp. Again there were long lines, rain, and mud everywhere. On a loud intercom system, the Red Cross announced the names of people reported missing. Children were looking for their parents, parents for their children, wives for their husbands, and on and on, all day long.

Like everyone else arriving at the camp, we were assigned a small place on the wet floor of a Quonset hut, cramped in between hundreds of other sad-looking returnees. We dropped to the floor and fell asleep immediately. I remember my mother waking me up and asking for Erwin. He was nowhere in sight. We decided to search for him separately in neighboring Quonset huts. My mother took the huts on one side; I took the ones on the other. How I managed not to get lost myself has remained a mystery to me. After a while, I decided to go back to our hut and was glad to see that my mother had indeed found Erwin. I think we stayed a few days at the camp before being assigned to another train. Again, everything moved at a snail's pace, with many intermittent stops and changes of boxcars. We had to stay at a few more camps before finally arriving in Düsseldorf.

Düsseldorf, like most other cities, was unrecognizable. Most houses had been reduced to piles of rubble. For many houses, only the facades remained standing, pointing eerily to the skies. When we arrived, most of the rubble had been moved off the streets, allowing some traffic to resume.

Trucks and cars, the few that there were, moved through the ghostly cityscape alongside sad-looking people, some riding rusty bicycles or pulling small carts of all shapes and sizes.

There were veterans with lost limbs, many on crutches. Some streetcars were in operation, though they were crammed full of people. At night the streets were dark, and it took years until streetlights, mostly lit by gas, began to function again. Düsseldorf's prewar population of nearly 700,000 people had been reduced by more than half. Those residents who had survived the bombing raids were joined by thousands of returnees, making a desperate housing shortage even worse. Some built temporary shelters amid the rubble.

When we arrived in late 1945, some utilities (power, water, sewage) had already been restored. Most immediately lacking were food and heating fuel, like coal. People were cold and hungry. Many died as a result, especially the old and very young. We were lucky to find my grandparents (my mother's parents) in one of the few undamaged houses in the section of Düsseldorf called Bilk, on Merkurstrasse. My grandparents had survived years of massive bombing, seeing their neighborhood slowly torn to shreds. After many bombing attacks, they began to skip going to the basement or the bomb shelters and tried instead to sleep through the noisy raids. My grandmother later told me that if Jesus was going to call her up, she wasn't going to stand in the way.

My grandmother was a devout Catholic, believing that the Lord was going to spare her life in this hell on earth. He had taken her only son, Heinz (the source of my middle name), early in his life due to diabetes A, and he surely wasn't going to punish her even more. My grandfather, a committed socialist and card-carrying member of the SPD (Sozialdemokratische Partei Deutschlands or Social Democratic Party), shared her sentiment. When the war was over and their house was still standing amid miles of ruins, she knew her faith had saved her and her husband. When my mother, Erwin, and I showed up, my grandparents were overjoyed and invited us to stay with them. We were all haggard, cold, hungry, and without any idea how to make it through the weeks and months ahead. But we had made it through the war alive and felt great relief sitting together, knowing no bomb would disrupt our daily life any longer. What we missed the most was my father. We had received mail that he was still a prisoner of war at a camp in Florida.

The winter of 1945–46 would turn out to be one of the coldest on record. People needed coal or wood to feed their little cooking stoves and to keep warm. But coal was scarce and wood was not available. Lack of food was another big problem. Food and coal were distributed to the public with ration cards but not in sufficient amounts. There were stories of babies dying because of a lack of milk or candles to heat the bottles. Foraging became a way of life. So did bartering. A caught fish could be exchanged for a bucket of coal. City folks would invade farm villages and offer jewelry, paintings, or carpets in exchange for potatoes, vegetables, and milk. After a while, there were no more valuables to offer, and the city folks started begging, stealing, and ravaging the fields. The German term for this activity was "hamstern," which refers to the pouches of hamsters. Farmers protected their coveted goods the best they could, including using local police patrols.

We, too, did our regular hamster tours, usually splitting up into two teams. Erwin, who was then around four or five years old, would accompany my mother, and I, around eight or nine, would go with my grandfather. We would walk for an hour to the ferry in Volmerswerth, which would take us across the Rhine. From there, we would walk on to the many little farm towns on the other side of the river: Norf, Nievenheim, Stürzelberg, and others. My grandfather was not good at stealing, so we settled on begging. Once we had reached a village or farmhouse, we would knock on doors. Usually, no one answered, knowing full well what we wanted. When someone did open the door, they would see two skinny and raggedy-looking figures begging for food. Most of the time they would slam the door shut in our faces. Sometimes they would hand something through the door, usually slices of dry bread. In rare cases, they would let us sit on a bench or low wall outside the house and feed us a sandwich. Once I remember knocking on a door that slammed shut as soon as we were identified as beggars. We walked off. But after a few minutes, I heard a noise behind me and saw a girl running with a slice of cake on a piece of paper. She stopped in front of me and offered it with her outstretched hand. She was about my age, blond, blue eyed, and smiling. To this day, I have never forgotten her understanding look. Begging is a humiliating business. She helped me deal with it.

Unlike my grandfather and me, my mother and Erwin were more successful in doing the real hamster work. They would find a potato field, hunker down, dig out the potatoes, and hide them in a bag at record speed. One problem was getting the bag across the Rhine on the ferry. It was one thing to get potatoes, or anything else, from the farmer himself. It was quite another to steal them from him. An inspector on the ferry had to make that call. If it looked like the potatoes were stolen, they were confiscated. This is where little Erwin came in. He had to look at the inspector with blue angel eyes while my mother stroked his golden hair framing his hungry face. It usually worked.

Later, there were two other breaks in our constant search for food and fuel. My grandfather got a job with the newly constituted power company RWE (Rheinisch-Westfälische Elektrizitätswerk). During the war, he had remained a loyal member of the SPD, the socialist party that had opposed Hitler. This membership helped him to get a job as a security guard. As a bonus, on top of his wages he was given a bucket of coal. I don't remember how often, but I do remember that it was a godsend during wintertime and a valuable currency to exchange for food during the rest of the year.

The second break we received was when our grandmother's sister, Olga Hauptmann, in Pennsylvania, started to send care packages. They did not come that often, but when they did, we had flour, rice, peanut butter, and other nonperishable goods for a while. Olga had met a Jew from Silesia, Siegbert Hauptmann, and following their immigration to the US got married in Manhattan, just at the outbreak of WWI in 1914. Both of their children, Dorothea and Erwin, were born there. A few years after the end of the war, the family moved to Germany, where Siegbert died of a heart attack in 1929. Olga, Dorothea, and Erwin remained in Germany. After the rise of Hitler, Dorothea decided to return to the US in 1938. Olga and Erwin decided to stay. Erwin eventually became an engineer. According to the Nuremberg Race Laws of 1933, he was a "half-Jew" and potentially subject to a number of degrading living conditions. But he was the son of an Aryan mother and looked like a model Aryan boy. Plus, he was born in the

US. As a result, his life during the Nazi years was not different from that of any other regular German citizen. But after the end of the war in 1945, Olga and Erwin managed to get back to the US in less than a year's time.

While we were struggling to survive like everybody else around us during those dire postwar years, we were hoping that my father would be released from his POW camp in Florida soon and come home to take the reins. He was taken prisoner in April 1943 in Kairouan, Tunisia, by British forces. Along with thousands of other German soldiers, he was handed over to the Americans, who shipped them to prisoner-of-war camps in the US. My father spent about a year at Camp Aliceville in Alabama, a year at Camp Van Dorn in Mississippi, and a year at Camp Gordon Johnston in Florida, where he was released in February 1946. He was then shipped back to Great Britain, where he was kept as a prisoner for another year at camps in Plymouth and Gloucestershire. The British, like other nations of the victorious Allies, used German POWs to rebuild their country and compensate for the damage the Germans had inflicted during the war.

Eventually, in March 1947, almost two years after the end of the war, my father was released and sent back to his hometown of Düsseldorf. We knew he was coming from letters he had sent, but we did not know when he would arrive. The dates were moved a number of times without stated reasons. And then, one day the bell rang and he walked into our small apartment. Everyone hung on his neck, except me. I had a bad case of measles, with spots covering my entire body, and was quarantined in the bedroom. Eventually, he came in to see me, surrounded by my overjoyed mother, grandparents, and a beaming Erwin. He looked well but was unsure how to deal with the spotty kid in bed. He was cautioned not to touch me and he awkwardly told me he would check on me later. The group went back into the kitchen and celebrated without me. In a strange way, that feeling that things in the family would happen without me would return in later years. But at the moment, there was joy all around. Father was finally home, and things were looking up.

Things then began to happen very fast. I remained in bed with the measles as my father went to the city's housing office to find a place for us to stay. The chances were slim. The city was filled with people living in desperate conditions and looking for living space everywhere. My parents were assigned a small garret, a one-room loft with slanted walls and an attic window in Benrath, a suburb of Düsseldorf. The apartment was too small for the four of us, so I stayed with my grandparents until we could find a larger place. I didn't mind. I had grown fond of my grandparents and admired their indomitable spirit in fighting daily misery with confidence and humor. For instance, when I had no shoes to wear and running around barefoot became too difficult with the encroaching winter weather, Grandma managed to exchange a bucket of coal for a pair of shoes. The only pair she could get were women's high heels. She cut off the heels with a borrowed saw while commenting on a topsy-turvy world gone "verrückt," laughing out loud for quite a while. I had to learn how to walk with women's high heels cut short. It beat running around barefoot in winter.

It would be two years before I moved in with my parents and Erwin when the housing office assigned us two rooms in a three-story house on Hauptstrasse in the center of Benrath.

One of the rooms was a small all-purpose room on the first floor. The second was a small garret with slanted walls, an attic window, and no electricity. My parents slept in one bed and Erwin and I slept in another. The all-purpose room had a simple table, four chairs, a coal-fired kitchen stove, and a few shelves. There was shared running water and a toilet in the hallway. We had to wash ourselves with cold water in a bowl placed on one of the kitchen chairs. Soap bars were a rarity. There was one small towel, one toothbrush (no toothpaste), and one comb that all four of us had to share.

Clothing was also minimal. We had, at most, two sets of clothing. Erwin and I wore short pants, even during snowy times, until Christmas, when we would get long, thin sports pants (Trainingshosen) that left us just as cold as the short pants. We had one pair of shoes that had to last from Christmas to Christmas, and they were worn on all occasions. They usually developed holes that had to be fixed by the shoemaker, if we had the money. Often, we would run around with the holes in our shoes for weeks, showing our toes. I don't remember ever owning a jacket during my school years. Worn-out sweaters that left me cold, yes. But no jacket. The same was true for Erwin. In short, we were poor and we were hungry.

After his return, my father first worked unskilled construction jobs for very low pay. He had been a typesetter, but in bombed-out Germany, there was low demand for printing shops and high demand for housing. Eventually, he was hired by a printing shop in Benrath. I remember the excitement of the news and the associated expectations of better living conditions. Perhaps even an apartment of our own. But we were soon disappointed. Not much changed. My father had a better job. He could walk to work. He liked what he was doing. But he didn't get more pay. This was odd because skilled workers got much higher pay than unskilled workers. And typesetters were at the top of the pay scale.

I only solved the riddle many years later. My father was hired as an "Angelernter," someone who had acquired professional skills while doing the job without ever getting certification. He had started an apprenticeship in typesetting after finishing primary school (Volksschule) in Fürth as an eighth grader in 1926. But he never finished it because the printing shop went broke. During the Great Depression (1929–33), he left the rural setting of Lower Bavaria for the industrial heartland of Germany, settling in Düsseldorf, the capital of North Rhine-Westphalia. There, he eventually got a job with the national railroad company Deutsche Reichsbahn, working in the baggage office at the main train station (Hauptbahnhof). He had a natural talent for entertaining people, playing drums with bands at bars and joining amateur theater groups. While in Düsseldorf he met his future wife, our mother, Helga Trümper. They married in September 1937, when she was twenty-one and he was twenty-six. They had their first child (me) in February 1938. Their marriage was delayed for a number of reasons, though. First, my mother was Catholic, and my father was a Protestant. So, she had to get special permission to marry outside her faith from the archdiocese in Köln, which she eventually received, provided that she would raise her children Catholic. The process took a very long time, not merely because of slow bureaucracy but also because of the national requirement to prove Aryan descendance. And here, my father had a problem.

He was born "illegitimate" and probably did not know it. His mother, Katharina Freyhofer, was a factory worker who had had several affairs and five children from different men. She eventually married a man named Prückelmayer, who, I later learned, treated his five step-children cruelly. I met Herr Prückelmayer only once, when I was four-teen, and had an unfavorable impression of him. Father's biological father was Friedrich Lakenmacher from Magdeburg. He eventually must have left Fürth for Magdeburg when my father was still a toddler. The story Katharina Freyhofer told my father was that his father had been a major in the Bavarian cavalry and had died while falling from a horse during a parade. In fact, I remember my father telling me that same tale when I was a teenager in Düsseldorf.

When my father and mother wanted to get married, my father needed correct information on his parents and grandparents from the registry of the town where he was born, just as my mother did. In her case, there was no problem. But my father really did not know much about his father or his family. And his mother couldn't tell him any-more because she had died in 1930. With his blond hair and blue eyes, Father could have been featured on a Nazi SS recruitment poster. But the authorities in Düsseldorf wanted to see it on paper. Apparently, at the birth registry in Fürth, there was no entry for his father, just his mother. The correspondence between my father in Düsseldorf and the registry must have been fraught with confusion. Time was run-ning short; I was on the way. Eventually, my father's half brother in Fürth, Ernst Freyhofer, took over. Ernst was a few years older than my father and was the "illegitimate" son of another man. Ernst did some research and found that my grandfather, Friedrich Lakenmacher, still lived in Magdeburg and was able to get a certification that he was the "Erzeuger," that is, the biological father, and an Aryan. The Düsseldorf authorities accepted the certification and my parents' marriage was al-lowed to proceed, albeit a bit late.

The story of my father's profession was similar. He said he was a typesetter, but we didn't know he had no professional certification (Gesellenbrief). The print shop that hired him turned this problem to its advantage. Father worked like a first-rate professional, as I could testify from personal observation. But he seemed to have lacked the confidence to demand appropriate pay. To make up for his low pay, he worked overtime. Coming home late became routine. He was missed at the dinner table. Sometimes he came home late because he joined his colleagues at the local pub.

When he came home and my mother wanted to discuss issues, Erwin and I were sent to bed early. We would lie in bed for hours unable to go to sleep. I tried to read books I had checked out from the local library, but our loft had no lights. I read by dim daylight when the sun was still up. Erwin was too young to read books. And because of the age difference, Erwin and I seemed to be worlds apart at times and could not easily commiserate. I tried to be a tough guy, showing him I could handle all the tension without saying much, while I should have been an understanding and consoling brother. I was not. My world was that of my friends, the guys in my neighborhood that I sat with in school and played with in the streets. That was more important to me than anything else. And Erwin was too young to be part of this. He had to find his own circle of friends.

FOUR

Growing Up: Family, Friends, and School Life

At the time, Germany still had a parochial primary school system. Schools were either Catholic or Protestant. I went to the Catholic Erich Müller Schule in Benrath, a primary school (Volksschule) that went up to eighth grade. After graduation, students were expected to start an apprenticeship in some trade. At Volksschule, I quickly made friends. Some were members of the Catholic Boy Scouts, which I also joined. These friends became the most important people in my life. I have remained in lifelong contact with some of them, even after my emigration to America.

My closest friend was Günther Aufmwasser, who lived a block away on the same street. His father had died during the last few months of the war, and his mother had problems adjusting to life without him. Günther's sister developed poor coping skills as well. As a result, it often fell on Günther to make decisions in matters pertaining to the whole family. Like many boys in our neighborhood, he apprenticed at a large local machine manufacturer, WEWAG, and became a certified tool-and-die maker. He worked his way up to production manager of a different local company, later becoming an activist in the powerful IG Metall ironworkers' union. He was trained to become a union representative in individual labor disputes at court and was appointed to the national board of the ÖTV (service workers' union), ultimately becoming a judge at the Düsseldorf Regional Labor Court. Not bad for a working-class kid from Düsseldorf.

Hermann Gutermuth, another close friend, also apprenticed at WEWAG and became a mechanic. He earned a high school diploma (Fachabitur) by going to night school after work, went to college to become a mechanical engineer, and worked his way up to become the CEO of a large bottled gas manufacturing company. However, in the early 1990s, when he was only fifty-five, the company was bought by a national chain that downsized and outsourced much of the operation and laid him off. He shared the fate of many successful managers of the time who were sent to greener pastures without ever finding a fulfilling management position again.

Werner Ramann, who apprenticed as a lathe operator at WEWAG, ultimately specialized in the operation of large boilers. His company exported all over the world. He supervised installations and was seldom home, but he saw more of the world, especially the Third World, than anyone else I know.

Rolf Maier became an electrician who emigrated to Canada, where he became a master brewer in Vancouver. Max Schwalenberg became a master plumber and had a small but efficient company, which he apparently ran by sitting every day in the Ürige, a well-known pub—and his favorite—in Düsseldorf's Altstadt (old town).

My school days were uneventful. I hated going to school for a number of reasons. Most teachers seemed unable to convey the most basic knowledge to us kids. That wasn't altogether their fault. Back then, teaching was still a male-dominated profession at all levels. But the war had thinned out the ranks of teachers considerably, and new ones had not been trained in sufficient numbers. As a result, older teachers were called out of retirement. Many had health problems, couldn't hear well, or felt lost. But this was only part of the problem. There was hardly any instructional material. After the war, the occupational forces (from the US, the Soviet Union, Great Britain, and France) subjected Germany to a rigorous denazification program. Much of the existing educational material was declared propaganda and was sub-sequently shredded. This was perhaps a defensible policy when it came to identifying propaganda in literature or history books but not in grammar or science books. But the Allied authorities had decided that all material that had a swastika on it, even if only as a rubber stamp, had to be destroyed, no matter its educational value. As a result, we had no books.

Teachers had to teach from memory the best they could. The consequences ranged from the pathetic to the comical. I remember one very old lady who dictated the rules of grammar to us, expecting that we would copy them into our notebooks. But it was difficult to get notebooks. Even the stores that were open had none. Some families had some paper at home, but they were the more well-off ones. And their children were a bit embarrassed to have notebooks while most other classmates sat by silently. Some teachers brought poems to class, dictated them to us, and had us recite them endlessly. Each one of us could recite Schiller's "Lied von der Glocke" or Goethe's "Erlkönig" in our sleep.

Other teachers gave instructions on subjects that remained murky to us because they were never well explained. For instance in Naturkunde (study of nature), teachers would often start the class with comments like "Today, we will talk about rivers" or "Today, we will talk about the four seasons" and then seemed to ramble on. I remember a teacher once asking what different types of music we knew. When one student volunteered "Samba," she threw such a fit and hit the poor guy over the head for such a long time that everything that followed remained a big blur. I remember one teacher playing music on his violin during various class hours without much comment.

It was difficult to associate teachers with subjects. It seemed that all teachers covered all subjects and talked about everything under the sun. I could identify only two teachers by the subjects they taught. Herr Brettschneider taught history and Herr Franke taught mathematics. Herr Brettschneider talked a lot about Stone Age people, early German tribes, and his favorite topic, the Huns, who almost overran Europe a long time ago but failed thanks to heroic deeds of the Romans and Germans working together. Herr Franke taught us multiplication tables, division, fractions, and basic geometry. He made the most sense but had few pedagogical skills. He had no humor and seemed bitter that Germany had lost the war.

No teacher approached the world, including the physical world, in a comprehensive way. There was no Galileo, Kepler, Newton, Linnaeus, or Koch. Though there was much talk about rocks, fish, flowers, and other familiar objects in nature, there wasn't much taxonomic or other organizational context. I envied the students who, after fourth grade, had transferred to the separate boys' and girls' high schools (the Gymnasium und Lyceum), for I heard that their teachers would explain how the world really ticked.

There was also religion. This was a Catholic parochial school, and once a week a priest from the local church (usually Kaplan Kelly) came and taught catechism, dealing with official doctrines of the church regarding faith, rituals, and human behavior.

I liked Kaplan Kelly. He was young, energetic, and had answers to questions for our education-starved minds. Plus, he was also the guidance counselor for our Boy Scout group, in which I was very active. His was the only class that encouraged discussion and allowed for some use of common sense regarding lofty topics. But whatever questions we had that he could not clarify with common sense, he would address with lots of references to scripture and the power of miracles. Sometimes he gave obscure answers to simple questions, but he did so without diminishing our faith. I must have been twelve when I asked him how it was possible for the entire human race to descend from Adam and Eve without incest. I think we ultimately settled on the catch-all phrase that it was a miracle.

There were times when I felt that my entire time at school was wasted. The little I learned about the world I learned from reading books. I had discovered the local library, situated in one of the old wings of the local castle (Schloss Benrath), a fifteen-minute walk from our house. A librarian would ask what kind of book you'd like to read and try to find one that matched that interest. The library had been spared from the heavy bombing, as had the castle as a whole, and it was full of books for general reading, including children's books. It also seemed that many, if not most, had been spared the swastika rubber stamp during the Hitler years and thus survived the denazification cleansing.

When I was first asked what kind of book I wanted to read, I said, "Jungenstreiche" (pranks of young boys). To my surprise, they had quite a number of those books. For a while, I read a book every week or two, usually sitting at the kitchen table or, when the weather was nice, on a bench in the large Schlosspark or sitting in the grass at the banks of the nearby River Rhine. After a couple of years, I had read all of the boys' pranks books, and the librarian introduced me to more demanding reading material. I think I started with Mark Twain's *The Adventures of Tom Sawyer* and *Adventures of Huckleberry Finn*, before reading works such as Charles Dickens's *Oliver Twist*, Daniel Defoe's *Robinson Crusoe*, James Fenimore Cooper's *The Leatherstocking Tales* (*Lederstrumpf*), and Robert Louis Stevenson's *Treasure Island* (*Die Schatzinsel*), all in German, of course. And I read a number of books by Karl May, as many youngsters in Germany did at the time. But my favorite author was Erich Kästner. I read every book by him I could lay my hands on, devouring *Emil und die Detektive* and *Pünktchen und Anton*. My favorite was *Das fliegende Klassenzimmer*, the story of friendship and betrayal among classmates of rival boys' schools.

When my classroom teacher, Herr Franke, assigned us to write a report on our favorite book, all of the students in our class wrote about books by Karl May, focusing on the heroic deeds of May's central characters, the noble Apache chief Winnetou and his courageous fur-trapper friend Old Shatterhand. Old Shatterhand's home was in Saxony, but he had followed his true calling and moved to the American West to hunt bears. I was the only student writing about a different author, namely Erich Kästner. I focused on the main point of *Das fliegende Klassenzimmer*, which is that young boys who were bitter enemies could become the best of friends in the end. We had to read our reports out loud. After I read mine, Herr Franke turned to the class and explained that students who let their parents write their reports would be severely punished, meaning they would receive a failing grade, which is what I got.

I could not tell my parents, who never knew what my homework assignments were to begin with, because they would invariably take the side of the teacher. To them, such things were always a matter of preserving authority. Whoever was in charge was right, no matter the issues. I hardly ever did homework and did not want this to be a part of any discussion, for many reasons. Among these was the paper problem. My parents did not buy me the necessary notebooks for classwork. My grandparents helped out occasionally and gave me money to buy them, and sometimes I would borrow writing paper from classmates.

My teachers got used to the idea that I would not do my homework regularly and gave me bad grades accordingly, even when I showed in class that I knew the material quite well. For instance, when Herr Franke asked the class how a particular geometrical problem could be solved, I was usually one of the first students to raise his hand. But he hardly ever called on me. I had similar experiences in other classes. Eventually, I got so upset that I refused to go to school altogether. I think I had just read an episode in *Huckleberry Finn* where Huck refused to go to school because he saw no sense in it. And I was going to do the same.

When I left home for school in the morning, I went to the city library instead, got an interesting book, and went to the Rhine shore to lie in the grass and read it. My parents had no idea. Neither did my brother Erwin. He left for school five to ten minutes before I did so that he wouldn't be late, which I mostly was. After about two weeks of this, one of the teachers asked him how much longer I was going to be sick, and the whole thing unraveled. My father subjected me to the usual beatings and teachers promised to fail me again. And they delivered on that promise.

I probably would have been an interesting case for a psychologist, but at the time, psychology was considered a clinical science designed to help seriously deranged people. And I was considered a regular guy, at least by most people, if a little odd sometimes. For instance, during those years I developed uncontrollable, nervous laughter when I was in the presence of seemingly nonsensical human behavior. The solemn expression on a teacher's face when trying to pronounce difficult French names or the pretentious gestures of a neighbor woman faking better breeding than her peers could set me off on a laughing spell where I lost complete control over my nervous system. I would collapse completely, unable to move a muscle, my mouth twitching. I would usually recover in twenty to thirty seconds, but during that short time I often lay on the ground, remained hunched over a table, or leaned against a wall, puzzling onlookers.

My friends got used to it and considered it to be a mild form of epilepsy, and they prepared the ground for me when they saw my laughter coming on so I could collapse comfortably onto nearby grass or a chair. But I did spill drinks sometimes and even put my face onto a full dinner plate at least once. Sometimes I had the feeling that Günther especially tried to alert me to situations that could easily cause my collapse, such as by pointing out an old lecher trying to get cozy with a pretty girl on the dance floor or a politician explaining on the radio why eliminating certain people somewhere, perhaps through warfare, would bring a lasting peace for other people somewhere else.

In later years, some doctors tried to provide a diagnosis for this odd behavior but failed. I just had to live with this momentary loss of control, prompted by the perceived surreal behavior of others, for many years. It slowly disappeared during my thirties, for reasons unknown.

When my friends and I turned ten or eleven and we advanced from fourth to fifth grade, we saw a number of classmates disappear. They switched to high schools to obtain a high school diploma (Abitur) after eight more years of schooling. The rest of us stayed in Volksschule for four more years to leave as eighth graders to either become trade apprentices or work in unskilled jobs without further training. It was no secret who would go to high school, and it wasn't us. It was the children of the middle and upper classes, that is, children of families with some standing in the community.

One time when Herr Franke wanted to take a count of how many of us would transition to high school, I stood up to be counted. He looked at me and told me in no uncertain terms that I definitely did not belong there and made me sit down again. Since I figured that I was at least as smart as the kids that remained standing (and in some cases considerably smarter), Herr Franke's command left an indelible mark on my soul. The same happened to my close friends. Our intellectual development was hobbled by a traditionally unfair, class-based education system. In our bones, we felt we had to find other ways to live up to our natural potential. And we did.

In general, I always felt that I would do all right given fair opportunities. I saw an uncertain future ahead of me but always felt it was going to be better than the present. Despite all the deprivations and daily struggles, I never felt hopeless or depressed. And while I had a very stressful relationship with my parents, it took only a few material things (a pair of new shoes or new underwear, for instance) to make me content.

My father used to give me a good beating every now and then, usually without saying why. If I indicated that I didn't know the reason, it made matters worse. Usually, it had something to do with what I did, something inappropriate (such as stealing an apple) that someone from the neighborhood told my father about. My father and I hardly ever talked about anything. If he wanted me to know something (that I shouldn't let the radio run too much, for example), he usually told my mother to tell me. Likewise, anything I wanted to let him know (like that I needed two marks for the Boy Scout trip), I had to relay to him through my mother.

He controlled all the money, little though it was, and I desperately wanted a bicycle. All my friends had bicycles. I was the only boy who didn't. So I started to put one together by myself with some spare parts. They were hard to come by, and I didn't know what I was doing. I tried to get a bit of money by collecting scrap metal and selling it to a dealer. In the neighborhood, that was a sign of being from a poor family, and my father forbade me to do it. I tried to do it in secret, but he found out and I received more beatings.

Against all odds, I eventually put together a bike. But it barely functioned. The tires were worn out and the inner tubes lost air. I couldn't get the handlebar to stay in place. One pedal always came loose. It was one thing after another. In my desperation, I tried to make some kind of truce with my father and pleaded with him to help me fix the bike. He looked at the bike, didn't say much, and never gave me a helping hand. I wish I had a different story to tell. But I don't. I needed many things then and didn't get any of them. But not having a bike meant separation from my friends. And nothing was more important to me than my friends.

My parents lived with a lot of tension back then. My mother, like almost all mothers at the time, was a stay-at-home mom. But there was little to do at home. So she visited other moms and commiserated. My parents had friends, other couples on the same lower social rung, with whom they got together occasionally, usually on weekends, and had a beer or Kaffee und Kuchen, when they could afford it. My father was usually the dominant figure, trying to entertain with jokes and funny stories. This was when I saw a side of him that I would not see when we were by ourselves. Unlike my mother, my father was very outgoing in public.

He liked the attention and tried to appear more educated than he was. He liked to drink beer and smoke cigars even when he couldn't afford it. To others, he had an honorable profession as a typesetter. He knew how to speak intelligently even though he was a bit loose on facts. He joined the local amateur theater group and played leading roles in popular, mostly comic plays such as *Der Biberpelz* by Gerhart Hauptmann or *Der zerbrochene Krug* by Heinrich von Kleist.

My father had genuine theatrical talent, and I am sure he regretted not having the opportunity to make something of himself in that respect. But it often seemed that his extroverted behavior covered up a deep-seated insecurity about his place in the world and a lack of confidence to change things. My mother shared the same problem but endured life mostly in silence. She did not join the theater club but seemed jealous of her husband's activities there and must have dreaded real or imagined affairs with the ladies.

At times, my mother showed impressive skills when handling numbers, but she was far from matching her husband's ability in handling words. She could be very gregarious with close friends but extremely shy with strangers. That was, I'm sure, also a result of her inability to work on her appearance as much as she wanted. Lack of money often made her look pale and worn out. Whenever she did manage to put on some makeup and wear a nicer dress, her potential to be an attractive woman became immediately apparent. And here, too, a little bit of money would have gone a long way toward making her life so much happier.

There was one area where my parents shared an occasional spark, and that was when they went on bus or river tours together. During the early fifties, this was a big deal. A group of people, usually members of private clubs (bowlers, seniors, gardeners, and others), school classmates, or coworkers, would go on excursions together in a touring bus or on a cruise ship, often to beer gardens or wine villages up the Rhine and Moselle Rivers. The employees of my father's printing shop saved up money in a piggy bank to go on these trips with their spouses.

Those trips generated a lot of not-so-sober escapades that my parents talked about for a long time afterward while planning for the next trip.

Our school classes also took such trips, usually to historic landmarks (Drachenfels, Kölner Dom, Wiehler Tropfsteinhöhle, and others) for educational reasons. I hated those trips because I became motion sick on the bus. I remained susceptible to motion sickness into my late thirties.

None of my friends had much money to spend, but I always felt I was the poorest. We boys soon discovered that one way to travel cheaply was to hitchhike. During the fifties, lots of people did it, especially youngsters. I must have been thirteen or fourteen when I started, at first accompanying larger boys from the scout group. We wore our Catholic Boy Scout uniforms and were usually going to some camp. Waving one hand up and down at cars going our direction (sticking up a thumb came later), we generally hitched rides quickly, especially when standing at an autobahn on-ramp.

Pretty soon I traveled on my own, using maps that showed all the youth hostels where one could stay overnight for 50 pfennig. The German youth hostel system was started at the beginning of the twentieth century to accommodate the growing number of young people exploring nature on foot and by using the spreading rail system, whose steam-engine locomotives began to connect remote villages with heretofore unimaginable speed. The first youth hostel was opened in 1910 in Bergisches Land at Burg Altena, a castle just twenty-five miles east of Düsseldorf. The quest to get in closer touch with nature had been spurred by the romantic artists of the late nineteenth century and created a pageantry of its own, perhaps expressed best in the Wandervögel (migrating birds) movement.

Wandervögel were youngsters who expressed their adoration for nature in songs while exploring it. Their well-known anthem was "Wenn die bunten Fahnen wehen" (When the colorful banners are unfurled). We in the Boy Scouts still sang many of their songs during the fifties, accompanied by guitars where possible. I would have given anything to be able to get a guitar. Those in the Boy Scouts who had guitars and who took lessons came from upper-middle-class families. But I am still glad they shared their skills and joy with us working-class kids.

I think I was fourteen when I decided to hitchhike to see my father's relatives in Fürth, Bavaria. It was a 500-mile trip and took two days. I met Ernst, my father's half brother, and his family (wife Emmie, daughters Luise, Helga, and Monika) and stayed for several days in their apartment on the couch. Ernst was a carpenter and, from all appearances, did quite well.

I also met Frida, Ernst's sister and my father's half sister. She was living in a small house without indoor plumbing. I only saw her briefly. I think her husband had died, and she had a daughter living nearby. The daughter and her husband were doing very well, raising two daughters. Her husband had a trucking business. They owned a large family home and drove two cars, which was nothing to sneeze at in 1952.

What I took away the most from this trip was the description my uncle Ernst gave me of my biological grandfather Friedrich Lakenmacher. According to the story my father told me, Friedrich was a major in the Bavarian cavalry and had died when his horse reared up during a parade. Ernst told me that Friedrich was a factory worker from Magdeburg, who had a long affair with my grandmother Katharina Freyhofer, also a factory worker. They had three children together (my father, Christian, and his sisters Elsa and Hannelore) but never got married.

Eventually, Friedrich went back to Magdeburg, leaving Katharina with four children to take care of by herself: Christian and Elsa, plus Ernst and Frida, two children Katharina had from an earlier affair with a certain Alois Tretter. According to my father, Hannelore died as a young child as a result of an accident on a public playground. Katharina must have lived a tragic life. She died in 1930 at the age of forty-three in the midst of the Great Depression, when my father was eighteen years old. He had to take care of himself. So did Ernst, Frida, and Elsa. When exactly my father moved to Düsseldorf, I never found out. He once told me that he had been referred to a printing business there by someone back home.

After he lost his apprenticeship because the business went bankrupt, he worked for a while in Erlangen, a university town close to Fürth, with the newly established Reich Labor Service (Reichsarbeitsdienst), which was a program of the Nazi regime. This labor service worked much like the Civilian Conservation Corps, or CCC, of Franklin

Delano Roosevelt's New Deal. He told me once that he had many odd jobs during that time, including playing drums in bands, before getting a steady job in the shipping department of the Deutsche Reichsbahn (German State Railway) in the mid to late thirties.

He worked at Düsseldorf's main train station. And after my mother and he got married in September 1937, they got a nice apartment a few blocks away. Erwin and I were born in the nearby St. Joseph's Hospital (in 1938 and 1942, respectively), and we lived there until we got bombed out by British night raids in 1943.

FIVE

Early Travels

After my visit to see my relatives in Fürth, I moved on to see some parts of the Alpine region that everyone dreamed of seeing; Berchtesgaden, Salzburg, and St. Wolfgang on the Wörthersee. At the youth hostel in Berchtesgaden, I met a guy who was a few years older than me. He was looking for someone to climb with him to the top of the Watzmann.

The Watzmann is the second-highest mountain in Germany at 8,900 feet, and it looms large in German folklore. I could not resist the invitation, and I agreed to accompany him. He had no climbing experience and was hoping to find someone who did, and he got stuck with me and my lack of experience, but we both agreed to get up very early the next morning and give it a try. We had no idea what we were getting into. The climb was very steep, but we were told that we could make it if we were not planning to go up the treacherous East Wall.

We were wearing the wrong clothes: short pants (Lederhose in my case) and a shirt. I wore the cheap, all-purpose low shoes that I wore all the time because I had no other shoes. I had a little pouch to carry a water bottle and a sandwich. We agreed to take several sandwiches and alternate carrying the pouch. If all went well, the climb up and down would take about sixteen to seventeen hours. Most climbers sleep in a hut below the peak and descend the following day. But we had no sleeping bags, ice axes, ropes, or other essentials, so we thought we would go up and come back in one day. After two or three hours of climbing, we met climbers coming back down who warned us of bad weather. But we remained undeterred. However, after another couple of hours, my hiking partner threw in the towel. We had already run out of water and food, and his feet hurt. I urged him to press on, but my request fell on deaf ears and I continued on alone.

The Watzmann has two peaks, and I reached the first one on schedule. Because of bad weather warnings, there were only a few other climbers up there. But they were all wearing the proper gear and looked at me with disbelief. Fortunately, the weather was clearing up again. So, after a much-needed rest, I should have begun the descent. But no. I had to make it to the second peak, negotiating a very pointed ridge. My slippery shoes became a real problem. I don't know how I made it, but after about another hour, I was sitting on the narrow top of the Südspitze.

The view was overwhelming, and I felt lighthearted, almost giddy. I prayed when I saw a plaque, mounted next to the cross that marked the high point, displaying the names of the climbers who had died trying to make it up the East Wall. A real mountain climber spotted me from a distance. He had a camera and took a picture of me leaning with my back against the cross. If ever there was a picture of me that I regretted never seeing, this was it. But I have held the mental picture of this moment in my mind throughout my life.

Years later, I could not believe how dumb I had been, but I still remember how good I felt when I reached the peak. In retrospect, I don't know why I didn't brag about it much. My triumph on the mountain has always been a very personal experience for me. I regret that I have never fulfilled my promise to myself to someday go back and repeat the feat. But it wouldn't be the same. I have heard there are carved-out paths in the rocks now and mounted steel ropes to hang on to.

So, I'd reached the top, but I still had to make it down. The shadows were getting longer, and I had to be fast in my descent. On the last stretch, I was climbing in the dark with no one else in sight. When I finally made it back to the youth hostel, just before curfew, I felt sick as a dog. There was a rule that one could not stay in bed after 9:00 a.m.

After that, the sleeping hall was closed for the day. Only the beds of guests who had already departed were made up. I stayed in a bed for two days, hiding under the blanket when I heard a noise. After two days, I wobbled out of the youth hostel and hitchhiked back home. I remained sick for quite a while but eventually recovered fully.

My next memorable trip happened a couple of years later. In the summer of 1954, our Boy Scout group of seven or eight took a train to Innsbruck, Austria, where we split up into smaller groups to explore the Alps for three weeks, planning to meet up again afterward. I decided to take off by myself, and rather than explore the Alps again, I went to Rome, hitting such dreamy towns as Venice, Florence, Siena, Padua, La Spezia, and more on the way. During the 1950s, Germans in particular flocked to Italy any chance they had, usually during their school vacation or, in my case, the three-week vacation given in my employment contract. Hungry for sunshine, these Germans not only tried to escape the dreary northern weather but also the long and difficult hours in dusty factories and stuffy offices and the depressing urban landscapes that were still full of ruins and rubble from the war.

At that time, I was an apprentice at a large department store, DEFAKA (later Hertie), in downtown Düsseldorf. I worked around fifty-five hours per week (the forty-eight-hour week was still in effect then, and we usually had to work longer, without compensation) and still lived in cramped housing conditions. Italy sounded like heaven to me, as it did to millions of other Germans. Italy as a sunny and romantic place to visit was popularized in many German movies and songs, sung by such well-known stars as Vico Torriani and Caterina Valente. Her "Komm ein bisschen mit nach Italien" (Come along a little to Italy) was on the lips of most Germans during the 1950s. And here I was, in Venice of all places, and I couldn't believe it myself. Using a simple street map of the city, I walked for hours along the canals, hitting the most familiar landmarks first: the Grand Canal, Rialto Bridge, St. Mark's Square with its famous campanile and basilica, the Doge's Palace, and many, many more. I felt a strange sense of adventure when I saw the Bridge of Sighs, having recently read Casanova's account of his escape from the inescapable prison the bridge led to.

In 1954, Venice was one of the most desired tourist destinations, and it still had its own charming, historic look. And there were sections seemingly untouched by time, along the major canals, but especially along the many side canals, some of them showing advancing decay. People had lived here for centuries. And they were still here, rich and poor. I saw a lot of garbage floating in the canals, especially in the minor ones, and a slight stench of sewage and debris hovered over the water of all the canals. But it did not distract from the mystery and absolute beauty one met at every turn wandering through town. I got lost many times trying to find my way out of a maze of canals I could not find on my map. Sometimes I was the only foreigner and no one spoke even a bit of a foreign tongue.

Many years later when I went back to retrace my steps, the town was not the same. The last time I visited with Sue, in 2015, Venice had assumed a bit of a Disney World feeling.

In 1954, I could have stayed (and probably died) in Venice, given the smallest chance. But I had to move on, and my next stop was Genoa, where I saw the fourth-century cathedral. Then I followed the Riviera route to Pisa, where I stood under the famous leaning tower and had to convince myself that it was indeed not going to fall on me.

Florence was next, where I saw Santa Maria del Fiore, the Ponte Vecchio, *David* at Michelangelo Square, and much more. Then it was off to the eternal city of Rome, where I stayed a whole week. Looking for the youth hostel there, I ran into a bilingual hitchhiker from Tirol who was twice my age. He had been a young German soldier in Italy and knew Rome quite well. He took me to several historic places and explained their significance to me at length, all the while conversing with the locals in perfect Italian. He knew all about Trajan's Column, Forum Romanum, the Colosseum, and other landmarks. When he took me up the Spanish Steps to the Trinità dei Monti church, he went silent. Inside the church, he nearly collapsed in a fit of crying. Memories of his stressful time as a young soldier, only ten years before, had overcome him. He left Rome the next morning but gave me a map of the city to find my way around.

Back at the youth hostel, I spent the rest of what little money I had on two upcoming events: seeing the opera *Aida* at an open-air theater and seeing Pope Pius XII at the Vatican. I wasn't particularly interested in seeing the opera, but a pretty German girl at the youth hostel was going and asked if I would come along. Of course I agreed. And I had promised my grandmother to see the pope and tell her all about it upon my return.

Both events were organized by a tourist office. I remember the bus ride to the open-air theater but little about the opera performance. The trip to see the pope was more dramatic. It was all part of a one-day excursion to see many things in Rome but mostly the Vatican. We saw the pope at his private residence at Castel Gandolfo, just outside Rome. We were part of a group of a few hundred "pilgrims," waiting in the courtyard when he opened the window and addressed us in several languages. His German was flawless, as he had been nuncio in Germany for many years before becoming pope. I was a devout Catholic boy and had the feeling he was speaking directly to me when he gave us his blessings. Tears ran down my cheeks. I have rarely felt so uplifted since.

Later our group visited the catacombs under the city. I had no idea they existed. Our guide explained that Christians had hidden in them during times of persecution, and again under Emperor Theodosius, and later used them mainly as burial sites. We saw stone graves, sarcophaguses, altars, and many frescoes depicting biblical scenes.

For the most part, there was no lighting in the catacombs, and we had to walk holding lit candles. The pretty German girl and I lagged farther and farther behind until we lost touch with the group. At first, it was very romantic, but we panicked when we couldn't see any lights. The catacombs were a maze, and we had been told that one could get lost and never emerge again. We stumbled ahead, and at forks in the caves we used our intuition to move ahead until we could hear the group at a distance. Soon we saw dim lights and said a prayer of thanks. No one had missed us, and we were told that the next group behind us would probably have picked us up again. The girl and I stayed in touch, writing letters for about a year. But we never saw each other again.

The next day, I started heading back home. I hit Siena, Florence a second time, Bologna, and Verona before linking up with my friends again in Innsbruck, broke, hungry, with holes in my shoes, and eager to swap stories. Everyone had exciting stories. But no one else had seen the pope.

We were all Catholic Boy Scouts (Sankt Georgs Pfadfinder), and on the train ride back to Düsseldorf, I enjoyed my hero status. When I finally told my story to my grandmother, I saw her eyes welling up. I am sure she was thinking of her lost son Heinz and how I had made the trip in his stead.

SIX

Entering the Working World, Doing the Draft, Living in Munich

I shared my summer adventures with my coworkers as well. In 1954, I was in my second apprenticeship year as a window decorator (Schaufenstergestalter) at the giant department store DEFAKA in downtown Düsseldorf. I had left the Erich Müller Schule in Benrath with a completed eighth grade education, as all students did. There was no graduation ceremony, just a completion ceremony (Abschlussfeier) in March 1953. My apprenticeship started on April 1. At that time in Germany, there were many more eighth graders leaving schools than there were apprenticeships available for them. And there was no recruiting process. Parents had to take their fourteen-year-old son or daughter to potential employers and hope for the best. Students' interests or talents were usually secondary to employers' needs or the wishes of the parents.

Many parents wanted their children to follow their own career paths and prepared them the best they could, usually by asking their

employers if there was a place for their child in their company. In that
way, many trades tended to stay in families. If that wasn't possible,
there were always large employers, mainly in the manufacturing industry, who hired a great number of apprentices. I lived close to many
large factories that trained young apprentices in well-organized programs to become skilled workers for their operations.

Many of my friends went to the factories and became lathe operators, mechanics, or welders. But the companies would not take just
any fourteen-year-old. In their search for the smartest kids, they considered two things: reputation (often based on letters of recommendation from teachers) and grades. I was a failure on both fronts. I could
not think of anybody who would put in a good word for me (except
Kaplan Kelly, who wrote a recommendation for every kid). But I was
also afraid to ask. Even so, my grades were deplorable, even in subjects where I excelled, like mathematics. But there was one area where
I was never given a low grade: drawing. I was without a doubt the best
drawer in class. Even my father showed appreciation for my skills,
partly because he thought I inherited them from him. His employer
did all the printing for DEFAKA, and my father recommended me for
an apprenticeship in their decorating department. When I had my interview, I impressed them with a command of German above what
they apparently expected of an eighth grader, and I got the position.

Later on, I learned that several other boys had interviewed for the
spot, and I thanked Jesus for giving it to me. Being a decorator meant
I was part of the white-collar world. As my friends saw it, I had escaped the drudgery of the blue-collar world. And indeed, many of my
colleagues came from better-off families, often having had to leave
high school for one reason or another, and for the most part envisioned themselves to be future artists. For a while, I too was drawn
into this atmosphere and made it my goal to get into the local art academy (Kunstakademie) and become a stage designer (Bühnenbildner).
Whenever I had extra time, I would sit in downtown cafés and stretch
a cappuccino for as long as possible, imagining being on the Left Bank
of Paris. I went to the theaters and opera houses whenever I could afford it, either with my friends or, if I had any extra money, on a date.

During those days, guys had to pick up the tab. In return, they
could hope for a kiss on a park bench on the way home. The Pill had

not arrived yet, and fear of having unwanted babies kept the screaming goodies under wrap. I wasn't a big success on the park bench either. I liked foreign films and could not get enough of the French New Wave, Italian neorealism, and of course Ingmar Bergman. My problem was that after leaving the theater with a date, I wanted to analyze the films over a cup of coffee, and that usually killed all prospects of a romantic ending for the evening. The Italian guest workers who had recently arrived in Germany in great numbers were mostly eager young men in desperate search of love. They seemed to be much more successful on the park benches, in part, no doubt, because their knowledge of German was very limited. Their actions spoke louder than their words.

If my pseudo-intellectual apprenticeship years taught me anything, it was that I was not a guy who could dress up windows for the rest of my life and stay sane. I also knew I had to leave my parents' home as soon as I possibly could. It was still cramped, and the older I got, the more I felt the limitations it imposed on everyone, including me. My chance to leave home came in the form of the military.

By 1956, Germany had joined NATO. I got a letter from the defense department stating that my age group would be the first to be drafted, but because soldiers were needed as soon as possible, I could sign up early and receive a bonus. Draft service was eighteen months. In July 1956, I signed up and was inducted into the artillery battalion stationed at the Klotzberg-Kaserne in Idar-Oberstein, 150 miles south of Düsseldorf.

By now I had finished my apprenticeship as a decorator and had the opportunity to escape the physical and mental confines of my home environment by running into the military. I quickly found that I had paid a high price for leaving home. Military life was stifling and boring, but I got along with the guys in my platoon quite well. We were told we were preparing to defend Germany and NATO from the Russkies when, not if, they came.

For the first time, I got to know American soldiers, or any Americans for that matter, on a personal basis. Their army garrison in Baumholder was close to ours. We met soldiers in the local bars and started talking with them. They were generally very friendly, and I learned my first few English words and phrases, such as "Hello," "What is your name?" and "How are you?" And I saw the old cliché

Kanonier Freyhofer, Idar-Oberstein, 1957.

that Americans on the whole get drunk quicker than Germans confirmed. German beer is much stronger than they were used to, and Americans had some problems adjusting.

One of the American soldiers, Hermann, spoke decent German, and we met frequently in the local pubs. His German father was a medical doctor in Pennsylvania, and he said he would arrange for me to emigrate to the US and work in his father's hospital. I was very interested. But the deal fell through when his father learned that I couldn't speak English.

One Sunday morning in the Klotzberg Garrison when I was on my way to meet Hermann, an officer stopped me and asked where I was headed. When I told him, he instantly assigned me to guard duty. He gave me a few minutes to appear in battle gear ready to go. I joined a few other recruits, and we were driven to a nearby secret ammunition bunker. For twenty-four hours we had to patrol a long fence, alternately walking for two hours and sleeping for two hours.

Before we went on the walk, we had to load our American semiautomatic M1 rifles with one clip and one bullet in the chamber, ready to fire. Returning from the walk, we had to unload the rifles again, try to sleep for two hours, then repeat the whole process eleven more times. At one point, I was so tired that when I loaded my rifle, it went off. The bullet, a .30 caliber, hit my left foot.

All pandemonium broke loose. The corporal in charge did everything wrong. He was unable to communicate with anyone outside the bunker who could give proper emergency directions. He tried to pull off my boot. The gushing blood eventually stopped him. Unable to get an ambulance, he decided to take me to the nearest hospital himself in his little military Volkswagen Bug. The hospital was in the middle of Idar-Oberstein, a town of about 30,000, winding along the River Nahe.

The corporal's Volkswagen had no emergency lights. So he drove through the busy Sunday traffic like any other slow-moving car, observing all traffic lights and stop signs. He had given me no medication, and I managed the pain as best I could by biting into the collar of my heavy coat.

At one point, I thought he was going to stop and get a heisse Wurst (hot dog) from an Imbiss (fast-food place) along the road. It seemed an eternity before we got to the hospital. He made me hobble in rather than wait for a wheelchair, to speed things up, he said. No one in the hospital was prepared for me. But they managed to take my boot off and give me painkillers right away. They called the attending surgeon, who took a long time to show up because it was Sunday.

My foot looked terrible. The surgeon amputated one toe, the second from the right on the left foot, and patched the rest together the best he could. But I healed well. A couple of weeks later, I was doing light office duties again. Four weeks later, I was hobbling around the fields with the regular troops. I was even honored for coming in first hitting targets with a bazooka. But I had had it and wanted to get out of the small-town barracks. I applied for a transfer to Munich because I wanted to attend night school classes that were not offered in Idar-Oberstein.

It was very difficult to get transfers approved, but mine was granted by my company commander because, I am sure, he was happy to get rid of a difficult case. Munich had no artillery division, so I ended up in a pioneer battalion stationed at the Freimann Garrison just outside the city.

I was very pleased with the arrangement, even though my superiors did not know where to place me correctly. I circulated among several military units, first the post office, then the field communication unit, before I was assigned to transportation. There, we learned how to operate all of the different vehicles used by our battalion, from heavy motorcycles to armored vehicles. I also found it comforting that a good friend of my father, Dieter Götze, whom I knew personally, was one of the instructors. It was a great coincidence indeed. After four weeks of training and a few days before taking our tests, I found that I had driven all of the different vehicle types at our garrison but one, a new kind of truck, the Borgward Kübelwagen, with a suspension that minimized shaking, helping it to carry sensitive radio equipment. I asked a fellow soldier who was driving one to let me take a few spins inside the garrison over lunch break.

After I returned the vehicle, Dieter, with whom I otherwise had no problems, wrote a formal complaint about me that prompted my immediate dismissal from the unit and barred me from taking my operating license exam, which would have allowed me to drive large trucks and heavy equipment for the rest of my life. Instead, I was placed in the mapmaking unit on account of the drafting skills I had acquired during my apprenticeship as a decorator. My father's "friend" was soon promoted from private first class (Gefreiter) to corporal (Unteroffizier). After his discharge from military service a few years later, he used the instructor's license he had acquired to open a driver's license school (Fahrschule) in our hometown, Benrath. If his intention was to demonstrate to his superiors that he could be relied upon to turn in a friend when military discipline demanded it, he obviously succeeded and was rewarded for it.

Still, I was glad to be in Munich. Munich is an exciting city, which I explored as much as time and my meager pay allowed. I never did sign up for evening classes even though that was the reason I'd given for my transfer. Instead, I frequented the beer halls, Tanzcafés, and bars, usually with other soldiers and mostly on weekends.

I was fascinated by Schwabing, a student and artist quarter near the university that featured jazz bands, cabarets, and music shows until the wee hours. I missed many curfews and got official warnings, reprimands, and detentions. I was also never promoted to even the lowest rank, which was rare for any soldier.

In short, I was not a model soldier. It didn't help much that I let everybody know that I was going to quit the military unless I was admitted to officer school. I had taken an admissions test for the officer program in Idar-Oberstein, but because of the foot-shooting incident and my subsequent transfer to Munich, the results were somehow lost. Eventually I requested an early discharge, citing my foot injury as the main reason. It was denied. After that I tried to wait out my time while engaging in interesting off-duty activities as much as I could.

Here is an example: While I was with the communication unit, I had to do occasional switchboard duty for the garrison. No call from outside could connect with any phone in the garrison directly. A switchboard operator answered all phone calls and made the connections or explained why a connection could not be made.

It was on a Saturday when the head of a boardinghouse for young ladies called and asked to speak with the commander. He was not in, so I asked whether she wanted to leave a message. She told me the matter was a bit pressing. The boardinghouse had a party that evening, and she wondered whether the commander could send over young officers to provide the ladies with some company. I told her not to worry, as a number of soldiers would show up that night and be on their best behavior. Somehow, I managed to have myself replaced as operator and got a few decent-looking guys to join me for fun.

We did not appear in uniform, and no one ever asked us for our ranks. The young ladies were celebrating something, and a small band was playing and inviting people to dance. I had to dance a few times with the housemistress who had called me, and I became painfully aware that she was at least twice my age. But things went rather well otherwise, and at the end of the evening, the head lady asked me whether we soldiers could contribute to the next week's musical performance. She added that many young ladies would play instruments and sing solos or perform in choirs. I said that we would be honored to contribute, that perhaps we could sing an uplifting military song. My comrades agreed. We did, in fact, get together a couple of times and practiced "Hohe Tannen" (Tall firs), an all-time favorite.

The evening came, and we sat in the back row. There seemed to be many dignitaries, all dressed up and looking somber. The young women performers all looked very professional. Some played Bach on the violin, and others sang romantic songs by Schubert or Weber. The longer we listened, the more we realized we were out of place. None of us could hold a tune to begin with. I told the guys we had been invited to represent the spirit of the new military and would not be judged by our performance.

When it was our turn, I tried to force the issue by getting up, walking to the front, and having the guys follow me. But they didn't. I stood up front alone, staring at the expectant faces in starched shirts and evening gowns. "Hohe Tannen" wouldn't go over well as a solo. The housemistress sensed my despair. Standing behind me with a guitar, she asked whether there was another song that I would feel comfortable singing myself. I thought of the Columbus song. It's a song that details the discovery of America by Columbus as much as it presents it musically. It has many stanzas, and I knew them all by heart from my Boy Scout years. I started, "Ein Mann der sich Columbus nannt, widewidewidbumbum, war in der Seefahrt wohl bekannt, widewidewidbumbum" (A man who called himself

Columbus, widewidewidbumbum, was known as a sailor far and wide, widewidewidbumbum). I got stuck shortly after the second stanza. But the head lady helped me get over it, pretending we had to stop so she could tune her guitar. I don't think I have ever received more heartfelt applause for anything I did later in my life than I did that evening. Everyone had felt my dilemma and was just as relieved as I was that it was over. I had earned the never-ending admiration of the head lady and the alluring gaze of some girls in the room. My army comrades who had left me in the lurch and I did not talk for quite a while. Instead, during the coming months, I talked a lot with a girl named Renate Ziegler, who had been in the audience and considered me a hero. We saw each other mainly on weekends. On one of those weekends, she invited me to a picnic with some of her friends at a green pasture outside Munich.

Lying on a blanket and sipping Coke, she casually pointed to a large building behind some trees in the distance and said, "Some people that I know were in that camp over there, Dachau. My parents barely escaped getting in there. They are Jewish. Now it's full of refugees from Eastern Europe." I had heard of the concentration camps during the Nazi regime and knew some by name, like Dachau. I also knew that many people had died there but not how they had died.

Given the wartime stories that I grew up with, my understanding was that the people who had it the worst during those years were the front soldiers and the civilians in urban areas who endured Allied bombings. I was one of them. People in camps, it seemed to me, were spared the worst. Even though I knew a little about the Dachau camp and that she was Jewish, Renate's remarks did not resonate much with me. I didn't give her Jewishness much thought. It was like if someone told me they were Protestant or Catholic. But I soon learned that she was deeply involved in restoring Jewish life in Munich. She was an employee of the Wiedergutmachungsamt, the German Office of Restitution, handling claims for losses suffered by Jews under the Hitler regime. Still, all that seemed very normal to me. I even picked her up from work in, as I came to find out, the old Jewish section of Munich. We did not talk about her work very much. Neither did we talk much about my dreary days in the Freimann Garrison. We focused on going to the movies and dance bars and sitting on benches in the Englischer Garten. In retrospect, that all seems strange. But at the time, I had no idea about mass exterminations in death camps. Renate must have, but she didn't bring it up.

Looking back on this affair, I wonder why she never told me not to pick her up from her office in uniform. That would have been odd. It is difficult for anyone who has not lived during those years to understand them from the perspective of that time. But I grew up in a world without television. I had never seen pictures of mangled corpses piled up in front of death camps. Nor did I know anyone who had. And at the time, my mind was occupied with other matters.

My military service was about to end, in December 1957, and I had to figure out what to do next. I did not want to return home but wanted instead to stay in Munich and find a job. That was not easy for a nineteen-year-old in a town that was not welcoming to non-Bavarians. This too was a part of living in the fifties.

I went to the employment office in Munich looking for a position as a decorator in one of the larger department stores. A clerk there told me in clear terms that Munich had no jobs for "outsiders" and that the best thing for me would be to go back to Düsseldorf. He used the local dialect, which I hardly understood, and which obviously pleased him. I tried to speak standard High German (Hochdeutsch), which many Bavarians consider a foreign tongue spoken by "Prussians." And for many Bavarians, a Prussian is any German who is not Bavarian.

Moving forward, I went to the department stores myself and was hired by Hertie, one of the largest stores around, located right across from the main train station. There were around twelve decorators in the window display department, and I was the only "Prussian." That did not make things easy for me. The two sign painters I had to work with did not talk to me at all, which was difficult when I had to give them work orders for the windows. But somehow I survived.

I also had to find an apartment, which was not easy. But I was lucky to find a furnished studio not far from Hertie. My salary was meager, but I made enough to get by. In all of this excitement, I somehow lost sight of Renate. We just stopped communicating. After a while, I started dating again, mainly salesgirls from Hertie.

At Hertie, I worked on a few projects with another decorator, also called Horst, who had just finished his apprenticeship and was a year younger than me. He was unlikely to be drafted because his father had recently died climbing the infamous Eiger-Nordwand in Switzerland. Very few people ever tried to do this climb, and those who succeeded became famous in the world of mountain climbing. But many lost their lives, and Horst's father was one of them.

Horst needed someone to talk to, so he opened up to me. We became good friends. He was from an upper-middle-class family and lived with his mother and sister in the suburb of Obermenzing, in a large one-family house. Soon, Horst invited me to rent a room in his house, and I accepted his offer. We found that we both shared a certain disdain for the stuffy middle-class life. He had lived it and hated its hypocrisy. As for me, I had not lived it but hated its pretentiousness.

Horst loved jazz and knew all the right clubs. We explored Schwabing's chanson bars, like Gaslaterne, and sat for hours in our favorite café, Mulhouse. Horst and I were different in character. He was the flirtatious southern type, and I was the thoughtful northern one, but we complemented each other well.

Horst had some high-society girlfriends but was painfully aware that their families would not approve of him as a serious suitor. Like me, he had no university education or prospects for a lucrative career. During the fifties, that closed many doors for aspiring young people like us. We talked ourselves into a "getting-out-of-here" mood and became less interested in our daily work and more in planning escapes. One plan was to go to Seville, Spain, where Horst had an uncle doing well in the orange-growing business. And true to Horst's flair for the extraordinary, we were going to drive there in an oldie.

We saved up for several months and bought a 1928 BMW Dixi, with spoke wheels and a crankshaft rod that could start the engine from the front by hand in case the electric starter gave out. Neither of us had any idea about car mechanics. We bought the car from a trusted mechanic, who explained everything to us laymen. He did warn us that it was unlikely that the car would make it all the way to Spain. But we tried anyway. We got as far as Belfort, a few miles south of Mühlhausen, in France, when our car gave out with a broken crankshaft. The engine leaked oil and became overheated. We had the crankshaft rebuilt, which took two weeks and cost us almost all of our money. We pressed on anyway, but the engine broke down again a few miles from where we started. We stored the car in the garage that had "fixed" it and headed back to Munich.

Later, we had the car shipped by ADAC (the German AAA) to a relative of Horst's near Stuttgart. It stayed there for almost a year until I towed it to Düsseldorf, where I ultimately ended up again. In Düsseldorf, I exchanged it for a motorcycle (a 350 cc Horex), which I used to explore the lower Rhineland region for several months.

SEVEN

Back to My Hometown: Düsseldorf

After we arrived back in Munich, we were broke. Horst, of course, had a home. But I had none. My parents still lived in the same cramped conditions they had when I'd left to join the military, and I would have rather remained homeless than go back there. Horst's mother made it clear that I could not stay at her house any longer. What followed were a few months of homelessness in Munich. I slept in used cars at dealers' lots, at the Chinese Tower in the English Garden, and in a certain niche at the central train station.

One night, a guard found me there and took me to the security office. I had to sign a statement that I would never enter the grounds of the train station again or face vagrancy charges and certain incarceration. Horst gave me a tent, and I did much better, until it was stolen. At one point, he handed me a letter from my mother. She still used Horst's address to reach me. My family in Düsseldorf had no idea about my vulnerable situation and assumed I was well off in Munich. But my mother pleaded with me to return to Düsseldorf because, after fourteen years of waiting, the Wohnungsamt (governmental housing department) had finally assigned my parents an apartment unit in a newly built housing complex in Düsseldorf-Eller, a few miles from Düsseldorf-Benrath. They asked me whether I could help them set it up, wallpaper and paint it, select and hang curtains, and buy furniture. After all, I was a decorator, and a decent one at that. However, I would have to share a room with Erwin. He was sixteen and a baker's apprentice. And I would have to pay rent. Nevertheless, I agreed, hitchhiked back to Düsseldorf, and started looking for a job.

Düsseldorf had always been considered the most fashion-conscious town in all of Germany, and Kaufhof, the most prestigious department store in Düsseldorf, located on the famous Königsallee (nicknamed "Kö"), hired me. I was twenty-two years old and on top of my game. My days sleeping under bridges were over, and I dressed again like a lounge lizard. I got in touch with my old friends, mainly Günther and Werner, and we set off to get our piece of "the big life." Eventually, I got a car (a used Ford 17M), and we explored places like Köln and Amsterdam. But our real passion became gambling, roulette mainly. Günther also liked the horses. The closest casinos were located in Spa, Belgium, a two-hour drive from Düsseldorf.

Situated in a late baroque palace, the casino had an elegant dress code that gave it a touch of old-fashioned splendor. This was also where the German military high command had its headquarters for the western campaign during World War I.

Roulette is primarily a numbers game. Günther and Werner played mainly on impulse, hoping that chance would favor them. I tried to beat the numbers statistically, sitting at the tables for hours tracking down trends, then betting against the numbers most likely not to appear in the short run. The system generally works if you stop playing when a short-term gain has been reached. But that is what most gamblers cannot do. They keep playing (after all, they are winning) until the trend reverses and their gains turn into losses. Anyway, whenever the trend favored me, I left the roulette table to go pay for our hotel and food before continuing with the betting. That generally worked. Afterward, we usually went to the disco Le Sanglier (The Wild Boar) and tried our luck with the Belgium girls doing the twist to Chubby Checker.

We should have been satisfied with our lives, but we were not. I was looking for a more challenging occupation. First, I quit my job at Kaufhof after working there for only six months, and I accepted a position at a fashionable boutique with ten display windows on Benrath's main street (Kaufhaus Thiele). I was the only decorator, doing everything myself, from design to execution. My budget was limited, but I managed. Soon the displays attracted wider attention, and lots of locals came window-shopping. These were the days when most people got ideas about what to buy from comparing displays in store windows. I was good at what I was doing. Still, I felt I had a talent for greater things.

Journalism had always been attractive to me, and I applied for any position offered at the major newspaper outlets in our region. The story was always the same; I had no Abitur.

The theater had always been attractive to me too. I had joined the amateur theater group my father belonged to and had major parts in two plays: N. Richard Nash's *The Rainmaker* and John Osborne's *Look Back in Anger*. I thought I was really something and *had* to enter the professional stage. So I went to a well-known acting school in Düsseldorf, where a well-meaning instructor told me that I really had no talent. Deep down, I had to agree. Perhaps I could start my own advertising business.

I quit my job with Thiele and started my own company decorating windows. I advertised my business in local papers and received many offers. I even got jobs at the Messe Düsseldorf, an annual international trade fair show. But I was not financially stable and I was also impatient. In the long run, I would have succeeded had I stuck with it. But I had little business sense back then.

When I was in a financial crunch, I took quick jobs to keep me afloat. For a while, I operated a crane at the DEMAG heavy equipment manufacturing plant in Reisholz. I delivered soft drinks for Canada Dry and Sinalco. I worked in a Thyssen plant, close to a furnace, in an asbestos suit that nearly cooked my blood, making seamless steel pipes. One of my friends, Erwin Kummer, was a typesetter and told me that if I worked as a typesetter at a large newspaper like *Rheinische Post*, as he did, I would make very good money. He told me that many papers looked for typesetters to do advertising pages. He also told me that it was simple work and I could learn it in a couple of weeks. So I did.

My relationship with my father improved during those days, though he never approved of my hop-on-hop-off attitude regarding employment. Still, he told me he would teach me to do typesetting work at his printing shop in Benrath. The shop owner, Herr Gather, didn't mind because he wanted to keep my overworked and underpaid father happy. And I set out to teach both Herr Gather and my father a lesson.

After acquiring a few basic typesetting skills, I answered a job ad in the *Düsseldorfer Nachrichten*. The paper was looking for a typesetter for its advertising section. I applied in person. When I was asked to submit the usual documentation (such as professional certification and letters of reference), I told the interviewer that I had recently applied for a job in Sweden, that I had sent everything to that company there, that I would not take the job if offered, and that I would turn the documents in as soon as they were returned. Back then, that wasn't as far-fetched as it sounds today because in 1962 the first photocopying machines (by Xerox) were just being introduced, and people generally had no copies of originals.

My excuse was accepted, and I started my job a few days later. The first few days were really nerve-racking, but I survived. Eventually, I could set the type for advertising columns in acceptable time frames, and I became more comfortable with what I was doing. But then I made a mistake. A typesetter union representative came to my workstation and asked me to join. I declined, thinking that the less people knew about me, the greater the chances that my deception would remain undisclosed. The representative wanted to know where I had done my apprenticeship, and I told him with the *Benrather Tageblatt*, a local paper where my father sometimes worked part-time.

For several weeks I didn't hear back from them. But one morning, as I entered the building on the Königsallee (situated a few blocks from Kaufhof, where I had worked as a decorator a year earlier), the union representative met me and took me to the management office. There were several people there already expecting me. My deception had been discovered. The union wanted my immediate dismissal. Management wanted to keep me because I did good work. Both sides compromised and agreed that I could stay, provided I would only do unskilled labor while assisting other typesetters. My pay was cut nearly in half. I accepted it for the time being because I already had other plans in mind.

Horst had also tried a few things in Munich and hadn't got ahead either. Eventually, he followed a plan we had discussed earlier: to emigrate to Canada. Many countries were competing for immigrants from Europe, particularly Australia, South Africa, and Canada, all former British colonies. The United States was not competing. Nearly all over the world, people who wanted to resettle someplace better overwhelmingly picked the US. As a result, the US put caps on immigration early. In 1924, the federal government set quotas for countries and nationalities proportional to their ratios of immigrants in the US population in 1890. As a result, there were long waiting lists for admission from all countries. But there were no waiting lists for Western Europeans who wanted to emigrate to Canada, Australia, or South Africa.

Canada almost immediately admitted Western European immigrants upon application, provided they passed a health exam and police record check. In fact, Canada would even pay the fare on a credit basis so that no waiting was necessary. This is how Horst got to Canada. He had left Munich on the spur of the moment. He wrote me letters from Toronto, praising his newfound freedom and large paychecks, inviting me to join him. I hesitated at first. But the more I felt boxed in in Germany, the more inviting his letters sounded. I also wasn't doing too well personally. I had very good friends, and I would feel like I was betraying them by going away for good. But my restless spirit, which my friends found so interesting, largely undermined all of my relationships with the opposite sex. I cannot say that I blame any of the women.

I did not give off a feeling of future security. When in the middle of 1962, a girlfriend of long standing told me it was over and she was going to marry an established guy who was a head shorter and more than twice her age, I knew the time to leave had come.

EIGHT

Off to the "New World"

One day, when I was driving in my 17M to a customer to dress up a window, something I did whenever I had extra time, the radio played an announcement by the Canadian government explaining the advantages of settling in a country full of opportunities for ambitious newcomers.

The next day, I showed up at the Canadian embassy in Bonn and got the application papers. After a couple of weeks, I returned them with all the required documents, including an extensive health check. A personal interview was the last step, and I was told I should not expect a bed of roses in Canada but only hard work. A few days later, I received the boarding pass in the mail.

Leaving Düsseldorf was more difficult than I thought it would be, as it was my real home. It was where my family lived. It was where I had friends who understood me better than anyone else. It was where I suffered as a child through American and British bombing raids that had killed many of my beloved neighbors but had spared me. I was having second thoughts. At the time, emigration to North America meant leaving for good. Most people who emigrated were rarely heard from again. Family members were considered lucky if they got an occasional letter. My grandmother's sister in Pennsylvania sent occasional Christmas cards with generic greetings in English. I could not tell my grandmother, the one person in my life who had always loved me unconditionally, that I was leaving, perhaps never to come back.

I walked through the Schlosspark Eller, pondering my decision, sat on a bench, and cried my heart out. When I drove to my grandparents to tell them about my departure, I told them I was going to Munich again and was planning to stay there for a while. They were sad to hear that, but they knew I had gone to Munich before and always returned. I remember waving to both of my grandparents, walking away from their place as they sat on their balcony waving back. It was the last time I saw my grandfather, who had taken me to the farming villages across the Rhine begging for food during the hunger years following the war. He died a few years later.

What I didn't know when I left was that I would be back six years later, in 1968, to see my grandmother again, who was frail and unable to carry on. She was overjoyed to see me, but unfortunately, life had other plans for her, and she died the following year.

My parents had a different take on my departure. They were very much preoccupied with their new addition to our family. My mother, at age forty-five, had become pregnant. She noticed it very late, thinking she was way beyond menopause. My father was fifty, and they decided to welcome their new life and start a phase of middle-class existence they had not had when they reared Erwin and me.

Udo was born at the Städtisches Krankenhaus on July 11, 1962, a few weeks before I left for Canada. I wished him well, knowing he would grow up in a much more secure world than Erwin and I had ever known. Later, my father found a printing job that paid him a regular wage as a typesetter, and my mother started working too, first in a factory and later cleaning offices. The German Wirtschaftswunder (economic miracle) had finally reached them too.

When I bid them goodbye, they both became sad, but I promised them I would stay in touch, no matter where I ended up. Erwin took my departure in stride, letting me know that we would do something together again one way or another. I had a last party with my friends. We all tried to downplay the importance of the moment, drowning it in as much beer as possible.

The ocean liner Arkadia. *On this ship, I sailed from
Bremerhaven to Montreal in August 1962.*

On August 5, 1962, I boarded the Greek liner *Arkadia* in Bremerhaven and arrived in Montreal on August 16. The Atlantic crossing was rough, and I got seasick quickly. For much of the trip, I lay in my bunk bed. During quieter days, I sat in deck chairs, reading books I had brought along. The *Arkadia* was an old cruise ship that was then used to transport mainly emigrants from Europe to North America and other places. I was glad when the trip ended, and Horst picked me up at the Montreal harbor pier. He found me a room in the apartment building where he lived in a section of Toronto called Yorkville, near the University of Toronto, which was full of students and immigrants.

It was August when I arrived, but Toronto was cold. Streets were wide and had few people in them. Shops were unadorned, screaming out for some flowers in the windows. Housefronts ran in straight lines to far-off points. The main drag, Young Street, was several miles long. This was a city made for big cars. But it also had a very efficient public transportation system. I used the subway for my first order of business, going to the city's employment office. Immediately, I had to deal with my new and overwhelming handicap. I spoke no English. I couldn't read signs. I couldn't ask for directions. All I had was a city map. It took a while, but I got there. The person at the counter gave me the address of a commercial sign-maker who spoke German.

I worked at his shop for a few weeks before getting a job as a window display man at a department store, Sayvette, in the suburbs. Sayvette was a chain, like Target or Kmart, and it advertised much of its merchandise in display windows. I was back in my element because my boss was German. He explained to me that he was a Jew from Berlin whose clothing store had been destroyed by storm troopers on Kristallnacht in 1938. He and his family subsequently fled to Canada, and he greeted me, in jest of course, with the Hitler salute. We got along fine because we spoke German all the time, and he explained my job assignments in great detail. We worked together for a full year until I left Toronto for California. I could see he was sorry that I was leaving. He had heard many compliments about my work.

My furnished apartment in Toronto had no television, but I didn't need one. I had grown up without TV. The first time it became part of my regular life was when I returned from Munich in 1960 to live with my parents again, helping them establish themselves in the new apartment they had wanted for so many years. At that time, only three public channels were available, one tending to the right politically, one to the left, and one that was supposedly neutral. In practical terms, it featured more cultural than political or economic programs. All programs started in the late afternoon, around 4:00 p.m., ostensibly not to interfere with daily work. The channels had similar formats. They included thirty-minute news summaries, feature stories on topics of general interest, and some more serious pieces of entertainment. On weekends, programs started earlier with occasional full-length feature films, music performances, and theater plays. There were no commercial channels. When I was leaving Germany, the channels allowed some advertising. But all TV spots were bundled together in one half-hour session per evening that most everybody ignored. Commercial channels would be introduced some years later, but they never reached the popularity of the public channels, even when, in the late sixties and early seventies, they tried to entice more viewers by showing soft-core porn late at night.

I grew up spending evenings reading or in pubs and coffeehouses with my friends. That is what I continued to do in Yorkville. After work, I usually went to the Café Anglais, a few blocks from where I lived on Wellesley Street. It was a meeting place for all sorts of immigrants and students from the nearby University of Toronto. The place was often packed, but there were many other hangouts nearby. I usually searched for people I had come to know. No matter where I went, I encountered tables with people speaking other languages. Some conversations were loud, often heated, usually dealing with problems people thought they had left behind. As my English improved, I started mixing with everybody who invited me.

There were Hungarians who lamented their betrayal by the West in their bloody uprising against the Soviets in 1956. Palestinians who had been forced off their land by Jewish settlers, many of whom had survived the Holocaust. Pakistani Muslims who had fled persecution in Hindu India. Canadians from Quebec bemoaning the Anglicization of their French culture. And then there were the Germans, probably the largest immigrant group in Canada at the time. The greatest number came from former German lands in Eastern Europe, which had been incorporated into countries that came under the control of the Soviet Union after World War II. Millions had fled the advance of Soviet troops at the end of the war, and many more had been removed forcefully (ethnically cleansed) after the war. Most of them had been farmers and welcomed the opportunity to acquire land in Canada, where they tried to rebuild their lives.

Others, like myself, joined the urban masses searching for opportunities that had eluded them back home. It seemed to me at the time that Canada was an assortment of ethnic groups that, while trying to integrate, also clung to their heritage in many obvious ways. Like other groups, the Germans had their own social clubs (Vereine) with oompah-pah brass bands, Kaffee Klatsch, Saturday dances, and much more. The radio had German stations that played such popular songs as Freddy Quinn's "Es kommt der Tag, da will man in die Fremde" (The day will come when you want to see foreign shores) or Hans Albers's "Ein Wind weht von Süd und zieht mich hinaus auf See" (A wind blows from the south and pulls me across the sea). And, of course, there were restaurants called Old Heidelberg and Wiener Wald. I went to them a couple of times and eventually thought I had left all that behind me.

I felt more at home in Yorkville's chaotic coffeehouse culture and be-came a regular there.

The waves of immigrants that invaded Canada after World War II dramatically changed the country's social character in many ways. The descendants of earlier immigrants, mainly from Britain and France, fenced themselves off, physically and mentally, often referring to themselves as "old Canadians." Most tried to stay aloof from the newcomers by socializing mainly with each other, regardless of class. I learned that even full integration did not mean one was 100 percent Canadian unless one was of British descent, much to the dismay of the French Canadians who made similar claims and insisted on speaking French only. I remember one angry German telling a British Canadian that Brits descended from the Angles and Saxons, and since he was a true Saxon, he was the truer Canadian. At the time, I was surprised how important such identity questions were for many people. I have always considered them silly. But they have by no means disappeared. I remember having a conversation at Café Anglais with some other German immigrants when suddenly a younger guy from an English-speaking table spoke in perfect German and corrected some remarks I had made about the rise of Hitler. According to him, I was ignorant beyond repair, and he let the whole restaurant know it, or at least those who spoke German. I figured out he belonged to a large group of Jewish immigrants, many refugees of Nazi persecution. It was the first of many such encounters I had with members of the Jewish commu-nity, and such encounters became a regular part of my life and that of the lives of most other German and European immigrants. But at the time, it didn't make much of an impression on me.

Eventually, I found a circle of friends I got along with quite well. We met often and did many things together. Of course, there was my friend Horst from Munich. But two years before I arrived, soon after he arrived in Canada, Horst had married a woman from Hamburg and now had two small children. Plus, his lifestyle took a nosedive. He dressed flashy, bought a Porsche, started associating with shady char-acters, and eventually disappeared somewhere in Montreal. Five hun-dred dollars I had loaned him earlier were gone too. But he had helped me so often when I was down and out in Munich that I considered it a repayment. We lost track of each other for good.

Later I met Peter von Stelzer, a wheeler-dealer from Vienna with an aristocratic flair. He worked in sales, drove a sports car, and had a pilot's license. He would rent a small plane on Sundays and invite his friends to fly along. Usually a group of four of us would split the cost, and he would take us on wild rides. We would see Lake Ontario and Niagara Falls from above.

As impressive as it was, I disliked those trips for two reasons. I got very airsick and had to throw up a lot. And Peter liked to scare us by shutting off the engine and letting the plane glide for a while. I don't think it was legal, and it looked dangerous.

Then there was Josef, whose last name I forgot. He was a Swiss waiter whose main ambition was to seduce the many pretty girls who frequented the cafés where he worked. He looked the part (a bit like Elvis), and we were glad about his presence, as it would mean we would usually have female company in an environment dominated heavily by immigrant males eager to please.

There was also Reinhold Nickel. He stood out at the tables of Café Anglais because he knew English better than any of us and because he had something none of us had, an Abitur. He had a job at a big bank, and his sights were set on climbing the corporate ladder. He did eventually achieve his goal, not in banking but in the manufacturing business. Twenty years later, he was the CEO of a company in Ontario with over 200 employees that produced industrial suspension systems. He lived happily with his German wife and daughter in a mansion outside Toronto.

A little later, I met Edwin Bockelman. He worked as a receptionist at a large hotel and had done his apprenticeship at the famous Kempinski Hotel in Berlin. Tall and definitely Teutonic looking, he had a way of making people look small without meaning to. He was a big talker, telling stories featuring mostly himself in different ways depending on his mood at the time. He came from a well-off family and had failed the Abitur. He was not good at math. His family didn't take it well, and he left them angrily. He eventually became general manager of the Atlanta Hilton, created his own tourism company, sold it profitably, and sailed the world on a dream yacht with his wife, Nancy, for many years.

These became my new and closest friends. All of us had arrived in Toronto during the summer of 1962. Earlier immigrants warned us about the cold winter climate, but we brushed it off as a mere scare tactic. Then the winter arrived. There was wet snow and freezing temperatures in early November that lasted until Christmas, when temperatures dropped to minus 4 degrees Fahrenheit and stayed there for months, with only intermittent thaws that caused havoc in the streets. The worst thing was the harsh wind blowing in from Lake Ontario, causing some people to wear two pairs of long underwear and still feel cold. I had brought no winter clothes from Germany and did not spend much money getting any in Toronto either. Because I had a plan. The same plan almost every immigrant in Canada had: namely, moving to California. The colder it got, the more we plotted our escape during our usual cappuccino hour at Café Anglais. California was a dream that would not leave us alone. The air seemed to be full of songs from the Beach Boys. Tony Bennett's "I Left My Heart in San Francisco" was on everyone's lips. Years later, I still got tears in my eyes hearing the Mamas and the Papas sing "California Dreamin'" and seeing ourselves sitting at Café Anglais, not knowing whether we would ever make it. We all did, except Reinhold, who saw his career opening up in Toronto and stayed despite the wind and cold.

One evening at Café Anglais, Edwin told me more details of his plan. Edwin was not just a big talker but also a shrewd operator. He could understand obtuse bureaucratic texts in English, which would take me many more years to grasp. Edwin could fill out complicated forms with ambiguous questions. He had familiarized himself with American immigration laws and changing immigration policies. He told me the following.

The 1924 Immigration Act had set quotas for immigrants based on their nationality and the ratio of that nationality in the entire US population as of 1890. The quotas heavily favored Northwestern Europeans, reduced immigration from the rest of Europe severely, minimized Asian immigration, and closed the doors to the rest of the world.

As of 1962, quotas from countries like Sweden, Britain, and Germany had not been filled. But a new immigration bill under consideration by Congress was about to change all that. Therefore, it was time to get into the US with no waiting period. But there was still one problem. One still had to have a sponsor, a US citizen who would vouch for the immigrant, that is, be legally responsible for them for five years. Typically this was done by family members or public organizations like churches.

The word at Café Anglais was that people with skills in high demand in the US, like nurses or chefs, would be given preference in the application process. Edwin and I figured we had to get more reliable information and went to the US consulate ourselves. There we were told that, yes, the German quota had not been filled. We were also told that Canadian residents applying for US immigration did not need a sponsor. They just had to show that they could enter the US with at least $1,000, which was a lot of money at that time.

The consular official pointed out that we would become full Canadian residents in a few weeks because we would have fulfilled the one-year residency requirement by then. On the way out, he gave us the immigration application forms and encouraged us to submit them as soon as possible, which we did. There was only one problem. I did not have $1,000 in my account at the time, only $500. I had loaned $500 to Horst, who had disappeared with it in Montreal. So I asked Reinhold to loan me $500 for a day so I could show $1,000 on my bank statement for the US consulate. It worked.

A few weeks later, we received our immigration papers in the mail and drank double scotches at Café Anglais all night long. The news spread quickly over the next few days, but our joy was not shared equally by everyone. Café Anglais was full of Eastern and Southern Europeans, Indians and Pakistanis, Moroccans and Turks, all from countries with low quotas. Some had applied for US immigration papers years earlier and were denied year after year. And here were some Germans who had hardly arrived in Canada and were already off to California. The US government was painfully aware of this inequity, and President Kennedy was pushing Congress hard to pass his much fairer immigration reform bill. But it would take three more years for it to become law. Peter and Josef followed our example, successfully applying for US immigration.

As planned, Edwin and I set our sights firmly on California, but now we had to find a way to get there. Edwin was usually a step ahead of me when it came to planning. He knew about the "Drive a Car West" deal many overstocked car dealers offered in the big eastern cities, especially Detroit. Dealers sitting on new cars that hadn't sold in a year needed the space for the latest models. They would have the unsold models driven to the West Coast and sell them as used cars. The dealers needed drivers, and they advertised for them in newspapers. The driver would pick up a car, usually in Detroit, and deliver it to a dealer in California, usually in Los Angeles. That took about a week, and the driver had to pay all expenses. And that's what we did too.

In August 1963, Peter drove us to Detroit, a four-hour drive from Toronto. The next morning we looked in a local paper for a "Drive a Car West" ad and found one. A Cadillac dealership gave us a new 1962 model. I think it was a De Ville. We had ten days to deliver it to a Culver City, California, dealership. We looked at the map and figured the quickest way was via Chicago, where we would take Route 66 across the US to Los Angeles. To see as much of the country as possible, we drove four to five hours every day in the morning and then explored all the new things there were to see during the rest of the day.

At the time, we did not know that the route had a special place in the hearts of the American people. Built in the early 1920s, it was the fastest route connecting Chicago and LA and was preferred by millions of travelers. An earlier song about the route, "(Get Your Kicks on) Route 66," enjoyed renewed popularity as we traveled on it while listening to Nat King Cole immortalizing it. We seemed to hear it on the radio every day, together with another song I could not get out of my mind for a long time: "Hello Muddah, hello Fadduh."

What struck us the most as we sped by so many interesting places was the vastness of the country. In Canada only Peter had a car, and we stayed close to home. Muskoka Lakes, about seventy miles north of Toronto, was about as far as we ever got. Now we had to travel a distance of more than 3,000 miles, driving eighty miles per hour. I figured going from Düsseldorf east 3,000 miles would take us to Siberia or Baghdad, Iraq. Germany, all of a sudden, seemed so small. We stopped in all of the bigger cities along the way (Saint Louis, Tulsa, Oklahoma City, Amarillo, and Flagstaff, among others) and many of the smaller ones and explored them as much as possible, usually by driving around the place, walking in the downtown area, and meeting people in local hangouts. We were impressed by the friendliness we encountered everywhere. Edwin had to do most of the talking. My English was still rudimentary. Our special interest was in Native Americans. We had both read Karl May and imagined finding Winnetou's descendants somewhere in the deserts of Arizona or New Mexico. There were several Hopi and Navajo pueblos along Route 66, and we visited as many as possible. When we got to Flagstaff, we drove to the nearby Grand Canyon and peered into the colossal abyss from the Bright Angel Trail.

NINE

California: Work, College, and Making UCLA

After our Grand Canyon visit, Edwin and I crossed the Mojave Desert and felt like pioneers or uprooted farmers of earlier days. As described in John Steinbeck's *The Grapes of Wrath*, this was where a lot of Okies and Arkies had struggled and perished during the Dust Bowl years, trying to make it to greener pastures in California. We followed the official warnings on highway signs and stocked up on water in case we got extra thirsty or our engine overheated. I guess we didn't have enough confidence in the power of our top-of-the-line, brand-new Cadillac. It only took a bit more than an hour to cross the desert in maximum comfort. It was still early in the morning when we arrived in Needles, a small border town by the Colorado River that divides Arizona and California.

In Needles, we learned that there had been a well-known government-run campground containing thousands of Dust Bowl escapees, making sure they would not overrun California. Edwin and I plunged into the Colorado River and swam to the Californian side, triumphantly celebrating the achievement of setting foot on Californian soil, despite the scorching heat. It was easily 100 degrees Fahrenheit and still getting hotter. But we were in California, shouting out that old German sailor song as loud as we could: "It's blow, boys, blow, for Californio, there is plenty of gold, so I've been told, on the banks of Sacramento!" I think we made it to Barstow that night and drove into Los Angeles the next day. We were still on Route 66 and faithfully followed it until the end.

In California, the road is better known as Will Rogers Highway and eventually merges with Santa Monica Boulevard, which leads to a bluff overlooking the ocean. We were in Santa Monica and I almost couldn't believe it—water and sand below, blue sky above. We parked our car and walked down to the beach. As far as we could see, there were girls, girls, and only girls, and they were all smiling.

I am sure there were guys too, but we blocked them out. School was out, and the beaches were packed. Edwin and I knew what to do. We went up the stairs of the bluff again and walked into the apartment building where our car was parked. It had a FOR RENT sign hanging outside. The building had a swimming pool. And again: girls, girls, and only girls.

We rented the apartment, and although it was a bit pricy, we managed. We had the car for three more days and tried to find jobs quickly. Edwin was lucky. Our apartment was across from the biggest hotel in Santa Monica, the Miramar. He applied for any opening they had and was immediately hired as a receptionist. My situation was more difficult. I introduced myself at the big department stores in Los Angeles and Beverly Hills and asked for a position as a decorator. But there were no openings. I found a position advertised in the want ads of the *Los Angeles Times* by a company with many department stores in larger shopping areas of the suburbs. They hired me, and I had to travel to all of them to take care of their window displays.

Someone in the apartment building where we lived sold me an old Ford Sunliner cabriolet on credit for $300, and things began looking up. But my English skills were still deplorable. I enrolled in a night course, English as a Second Language, at the Los Angeles City College. After two or three lectures, the teacher took me aside and said, "Don't come back here anymore. You will not learn English but Spanish." Indeed, almost all of my thirty-plus fellow students were Latinos, and they spoke almost exclusively Spanish with each other.

Arrived in Santa Monica, fall 1963.

The teacher told me to enroll in a course offered for American high school students who had failed basic required English for graduation and had to make it up. Students called this course "Bonehead English." I enrolled and was in a class with native speakers. We worked from a textbook that was clear enough for me to understand, but I scored miserably on tests. I routinely missed the spelling quizzes, which resulted in a failing grade for the course. "Not to worry," my teacher said, "just take it again." That is what I did, and I received a D. Despite the low grade, my English improved drastically because I was working in an English-speaking environment, and unlike in Toronto, my boss didn't speak German.

Soon life took on a regular pace but remained full of challenges. Edwin and I stayed around the swimming pool of our apartment, flirting with the stewardesses. Eventually Edwin fell for the prettiest one, Nancy. They often went on trips to Las Vegas, and one day they came back married. Nancy moved in with Edwin, and I had to move out.

Luckily I had somewhere to go. Peter had shown up from Toronto several months after Edwin and I arrived, and he immediately got a job as a car radio repairman with a large LA car dealer. But he always wanted to go to San Francisco, and since he had made plans to move, I was able to take over his lease. True to his style, he lived in a posh apartment in Hollywood at the corner of Sunset Strip and Doheny Drive. He had six more months on his rental lease and could lose a big security deposit if he moved out early. He convinced the landlady that I would take over the lease, and she would pay him back the security money in six months.

So I found myself in an expensive apartment complex in the middle of Hollywood with all sorts of would-be actresses and actors around the obligatory swimming pool. And I was dating. But it was not as exciting as it sounds. I was a nobody with a German accent. And everybody was looking for somebody who could advance their career. Some of the movie folks had bit parts in B movies and sat around the pool a lot, nurturing their perfect tans. I had no idea tanning was considered a science by some folks in Hollywood until I moved there.

I got to see people like Trini Lopez at the famous Whiskey a Go Go around the corner, Ella Fitzgerald at the Hollywood Palladium,

Shelly Manne at a jazz club in Huntington Beach, and many more well-known performers of the time.

Soon after Peter left, Josef showed up. He, too, wanted to live in San Francisco and followed Peter. Josef had always been a bit of a gambler and occasionally flew on the "gamblers' special" to Las Vegas. On one of those trips, a passenger shot the pilot and took more than thirty people with him to the ground. Josef was one of them. He was not even thirty years old.

A year after I started working as a decorator, I was laid off. The company eliminated the position and had the salespeople in the stores do their own window displays. Since I could not afford the expensive apartment on Sunset Strip anymore, I asked around for a cheap place to live and found a small room in a run-down one-story apartment complex on Pacific Coast Highway, right on the beach in Santa Monica. It was so small, the shower was on the outside. But I was only a few feet from the sand and a short walk from the famous Santa Monica pier. I took the room and fixed it up.

Many years later, during the 1990s, Hollywood made a TV series right in front of where I used to live that was watched by millions of people around the world, including in Germany. It was called *Baywatch*. By then, the area along the beach had been gentrified, and it would cost a fortune to live there. At the time, I rented it for $60 a month.

In the summer of 1964, I was twenty-six, unemployed, and lived by the famous Santa Monica beach. My motivation to rejoin the rat race took a severe beating every time I stepped out onto the sun-drenched white sand in front of my door and listened to the waves of the Pacific Ocean. But I had to pay bills and eventually had to think about a suitable career. I'd had it with window displays and considered an old dream from my coffeehouse days in Düsseldorf of becoming a stage designer or, better yet, a movie-set builder.

I lived a short walk away from Santa Monica City College (SMCC) and heard they had a well-known commercial arts program. I went there and learned that admission to the program required a high school diploma. I had been there before, in Düsseldorf, when I could not enter the Kunstakademie to study stage design because I had no Abitur. With that discouraging but unsurprising news, I went to the college cafeteria and ordered a hamburger. As I was shouting out my order, the guy in line behind me asked, 'Wo kommst du her?" (Where do you come from?) I turned around and he said, "Dein deutscher Akzent ist nicht zu verwechseln. Ich bin Peter aus Mannheim." (Your German accent is unmistakable. I am Peter from Mannheim.) "Ich komme aus Düsseldorf" (I am from Düsseldorf), I replied, and we sat down to talk.

Peter Arnold was a trained cook who came to the States under the "desired professions" clause of the immigration law, and he studied political science at SMCC. "How did you get into college?" I asked. He explained that he, too, was told to show a US high school diploma or the German equivalent. He presented his cook apprenticeship papers and the report cards of his trade schoo! (Berufsschule) in Mannheim. All apprentices have to attend one day of schooling per week to learn theoretical things about their trade. At the end of three years, apprentices graduate with a certificate and receive a report card. It does not have the standing of an American high school diploma. But the college admissions officer accepted it as an equivalent, provided Peter could pass a number of high school graduation make-up courses in various fields, all offered by the college.

Peter passed all of the courses with a grade of C or better and was matriculated as a bona fide full-time student. He told me to do the same. That particular admissions officer had bent over backward a lot to help Peter, and Peter told me how I could get the same treatment. First, I should not go to any other admissions officer. Second, while talking with him, I should wear tight pants and an open shirt and shake my blond beach hair a lot. It worked. The officer did try to grab my knees under the table, but I fended him off. He admitted me as a full-time student, pending the passing of some make-up courses.

I left the office feeling strange. I knew my life was about to turn a big corner, practically by a fluke. Later on, Peter and another German friend, also called Peter, who had also made it into SMCC by presenting himself in very tight pants to this particular admissions officer, celebrated my promotion to the academic world with a few tequilas. All three of us had made it from eighth grade straight into college, skipping high school altogether.

There was, of course, the money issue. The college was tuition-free for California residents. Residency required at least a one-year stay in the state, usually verified with a driver's license. I just made it. I had moved from Canada to California exactly one year before, as if I had planned it. There were, of course, the usual living expenses I had to pay somehow. Peter gave me some good advice about that too. He worked as a waiter and encouraged me to do the same. It's an ideal job for poor students. You work at night and study during the day. I had no idea about handling food and drinks in upscale restaurants, and I had to learn by doing it.

First, I worked as a busboy for a few weeks to learn the basics of table service. Then I applied for a job as a waiter at the Hungry Tiger Restaurant in Culver City, but I barely lasted a week. I made so many mistakes that the manager had to let me go.

A new restaurant—Trancas—opened at Zuma Beach, north of Malibu, and it was extremely upscale and expensive. Waiters had to wear tuxedos. Peter applied and was hired. Having worked in fancy places in New York City, he had an impressive résumé. Peter took the other Peter (the German who also made it into SMCC) and me along and introduced us as expert waiters. Then he told us to watch him and ask questions if we got stuck. We watched and learned. The other Peter had some experience and did better than I did. I was bad, but I didn't get fired. I could tell many stories testifying to my ineptitude, but here is just one that stands out.

To justify its outrageous menu prices, Trancas specialized in flambéing every dish possible. One was shish kebab on rice. The waiter rolled a cart with the dinner plates and several instruments next to the dining table. Then he took two soup spoons together in one hand, clapped a cotton pouch between their tips, dipped the pouch into a bowl of liquor, and held the soaked pouch over a burning candle until it caught fire. With the other hand, he lifted the skewer with vegetables and pieces of meat, subjected them to the flames by moving the burning pouch a few times back and forth underneath the skewer, drowned the burning pouch in a bowl of water, and voilà, your wallet was empty. It is, of course, crucial that the tips of the spoons holding the pouch point downward. Otherwise, the burning fluid of the pouch would run onto your hands. Well, that's what happened to me. To make things worse, rather than let the spoons drop to the floor, I tried to extinguish the fire in my hand by shaking them wildly back and forth. As a result, burning drops of alcohol flew all over the place. Peter watched me in horror and rushed to my aid. He got a burning drop in one of his eyes. I grabbed a glass of water from a table, threw it in his eye, and tried to minimize the damage. One of the burning drops had landed on his tuxedo and left a smoldering hole. He ran to the kitchen holding his eye. I saw guests stomping out little flames on the floor where the spoons had landed.

I joined in. So did the manager. None of the guests were hurt, so the manager told me to look after Peter, who had recovered. With a reddish eye and borrowed tuxedo, he entered the dining room. I had some minor burns on my hand and followed him. The whole dining room applauded. I did not, as I had expected, get fired that night. Perhaps another restaurant would have let me go immediately. But this was Trancas, a favorite hangout of many famous movie folks. And movie folks, I came to learn, like drama. It gives everyone something to talk about. Weeks later, one of my favorite movie stars at the time, Kim Novak, sat at one of my tables with a lucky boyfriend and gave me that look that said, "Okay, you are the one who is firing up the place around here. Keep it up." And I did.

At Trancas, we worked mainly on the weekends. While the tips were good, we needed more money to cover our daily expenses. Peter suggested joining the service workers' union. The union would refer members to employers. The best referrals were those for banquets in large hotels, like the Marriott or the Beverly Hilton. They would pay a 15 percent gratuity for, in many cases, very expensive meals. The fanciest place I ever worked was the Hotel Bel-Air. I only worked on room service and at the swimming pool. There, I met many stars. One in particular helped me out in a big way: David Niven, best known at the time for the classic film *Around the World in 80 Days*.

I was working as the waiter at the pool, and Mr. Niven came with his entire family (wife, three kids, plus a nanny) to swim and eat. They gave me their orders, and when the food was ready, I stacked the plates on a cart and wheeled it out to the pool. On the way to the table, one wheel dropped over the edge of the pool, and all the plates slid into the water. The lifeguard jumped in, trying to rescue the steaks, baked potatoes, and ketchup bottles. The Austrian maître-d' came running like a madman, ordering me back to the kitchen. After a while, he came to find me. He was red in the face and told me that he was going to fire me on the spot but that Mr. Niven had made him promise not to. The maître-d' wanted to know how I knew Mr. Niven. Of course, I didn't. I think Mr. Niven was just the kind of British gentleman he usually portrayed in his movies—reserved, understanding, and helpful.

I worked at the Hotel Bel-Air for quite some time and even got a friend, Fred Blumenstein, to work there too. I met Fred the way I met Peter, in the food line of the SMCC cafeteria. He was ordering, and I noticed his French accent. I was taking a French course then and tried some phrases on him. He laughed and said switching to German would be easier for him. We settled on English. He was a science major from Cannes, new to the area, and he lived with his grandparents in Beverly Hills. We decided to meet again and speak half French and half German. He liked jazz, and soon, on my days off, we would go to Hollywood bars to hear live jazz. Like me, he liked the French singer Charles Aznavour, and we took two pretty college students to see him when he performed at the Hollywood Palladium. What Fred liked best was using his French accent to bedazzle American girls, with mixed results.

I figured his worldly manners would match the posh style of the Hotel Bel-Air, and I asked him to join me working in room service. I told him he would see lots of movie stars. That interested him, and we worked there together for about six months.

Eventually, he invited me to his home, and I met his grandparents. I learned that they were Jews from Vienna. That explained Fred's initial hesitation to invite me. They lived in a large mansion in the middle of Beverly Hills. Fred's grandfather, Dr. Jodl, was a psychiatrist who personally knew Sigmund Freud and many of the other noted psychiatrists in Vienna before World War II.

After Hitler's takeover of Austria in 1938, the Jodls fled with their entire family to Cannes. They survived Vichy France and, after the war, emigrated to the US. I learned this bit by bit. The Jodls invited me over for dinner several more times and served schnitzel and Kaiserschmarrn before letting me know how much they missed Vienna.

Fred was an excellent tennis player and made the SMCC tennis team, an amazing feat considering that, at the time, California had more than half of all the tennis courts in the world and produced some of the best tennis players anywhere. Fred taught me some basic strokes before he left to continue his studies at the University of Colorado campus in Boulder, where he entered medical school and received his MD. Before he left, he married an Anglo girl from a conservative family steeped in the teachings of the Church of Christ. Afterward, we lost touch. I found out later that he practiced psychiatry in San Diego.

I kept working as a waiter, making enough money to stay afloat. My grades at SMCC improved, and things generally moved in the right direction. Soon, I got a note from the academic office asking me to see a guidance counselor. He wanted to know what I intended to major in. My first reaction was to say commercial arts. But thinking about my conversations with Fred, I said psychology. The counselor gave me a list of courses that would lead to a two-year associate of arts degree. It leaned heavily toward the natural sciences, which were required for admission into a bachelor of science program in psychology at any four-year college or university.

I quickly learned that I had stepped into quicksand. I had never gone to high school and therefore had never taken courses in chemistry or biology. I survived the make-up courses I had to pass to get admitted as a regular student, but just barely. I only passed biology because I cheated some on the final. But extensive knowledge in such fields was essential for getting the high grades needed to stay on the degree track.

Something else worked against me as well. Grades were given on a curve, even in many science classes. There were too many science students aiming for UCLA, and they set the curve so steep that I had trouble getting a C. I learned I was competing with students who had aced similar tests in high school, while the material was completely new to me. I would never outperform them, especially not with the then-popular multiple-choice tests, and therefore I would never get an A. Plus, the behaviorist psychology that dominated college teaching at the time, and the strict physical causality approach on which it was based, seemed to drain it of what interested me most, namely human mystery and soul-searching.

On the other hand, I got excellent grades in the humanities, particularly history and philosophy. Those tests were based more on essays, and I rapidly became a decent writer. Professors told me they liked my provocative way of putting things into novel perspective. I remember writing a term paper for American History in which I tried to show that it was perfectly logical for the Japanese to attack Pearl Harbor in 1941, given the behavior of the Americans in the Pacific before the attack. Well, what I did not fully realize then was that certain things, like the idea that the Japanese perpetrated a sneak attack on that "date which will live in infamy," became part of America's mental DNA and were better left untouched. My professor, belonging to a Lebanese immigrant family, liked the paper and gave it an A+. He and my philosophy professor suggested that I should consider a career in the humanities. So I went to the academic office and switched my major to history. It was a wise decision. My GPA at the time was barely above a C. The guidance counselor pointed out that any student who graduated from SMCC with at least a B average (3.0 GPA) would be automatically admitted to the University of California. My goal became clear.

In the spring of 1967, I received my AA degree from SMCC in social science with a high GPA and immediately applied for admission to UCLA and Berkeley. UCLA admitted me without reservation, but Berkeley wrote that I needed two more courses, which I could take at City College of San Francisco (CCSF). I wanted to go to Berkeley to experience San Francisco. Also, Berkeley's academic reputation was even higher than UCLA's, and it was consistently ranked among the top ten best universities in the US. I couldn't wait to go.

Additionally, Peter von Stelzer, my friend from Toronto, had a small car radio installation business in San Francisco, and he'd asked me if I could run it that summer so he could see his family in Vienna. I planned a farewell party with my friends in LA and left for San Francisco. Peter showed me how to run his business before he took off with his spicy girlfriend to Vienna. I stayed in his large apartment in the Mission District and drove his car.

For the next four months, I was supposed to collect all the money the business would make and pay all of Peter's bills. Peter's garage was near downtown. There, he installed car radios with huge speaker systems. He had a mechanic who did all the work. Peter did the managing, which, as it turned out, was a bit tricky. A customer dropped off their car in the morning, selected a radio with speakers from a catalog, and picked up the car again later that day with everything installed. Peter himself had no radios in stock. He would go to a large wholesaler in town, get the unit the customer had chosen, and have his mechanic install it. If the wholesaler was out of the unit the customer had ordered, Peter would call them and discuss their options; it usually worked.

Peter was dependent on the loyalty of his one employee. He was an excellent and fast worker and had been trained in the military, but he looked a bit like trouble to me. He gave Peter his word that he would stay with me until Peter returned from Vienna, but he didn't. Peter was hardly gone when his mechanic accepted a better-paying job at a large company. I called Peter about it, and he told me to hire someone else. I tried but couldn't find anyone. I closed the business and applied for a window display job. The famous department store City of Paris in downtown San Francisco hired me, and the pay was also good. However, that summer, CCSF did not offer the courses I needed to enter Berkeley the following fall. So I decided to enroll at UCLA. I went back to Santa Monica. I drove a brand-new car. Because of my secure job at City of Paris, a VW dealer sold me a brand-new VW Bug on credit, a car that would last me ten years.

UCLA admitted me as a regular student with a major in history. I received some financial aid, which covered part of my expenses. I returned to waiting tables to cover the rest. Things got much harder because UCLA was very demanding. I had to work at least twenty to twenty-five hours a week waiting tables to make ends meet.

Getting my footing at UCLA was difficult. Everything was extremely competitive. Top scholars, researchers, internationally known experts, excellent teachers, and about 25,000 eager students mingled on a small campus. Standards were extremely high, and I was intimidated. I no longer attended a small community college. My academic advisor reviewed the courses I had to take to graduate with a BA in modern European history. Aside from courses in my major, I had to take a number of courses in different academic areas, like natural sciences and literature. I had faced this challenge at SMCC and figured I could manage at UCLA as well. But it was more difficult.

For instance, my advisor suggested that I enroll in an "easy" logic course with a subject that overlapped with subjects taught in the humanities: Symbolic Logic, which would fulfill a natural science requirement. The course was taught by Alonzo Church, who had taught at Princeton for many years before coming to UCLA. He had also studied in Göttingen for a while, where Planck and Heisenberg had developed quantum mechanics and Einstein was a guest lecturer. I should have taken that as a warning. But I didn't. Church had written the textbook used in the course. Teaching assistants tried to guide us through the material that even advanced math students struggled with.

After two weeks of struggle, I went to Church and asked him if he thought I could get a C in his class. He would give me no guarantees. After two more weeks of burning the midnight oil, I gave up and dropped the course. Later, I took History of Biology instead and did much better. As I said, you had to find your footing at places like this, and that took time. To help me with this, I took several German literature courses, mainly for two reasons. I finally got to read German classics like Goethe's *Faust* and Schiller's *The Death of Wallenstein*. My favorite writer came to be Bertolt Brecht. The second reason was that these courses boosted my GPA. That was probably not fair. The courses were geared toward native English speakers, not German speakers. On the other hand, I had to work harder in the other courses precisely because I was not a native English speaker. And a high GPA was essential for getting into graduate school later on; I had to survive somehow.

TEN

Study Abroad: In Göttingen?

One day when I was visiting someone in the German department, I read a flyer hanging on the bulletin board inviting students to apply for a year-abroad study in Göttingen. Requirements were good academic standing and advanced knowledge of German. I met both and wondered if I should apply.

Of course, the flyer was not meant for people like me. I was a German citizen living in America with a green card. I had been raised in Germany and did not have to be introduced to the German way of life, as the flyer promised. But something else was on my mind. It had always irked me that back in Benrath I had seen many youngsters who went to university not because they were smart but because they belonged to the right class. Some of them were numb brains. I would have given anything to go back to Germany and tell the political establishment and educational leadership how backward German institutions were regarding equal opportunity, closing doors to talented and eager youngsters while opening them for less deserving ones, not only in education but in most other areas of society as well.

As a result, many young people left and tried their luck elsewhere, as I had done, which was a big loss to the nation's well-being. It was the spring of 1968, and many nations were full of civil strife for a number of reasons. The lack of equality at many levels of society was one of them. Unlike in Germany and Europe in general, in the US, inequality was not class-based as much as race-based. In the US, the Civil Rights Movement, led by Martin Luther King Jr., focused on removing legal and cultural barriers Blacks faced when trying to enter mainstream American life.

For instance, King repeatedly pointed out how discriminatory practices and laws denied Black children equal education, despite the Supreme Court's landmark decision in 1954 (*Brown v. Board of Education*), which led to the desegregation of schools. The German situation was less dramatic and ultimately resolved through a number of educational reforms at the political level, but not before students loudly voiced their demands in public protests. I felt I would also have to say a word on this issue. So I applied for the study abroad program and wrote a long essay supporting my desire to function as a living example of how the more equitable education system in the US, despite its obvious shortcomings, had allowed me to excel while the German system had held me back. I said that Germany needed to do much more to ensure equal educational opportunities for all of its citizens.

I had an interview with the study abroad selection board. They told me they had lots of applicants, and UCLA had only ten spaces available. But I knew I had them hooked because I told them something Americans like to hear. I said, "The US is the beacon of democracy in the world. By sending me to Göttingen, you can show the Germans that you gave a German an opportunity they had denied him." I truly believed what I said. They sensed it in my voice, and they granted me a spot in the study abroad program. I waited very long to become a US citizen, until October 2013, to be exact. But I have never felt as ready to become one as I did then.

Students had to pay some of the study abroad program costs themselves. So during the spring and summer of 1968, I looked for a better-paying job and applied for the position of head waiter at the Host International restaurant in the Theme Building at the center of Los Angeles International Airport. I got the job. The restaurant appeared to be hanging from two crossed arches like a flying saucer, with the four pillars representing the world's four corners. Sitting in the restaurant, one had an impressive view of the airport. When I started working there, *The Lucy Show* was producing one of its episodes at the restaurant, and I saw Lucille Ball up close.

The restaurant tried to have an elegant ambiance, and it featured a string quartet with a harpist playing popular film themes. But it also seemed to serve as a meeting place for shady characters. I remember an overdressed man with two underdressed women (see-through blouses were in vogue then), paying for dinner with a single hundred-dollar bill that he pulled from a case stuffed full of hundred-dollar bills. He shouted, "Keep the change!" as he disappeared into the elevator, flanked by his two beauties.

This restaurant saw many people going to or returning from Las Vegas, a twenty-minute airplane hop away. Many of them flew to gamble. Others went to party and get a weekend tan. Most of them were great tippers, especially when they weren't sober. My summer earnings were excellent, and I was looking forward to spending them in Germany.

Of course, everyone I knew in Germany was on high alert about my coming. I had left six years before, and no one knew whether I would ever come back. And there I was, landing at Frankfurt Airport with about fifty other University of California students in early August 1968. My best friend Günther picked me up and drove me to Düsseldorf while the other students boarded two buses to Göttingen. My parents and Erwin were overjoyed to see me, but the big surprise was Udo.

When I left, he was only a few weeks old. Now he was standing there with friends his own age. I remember grabbing the one six-year-old who I figured looked most like Erwin and giving him a big bear hug. But I had grabbed the wrong kid. Erwin pointed out the real Udo, and I have been trying to make up for this mistake ever since. Naturally, we had Kaffee und Kuchen, and we swapped stories as long as we could stay awake.

The next day, Günther and Hermann drove me to Göttingen, where I received a serious reprimand from the study abroad director, Reinhard Bendix, for having left the group at the Frankfurt Airport. The group had some meetings, and I was told that I underestimated the importance of those meetings, especially because I was a special case. Reinhard Bendix told me that the Ministry of Education and

Cultural Affairs of Lower Saxony had informed him that I could not attend the University of Göttingen because I was a German citizen and did not have the Abitur. No one had anticipated this problem before. If I had been an American citizen, like all the other California students, this would have been no problem. But being German, I had to apply for a Sonderregelung (exception), which had to be approved by the ministry. And that could take weeks if not months. In the meantime, I was allowed to enroll on a provisional basis. At least I could register for courses. Reinhard Bendix told me not to worry.

He understood the German bureaucratic mindset better than I did, and he promised to take care of things. Born and raised in Berlin, he was a professor at Berkeley and a globally recognized expert on Max Weber, one of the founders of modern sociology. Being of Jewish background, he and his family left Germany in 1938. And he started a remarkable academic career at the University of Chicago. He, too, was another example of how Germany had driven so many talented citizens to seek refuge in other countries, often because of persecution. I thought of my first boss in Canada and my first boss in California, both of whom were also Jewish.

In Göttingen, Bendix had a staff of several people situated in the large office of an impressive baroque building across from the university's main administrative building (Alte Aula). A small plaza (Wilhelmsplatz) separated the two, in the middle of which stood a large statue of Georg II August, elector of Hanover, who had founded the university in 1734. At the bottom of the plaque, it listed the elector's other titles, including king of Great Britain. My American fellow students repeatedly stopped at the statue, making sure they'd read it correctly. It was George III, George II's grandson, also elector of Hanover, who lost the American colonies to the revolutionaries and George Washington.

We lived in a nice student apartment building at the edge of town and could walk to class. As we were settling in, a political event occurred a bit more than 200 miles east that turned out to be of tremendous global importance. On the night of August 20–21, Soviet military forces invaded Czechoslovakia and occupied the city of Prague. In many Eastern European countries, the ruling Communist parties had run a tight Stalinist ship but had been facing calls for liberal reforms from the citizens and even many high-ranking party members, calls for greater autonomy from Moscow and more decision-making power at all levels of their respective societies. In Czechoslovakia, the reformers rallied around the party leader Alexander Dubček and called for "socialism with a human face." Their public demonstrations for liberal change and early successes in allowing more freedom of the press in early 1968 quickly came to be known as the Prague Spring. It had threatened Moscow's power monopoly over Czechoslovakia and all Eastern European countries. As a result, Moscow intervened militarily and put the Moscow-friendly Gustav Husak in power.

The world watched on television as courageous Czech citizens fought Russian tanks with rocks, sticks, and bare hands. More than a hundred people died within a few days. Many more were wounded. There were calls for the West to intervene. But as in 1953 in East Berlin and 1956 in Budapest, the West merely watched, wary of risking an atomic war. Many of us students felt that war was in the air. The Iron Curtain separated West Germany from East Germany just a few miles from Göttingen. People flocked to see the barbed wire and wondered what would happen next.

Göttingen was on the front line, and many public demonstrations in support of the civilians fighting in the streets of Prague were organized quickly. I participated. At one of the California student meetings, Mr. Bendix reminded us that we had signed papers stating we would not participate in any kind of political activity and could be dismissed from the program. I took that chance. A couple of other students did too. But for the most part, the California students kept their noses clean. They had come to learn the language, study German culture, see the beautiful countryside, and visit historic places, and not participate in politics. They were aware that most UC campuses had become places of student unrest. Berkeley in particular was an early center of student demonstrations, where the free speech movement of Mario Savio supported the Civil Rights Movement and called for an end to the Vietnam War. But for the most part they kept their mouths shut.

The events at the Berkeley campus had encouraged students at other campuses, in California and around the nation, to demonstrate too. I had joined several student-led antiwar marches at UCLA, always spontaneously, without a special focus, merely on the gut feeling that children should not be killed with napalm, as was increasingly shown on the evening news. After all, I had my own experiences in this area. From what I could gather during those days in Göttingen, I think I must have been the only California student who consistently joined the ranks of the demonstrating German students. The issues that German students demonstrated for, aside from liberalizing Eastern Europe, were the same that American students in the US were demonstrating for, with a strong focus on ending the war in Vietnam.

In addition, Germany had its own issue that loomed large, especially in student demonstrations. Students wanted to get rid of an entrenched "establishment" full of old Nazis and die-hard conservatives. I was drawn into this fight by German students. Eager to make friends quickly, I went into Brieke, a typical German pub on a main Göttingen drag. The pub was around 400 years old and looked it. It was packed with students drinking beer. I ordered a round of beer for everyone, and a second, and a third. I got their attention. And I had interesting stories to tell.

One student in particular, named Hans Glowka, couldn't get enough of it. He was a revolutionary type and he introduced me to his lefty friends. From then on, we met regularly at Brieke, and I learned how to identify students' political views and affiliations. The gamut ran from anarchist to conservative, and Hans leaned to the anarchist side. He introduced me to the leader of the Jungsozialisten (youth organization of the Social Democratic Party or SPD): Gerhard Schröder. Schröder, like Glowka, was one of the few people in the room who did not come from solidly middle-class stock. He had gotten his Abitur attending night school while apprenticing as a retail sales clerk during the day. His father had died during the war, and his mother worked as a cleaning woman in Hanover.

Schröder eventually became a lawyer, and in 1998, he became chancellor of Germany. He won reelection and served eight years before President Vladimir Putin helped him become a leading figure in the large Russian energy enterprise Gazprom. When, later in life, I was a professor at Plymouth State University in New Hampshire, I invited Chancellor Schröder (Gerd, I called him) to give a talk to our students and receive an honorary doctorate in return. He wrote back that he was strapped for time and would have to take a rain check. But in the

summer of 1968, none of us drinking beer at Brieke knew of our future. At the time, I stuck close to the lefties and became politically
involved myself.

I tried to visit my family in Düsseldorf as much as I could, but
it was a four-hour drive from Göttingen. I bought a cheap VW Bug
with the money I had earned waiting tables in Los Angeles, and off I
went. Whenever I had enough time, I took trips, usually with friends.
I traveled to Paris and Amsterdam a few times and also to Hamburg,
Munich, and Berlin. Berlin was a divided city, an island in the middle
of East Germany, with a western section (West Berlin) and an eastern
section (East Berlin).

From outside East Germany, Berlin could only be reached on des-
ignated roads. I visited East Berlin a few times and walked along the
infamous wall on the Communist side for hours, feeling surreal. The
wall ran through the middle of the city. And when the East German
government erected it in 1961, it divided closely knit communities
overnight, splitting many families. Anyone trying to cross the wall was
shot by border guards. More than 100 people shared this fate. Some
managed to get out by hiding in cars of mostly Western visitors and
some by building tunnels. When I saw the watchtowers along the wall
with machine gun–carrying guards, I could not shake the feeling that
they were harbingers of a coming war. I had a similar feeling when
traveling to Prague in March 1969.

Moscow had squashed the uprisings in reform-minded Czechoslovakia and installed a Russian-friendly hard-line regime propped
up with tanks. The invading forces remained. Russian patrols were visible in the center of Prague, while the country tried to project an image
of normality. Tourists were encouraged to visit again, though few did.
We were a bus full of students from Göttingen, eager to see what the
famous city looked like, despite Russian control. We figured control
would be tight when crossing the border, and indeed, one of us had
to shave off his beard because it was not on his picture ID. But once
in Prague, much to our surprise, we were largely free to go anywhere
without much supervision. We listened to the instructions of the tour
guide and then were on our own, splitting up into several groups.

There were not many tourists visible, and we were quickly spotted
by entertainment promoters, escort providers, and currency exchangers.

Our group stayed focused on the many famous sights, mainly Prague Castle, St. Vitus Cathedral, the Charles Bridge, and the glockenspiel of the large, 600-year-old astronomical clock outside the city hall on the old town square. We explored the house of Franz Kafka and listened to Mozart's music at the Laterna Magika, and much more besides.

Because of the very favorable exchange rate, everything was very affordable. I even bought the collected works of Marx and Lenin in one of those charming bookstores that served coffee and strudel and spoke of another world. Prague, in many ways, was still raw, smelling of centuries of rich history that seemed to make the present look surreal. I remembered that I had similar feelings when visiting Venice years earlier, at the time also a city without too many tourists. In both cases, I got the impression that the quiet sense of grace and beauty these cities emanated would soon, perhaps within my lifetime, be crushed by hordes of noisy pleasure-seekers looking for Starbucks.

A week later, we were back in Göttingen, hitting the books again for our classes. Among them were Marx's *Das Kapital* and Lenin's *Imperialism*. I fell deep into my studies. Initially, I had some problems finding the right courses in which to enroll. The German system and the European system in general (except in Britain) do not always distinguish clearly between undergraduate and graduate courses. My fellow Californian students, all undergraduates, were advised to take less advanced courses and worked with tutors provided by the program. As a native German speaker, I figured I would try some advanced (graduate-level) courses, but I found out quickly that the material was over my head.

For instance, I enrolled in an advanced seminar, The Russian Revolution. The professor smiled at me when he realized I could not handle Russian. I switched to The French Revolution at a lower level. The few French classes that I had taken at SMCC allowed me to at least read the French source material. I also took German Constitutional History and found my German colleagues were mostly law students.

I also had problems adjusting to the traditional lecture style still used in Europe at the time. Professors lectured continuously from lecterns, usually reading from prepared manuscripts, while students took notes. The manuscripts were often soon-to-be-published articles or books. It was difficult to follow the material presented unless one was highly interested in the subject matter. For questions about the material, one had to wait for the smaller seminars offered, perhaps the following semester.

I once interrupted a professor—a nationally known former Supreme Court justice lecturing on constitutional history—to ask for clarification of a term. One could hear a pin drop as students turned toward me. That just was not done. However, this was 1968, and as Bob Dylan informed us over the airwaves, "the tiiimes they aaarree chaaanging."

Some members of the SDS (Sozialistischer Deutscher Studentenbund) invited me to participate in their efforts to demonstrate against the hierarchical system of higher education, and I did. With signs reading UNTER DEN TALAREN, DER MUFF VON TAUSEND JAHREN (under professorial gowns dwells the stench of a thousand years), we demanded open communication structures, with professors and students sharing the same platform. As a representative of the Fachschaft Geschichte, I participated in a weeklong conference of many student groups calling for an end to the old lecture system.

The conference produced a lengthy summary statement titled "Hat die Vorlesung noch eine Chance?" (Does the lecture system still have a future?). I was cited as one of the four authors. I sent an original copy to Chancellor Gerhard Schröder in 2000, when I invited him to give a lecture to our students at Plymouth State University, to show him that once we had been in the same fight. I don't know how much of my lefty activities were known to the administrators of our study abroad program at the time, especially Reinhard Bendix, but I was never approached about anything. One night I took out Bendix's daughter, who participated in the program as well, and she assured me I was safe.

I took two more noteworthy trips during my year in Göttingen: one to Turkey and Greece during spring break and one to Spain and Morocco in the early summer. In California, I had to read Homer's *Iliad* for my ancient history course, and I wanted to see the city of Troy immortalized in that epic novel. I had also always been fascinated by the life of Heinrich Schliemann, a German merchant who, with no archaeological training, used his acquired fortune as a fur trader to dig for the lost city that had alluded experts in the past. He found it by taking the right cues from Homer's writings. I also wanted to visit the ancient cities of Ephesus, Pergamon, and Athens. Günther decided to come along.

Years earlier, Günther had hitchhiked his way around Greece and Turkey and stayed several months in Istanbul, where he picked up some Turkish phrases that later came in handy. We traveled by train, bus, and boat, constantly searching for the cheapest routes. We spent a couple of weeks in Istanbul, which looked like one big, noisy bazaar where everyone wanted to sell something and nobody wanted to buy anything.

Günther knew the city and took me to corners even Turks tried to avoid. We got lost in the maze of narrow streets and had to ask little boys, in Turkish, how to get out. Of course, we visited the Blue Mosque, Hagia Sophia, Topkapi Palace, and much more.

Our next stop was Troy, and despite our maps of the region, it was hard to find. We only succeeded because Günther knew how to ask bus drivers how to get there.

When we got close, the bus driver told us we had to walk the last few miles. There were no signs: just a barren landscape and a few mud houses. We were on the road to one of the most famous cultural sites in Western history, but it was difficult to find. A small wood-framed building where we could buy tickets and a little booklet awaited us. We spent many hours there and only came across two other visitors, also students from Germany.

Getting back was difficult because buses did not seem to follow a schedule, if they ran at all. One had to wait by the roadside until a bus showed up, which could take hours. Our experiences in Pergamon and Ephesus were similar. I remember a handful of tourists at Ephesus. When I went back there in 2016, thousands of tourists were processed through a row of turnstile entrances and, like cows in a herd, shuffled through the main street of this ancient town without much of a chance to rest and contemplate the sites without being run over by the people behind them. I assume the same happened to Troy and most other historical places in the region and around the world.

Later in this trip, Günther got robbed in Istanbul, and we had to continue with only half of our travel budget. On the way back to Germany, I got stuck in Athens for a week, waiting for Günther to wire money to me at the Western Union office there. He had friends from whom he could borrow money in Bari, Italy, and we had had barely enough money for him to take a ferry there. The plan never worked, and he couldn't get ahold of me. Eventually, I learned how to get money by donating blood at a hospital. I figured that giving 400 ccs, twice the allowable amount, would pay my hotel and train fare to Düsseldorf. The folks at the hospital went for my sob story, and I soon boarded the train, drained but still standing.

My trip to Spain and Morocco was equally adventurous. I traveled with two friends from my Göttingen exchange student group. We went in my VW Bug and hit some familiar towns in Spain first (Barcelona, Valencia, Granada, Málaga), then crossed the Strait of Gibraltar and were off to Fez, Marrakech, and Casablanca before heading back to Spain. Marrakech, in particular, made a lasting impression on us. It seemed like an enchanted town of yore such as I had encountered in my readings of *The Thousand and One Nights*. And I see it vividly before me every time I hear Maurice Ravel's *Boléro*.

One other thing stood out. At a beach close to Casablanca, we were putting up our tent when I decided to go for a short swim. I swam quite a way out and tried to get back when I noticed I had drifted farther away from land. No matter how hard I tried to make it ashore, I was pulled farther and farther away. I panicked and screamed at my two friends, but they didn't notice me. All the while, they became smaller in size. Obviously, I was in the middle of a current pulling me out into the ocean. I tried to swim parallel to the shoreline, hoping to escape the current. Then I frantically swam to the shoreline at an angle. It didn't seem to work at first, but I had no choice but to continue, despite my aching arms. After what seemed like an eternity, I noticed the land was slowly getting closer again. I had left the current. When I returned to our campsite, my friends were not surprised that I had stayed out over an hour. They thought I was a good swimmer and knew what I was doing. I looked fine, and they didn't take my story too seriously. But it still scares me today.

When we crossed back into Spain, the border guards found a long hashish pipe in my car, an art piece I had bought as a souvenir. That was not what the guards wanted to hear. In 1969, Spain was still a fascist regime, run by Generalissimo Franco. And we did indeed look like a bunch of dopey hippies. As a result, they took my Bug apart.

We spent hours answering questions, sweating in the sun. When they found nothing else incriminating, they let us pass. Off to Seville we went. Then came Córdoba, Toledo, and Madrid. We saw all the sights, and everything was impressive.

What mostly stuck in my mind was the music the Roma played in Granada below the Alhambra and along the street that went up the hill to the caves where most Roma lived. I can still hear their passionate flamenco guitars today.

After my return to Los Angeles, I went to many Spanish guitar concerts but could never find the same authentic spirit displayed by the Roma of Granada. When I returned in 2016, little of that spirit remained in the public areas, and only a few high-priced establishments promised fiery performances to weary tourists in search of excitement.

Back in Göttingen, I had to accept that my time as an "American exchange student" was coming to an end. Göttingen had grown on me. I would miss my friends, especially Hans, and some girls I had met as well. For a while, I considered staying, getting a German degree and perhaps working as a high school history teacher. But there were two things strongly working against that idea. To continue my studies in Germany, I would have to pass the Kleines Latinum, a comprehensive language exam in Latin required of almost all students during the early part of their curriculum. My friends told me there were courses I could take to prepare for it and that they would help me. But the same friends also told me that they would give anything to be able to go to California and study at UCLA. They played "California Dreamin'" by the Mamas and the Papas to me while getting high and told me they would visit me at the Santa Monica beach. So I went back, and Hans came to see me a few years later.

ELEVEN

Back in California:
Trying to Cope

When I arrived at the Los Angeles airport in August 1969, the papers were full of articles about public protests nationwide, especially on college campuses, most of them demanding an end to the Vietnam War. Many articles focused on how the White House tried to obtain a victory by subjecting Vietnamese civilians to heavy napalm bombing. President Nixon had been elected in November of the previous year with the promise to bring "the conflict' to an end. But all indications showed otherwise. Also, the civil rights struggle of the early sixties was far from over, and large crowds were moving, especially in urban areas, demanding peace, justice, and equality.

There were also other headlines dominating the papers and TV news hours at the time. A string of murders had just been committed by a group of young people centered on a cultish leader called Charles Manson. They had entered homes, apparently at random, in the well-to-do sections of LA and slaughtered people in cold blood, bragging about what they'd done. Welcome home, I thought as I called my old roommate in Santa Monica, Peter Arnold, to pick me up at the airport.

He had kept the old flat and cared for my VW Bug while I was gone. However, his newest girlfriend had moved in with him, and I had to find my own place quickly, which I did. Peter had a waiter's job lined up for me, and soon I was back to normal.

Classes at UCLA started a few weeks later, and I had to make sure my studies for my BA in history were complete by the end of the 1969 fall term. All went well, and I had to decide where to apply for graduate studies. I considered some fancy schools like Berkeley again and Stanford, as well as East Coast places like NYU and Rutgers. But I knew that even if I was accepted, I could not afford to attend those schools. But UCLA was possible because of connections I had for easily finding work in fancy restaurants with good tips. I applied to the UCLA grad school first, got excellent recommendations from my professors, and did well on the required entrance exams, and I was in. I even got some financial aid, a low-interest student loan and a work-study budget, meaning I could work up to twenty hours a week on campus for student wages.

In January 1970, I enrolled as a proud graduate student of history at the by now very familiar UCLA. Though I was prepared to take on the challenge, I had no idea how tough things would become.

I had made up my mind to concentrate on modern European history with a focus on Germany. The expert in the field was Peter Loewenberg. I introduced myself to him, and he agreed to serve as my advisor and help me to earn an advanced degree. After I had taken some courses with him, I told him of my critical view of his historical methodology. He explained historic events primarily as results of mental dysfunctions of principal individuals and groups, using Freudian psychoanalysis as his tool. The main focus of his studies was the Holocaust, and he based his views on such scholars as Erik Erikson, Peter Gay, and Bruno Bettelheim. It was a very popular approach at the time, especially in academic thinking at elite universities. But as much as I tried to apply the psychoanalytic method in my work and papers, Freud's descriptions of the human unconscious and subconscious collided with my general desire for more clarity. Loewenberg sensed my critical attitude, and we soon had a falling out.

I came to lean on Professor Peter Reill for help navigating the academic maze of the history department. His expertise was the history of the German Enlightenment, and we hit it off quite well. He eventually advised me to take courses with a new professor in the department, Hayden White, who focused on the intellectual history of modern Europe. He warned me that White was very demanding and dropped students without qualms if they didn't meet his standards. I decided to try it, and in retrospect, it was one of the best decisions I have ever made. From day one, I was impressed by White's clarity of thought, depth of knowledge, inquisitive reach, and sheer delight in probing uncharted and controversial territory. I got hooked quickly.

Trying to keep up with my studies, I was immediately pressed for time like I had never been before. I took the usual full-time course load and could not always find enough time to meet deadlines, for two main reasons. To make money, I had to spend most weekends waiting tables in fast-paced Hollywood restaurants. Also, I became more politically active than I could afford to be.

Shortly after my return from Göttingen, I walked by a table at the Student Union building that was recruiting members for a group called SWAC (Students and Workers Action Committee). I had been politically active in Göttingen but refrained from joining any organizations there because it could have meant dismissal from the exchange program. Back in the States, I also faced problems as a green card holder who could be deported if I were to engage in unconstitutional activities.

I got into a discussion with some SWAC members about their views and activities. SWAC was a campus-based Trotskyite group of mostly students who tried to link up with working-class people to form a worker-student coalition to establish a highly egalitarian society by dissolving the existing socioeconomic class-based system. The ultimate result would be a classless, democratic, and communist society.

I got into a heated discussion with them, trying to explain contradictions in their presentations. But they had studied Marx, Lenin, and Trotsky and insisted that the capitalist system as it existed was doomed to fail. The question was only when and how. They argued that lasting change for the better could only be achieved at the hands of exploited workers through organized collective action. Workers needed enlightenment about their state of exploitation in a profit-driven society and instructions on possible ways to change it, which was where students could be of help.

SWAC had a newspaper that regularly reported on labor issues in the LA area and encouraged workers to take action on their own behalf whenever possible. I was told that SWAC strongly rejected any dictatorial Stalinist notions found in many programs of other socialist and communist organizations. This was all familiar to me. Given the political climate of the US and elsewhere at the time, talk about the collapse of Western capitalism was gaining more and more ground, especially among younger people. I joined SWAC and soon became the "expert" dealing with the corrupt practices of labor union bosses in the construction business of the LA area. None of the thirty-plus SWAC members had a working-class background. Most had gone to elite schools and couldn't shake off their bookish knowledge of Marxian dialectics. Probably half came from Jewish homes and felt a duty to fight growing signs of fascism they detected in the apparent efforts of capitalist leaders to maintain an unsustainable race for ever higher profits. Such signs were manifest in the brutal destruction of the Vietnamese people and the continuation of Jim Crow racism despite the passage of the Civil Rights Act of 1964.

SWAC members were impressed that I had been a steelworker and typesetter, among other things, in Germany. They put me in touch with union members who had the inside scoop on corrupt union practices. I became close to some members of the construction workers' union LiUNA Local 300 in East LA.

Local 300 was run by a Mexican family that considered the union its little kingdom. My biggest problem reporting on union events was my lack of Spanish. The SWAC news came out every few weeks, whenever we could manage, and was distributed by us in front of the establishments we covered in the paper. We were threatened by the management and security guards of these establishments, which we expected. Most incidents ended peacefully, and only one is noteworthy.

A mechanic of a large machinery manufacturing company contacted us and asked whether we could write a flyer about unsafe labor practices that ruined workers' health and distribute it inside the factory directly to the workers. We agreed. I and another person decided to do it. This would be a raid, and we developed a plan. It required us to enter the secure premises unnoticed and exit safely after distributing the flyers. We had to look like factory workers, including wearing the company hard hat, and we had to act like we were familiar with the place. The mechanic smuggled us in with his closed-in pickup truck and told us the front gate and its side door were always open. We just had to be fast enough to distribute the flyers and get out before management got alarmed, fifteen minutes tops.

After about ten minutes, someone identified us as fakes and called for security, and we quickly walked toward the front gate, which was about a hundred yards away. Security guards tried to stop us physically while they read the flyer. They started to punch us and yelled obscenities. We did not defend ourselves, but we threatened them with lawsuits if we were harmed. We got out through the gate largely intact. But the road to the factory was half a mile long, with fences on either side. Still, we were on public land and we were safe. Except the security guards tried to provoke us, including by running their car into us. They also took pictures. We continued calmly, dodging all provocations, and told them that touching us would cost them dearly.

Eventually, we made it to a busy area, split up, and roamed around until we thought they had lost us. The mechanic told us later that the raid had been a great success, and workers were seriously discussing safety issues. However, I decided never to expose myself in such a fashion again, as I didn't want to risk losing my green card and being deported for "communist" (that is, unconstitutional) activities. SWAC was a self-professed Marxist organization. For the government, that was sufficient grounds for proving its unconstitutionality.

I continued working for SWAC, which included some appearances on the lefty radio station KPFK. I stopped working for KPFK when I realized that the airwaves were the first thing government agencies would surveil. I was also falling behind in my studies. And I needed to work more shifts as a waiter to pay my bills. In those days, I often felt torn. During the day, I studied corporate greed leading to the downfall of capitalism and wrote articles for SWAC about LA construction workers—many of whom were illegal immigrants who had to pay the bill for this greed—and at night I would play the well-behaved servant of people I blamed for the mess we were in. I worked in some of the most elegant places in LA and sometimes couldn't hide my dismay. My sloppy work wasn't always a result of inefficiency. It was mostly emblematic of my "I don't care" attitude.

I could write a long treatise on many fumbling experiences I had working in the service industry. But here I will note just one more that occurred at the exclusive California Yacht Club at Marina del Rey. In 1968, the club hosted the crew that had just won the prestigious America's Cup. One of the crew members was Black, and the club was known for not admitting Black members. When the crew entered the decked-out hall, the Black crew member asked for a separate table, where he sat by himself in protest. I was assigned to be his personal waiter. As much as I tried to let him know that I, a lefty student from UCLA, was on his side and fully understood his action, he completely ignored me. He sat silently throughout the ceremony, away from his fellow crew members, not touching anything. I am sure I was just another privileged member of the white establishment to him. Later, I often wondered whether he was not completely wrong. This experience motivated me even more, trying to understand what was wrong with society and how to fix it.

TWELVE

Getting Serious Academically: Starting the Dissertation

By early 1971, I had become a member of Hayden White's coterie, a circle of about ten students, mostly PhD hopefuls. Only one was a woman, and she assured everybody that, in case anyone thought otherwise, she was not looking for amorous attention and was as serious about studying history with the demanding Professor White as everyone else. She obviously felt it important to let us know that philosophic issues should no longer be thought of as a male domain. All of us were driven by a desire to understand the world and our place in it as best we could by using the ideas of the best minds it had produced. Our interests were highly interdisciplinary, with a strong bent toward philosophy and literature. Most of my fellow students had enviable educational backgrounds and could talk at length about the great works of Western civilization. They generally thought of themselves as radical anti-authoritarian thinkers and subscribed to various revolutionary doctrines based on such thinkers as Sartre, Heidegger, Nietzsche, Jung, and Marcuse.

White thought of himself mainly as Hegelian and explored new modes of consciousness with the help of literary critics like Kenneth Burke and Northrop Frye and critical thinkers like Jacques Derrida and Michel Foucault. Seminar discussions were often heated, with everyone trying to show that they understood the subjects more deeply or more originally than everyone else. White encouraged all statements and objections and had the gift of showing the merits and faults of each argument with comments that left everyone feeling as though they'd really learned something of significance. He generally supported any presentation as long as it showed some clarity of thought or poetic vision. If either was missing, he could be outright nasty. He once returned a paper to me that I had worked on for weeks and, in front of the entire seminar, exclaimed, "Horst, reading this paper is a waste of time. Write it again. And put some thought into it." I wasn't the only one who was crushed in this way. But White appreciated it when you returned and shined with fresh ideas and greater clarity. He would reward it with increased attention. However, some students could not take his honest approach. They enrolled in one seminar and never came back. He liked small seminars with students he could challenge and engage personally.

At the time, we didn't know that White was writing the book that would make him famous: *Metahistory*. We just knew he was working on something that took up most of his time. He once explained the larger scheme of his book to me, its many layers of interpretative strategies, ultimately based on linguistic categories, but it was too complex for me at the time. However, when the book came out in 1973, I recognized all the important elements in it—philosophical, ideological, literary, and linguistic—because he had discussed them with us in his seminars. The book weaves all of them together in one all-encompassing mental construct that reads like a declaration of war on the historical profession. It should have come as no surprise to us, especially given his views about history as expressed in his article "The Burden of History," published in 1966 in the journal *History and Theory*. There and in *Metahistory*, White tries to show that, ultimately, history as an academic field has no standing on its own and, at best, is an exercise in presenting human experiences in narrative form with the help of literary tropes. History is not what people discover in the past but what they create in their minds using facts of their choosing.

Therefore, understanding history has to start with examining the process of its mental creation. This is ultimately a Kantian position, and White left no doubt about his indebtedness to this great philosopher.

Metahistory indeed established Hayden White as one of the great American thinkers and cultural critics along the lines of Arthur O. Lovejoy and Kenneth Burke. This newly acquired attention also meant increased demand for his time. My efforts to hunt him down for serious talks on my dissertation plans became more difficult. White also did not want to waste time on students with uncertain prospects. I had told him in 1971 that I wanted to write a dissertation on the German Marxist thinker Walter Benjamin, who died in 1940 trying to cross into Spain while fleeing Nazi Germany. Benjamin had lived a colorful life as a cultural critic and had been associated with the left-leaning Frankfurt School. Writing about his life would have allowed me to delve deeply into the nature of the most dramatic conflict of the twentieth century, the struggle between communism and fascism, exemplified by the life of one wise individual. White initially agreed, but he later told me that the conflict so far had been explained almost exclusively from communist and liberal perspectives, ignoring fascist perspectives, which should be taken into account if it was to be properly understood. He suggested writing about an event, movement, institution, or figure that would help me to understand "right-wing" thinking based on "right-wing" principles as presented by "right-wing" thinkers. He gave me a couple of weeks to come up with something.

When I returned, he could see that I objected to his suggestion. He engaged me in a conversation about the scholar's obligation to probe new territory through personally acceptable lenses as well as objectionable ones. In other words, if you want to understand Hitler, do not only read Marxists or liberals, and if you want to understand Marx, do not only read fascists or liberals.

More to the point, try to understand why Marx made sense given the philosophical principles he used to construct his worldview. Do the same for Hitler or anyone else. Failing that, I could still become a learned scholar but not an understanding one.

White brought up a scientist, the originator of German vitalism, Hans Driesch. He said he had always wondered whether there was a conceptual affinity between Driesch's theory of vitalism and fascism.

He told me this would make a great dissertation. My gut response: absolutely not. Driesch was an early twentieth-century experimental biologist. And the only biology course I had ever taken was the make-up course at Santa Monica City College, which I barely passed with a C, and that was *after* some cheating on the final. Moreover, to see fascism through the lens of a fascist writer, as White suggested, seemed objectionable to me.

White gave me a few days to think it over. I rushed to the library and found that Driesch was one of the earliest embryologists, had studied under the famous Darwinist Ernst Haeckel, and ultimately tried to disprove the Darwinian theory of evolution by demonstrating that life, in all its facets, was the result of an intangible force, "élan vital," creative throughout the universe. He echoed the principles of the earlier Naturphilosophie (natural philosophy). This theory argues that nature manifests a grand design and does not result from random actions, as Darwin's law of natural selection suggests. I saw a real challenge here when White told me that most of the source material was in German, and I told him I would do it. Then White suggested I should shed some needed light on the matter by first explaining Driesch's theory of life formation based on his biological experiments and show the wider implications for other areas, including political ideologies. I agreed, but I had a few things to take care of first.

My scientific background was deplorable. Driesch was a trained biologist/zoologist, and his theory was based on observational data gained in the laboratory. To learn more about the field of biology during Driesch's time, I enrolled in upper-level history of science courses, where I sat mostly with science students needing to fulfill a history requirement, while I was a history student needing to fulfill a science requirement. Fortunately, no one had heard about Driesch. However, some had heard of Henri Bergson, his French counterpart.

Driesch had performed and published embryological experiments on sea urchins. In 1892, he discovered that when sea urchin embryos were separated at the two- and four-cell stage, they would grow into two or four fully developed, though smaller, sea urchins. He concluded, first, that all cells had equal potential to grow into an adult specimen and, second, that this could only be the result of an intelligent agent directing this growth, a vital spirit, "élan vital" according to Bergson, or "entelechy" according to Aristotle. Driesch called the theory he built on these findings "vitalism."

To see the full truth of his theory, he developed his own methodology. The modern scientific method of hypothesis, experimentation, and conclusion was unreliable, he argued. This method worked on the assumption that the human mind at birth is an empty slate, a tabula rasa, according to David Hume, on which experiences leave their mark throughout life a posteriori. But Driesch argued that, according to Kant, the mind organizes these experiences with principles given to it a priori, that is, preceding the experiences. Accordingly, hypotheses describing experiences considered to be true had to be grounded in these categories. Kant had made it his life's work to put together a final set of categories, such as unity, plurality, and totality. According to Driesch, the existing scientific method had to be restructured accordingly. But he also argued that Kant had missed one category crucial to understanding life, namely uniqueness. The category of uniqueness gives the mind the ability to recognize an object intuitively as something that is unlike any other object without having to refer to any other object. Since no two objects in the world are identical, this seemed to be a logical position. But Driesch had to show how his new category fit into Kant's finite table of categories. That was not an easy task.

Those who, like Driesch, have studied Kant in detail generally agree that the world was not the same after him. Much like Copernicus, he had turned the world downside up. After Copernicus, no one argued that the sun moves around the earth, but that, in fact, the reverse is true. And after Kant, no one argued that the world is what the senses perceive it to be but rather what the mind tells us it is. And when Driesch attempted to show that Kant had missed a crucial category, he was up against something big. To follow his arguments, I had to read Kant's *Critique of Pure Reason*, among other works, explain Driesch's critique of the *Critique*, and then show how Driesch corrected Kant's assumed errors by adding the missing category of uniqueness. This was only one aspect of coming to terms with Driesch's vitalism.

Driesch tried to show that his vitalism disproved Darwin's theory of evolution. According to Darwin, life evolved and progressed through endless struggles for existence in which the strong prevails and the weak perishes. In this way, nature blindly selects what stays and what goes. Darwin called it the "law of natural selection." This, Driesch maintained, was a mechanical process where life, in all its manifestations, was the result of physical laws acting on dead matter. Darwin and his followers, including Driesch's mentor Ernst Haeckel, did not tire of pointing out that philosophers and scientists through-out the ages had failed to provide scientific evidence that life had an independent existence of its own, leaving the subject to faith and spec-ulation. Driesch thought he was one of the first scientists to produce such evidence.

His works received wide attention, even though his experiments on sea urchins could not be duplicated on other animals, such as frogs. His theory that life was a manifestation of nonmaterial vital forces op-erating in the material world and not a result of laws that inhered in the material world itself got wide attention both in and outside aca-demia. Some of his many works were translated into several languages, and he soon assumed full professorships at Köln and Leipzig. The ram-ifications of the theory spread quickly and widely. He lectured in many countries, including the US. His ideas appealed to people who believed in and searched for something meaningful beyond the often oppres-sive and seemingly random trappings of the material world and estab-lished religions.

In my dissertation, I tried to show the larger context of Driesch's theory, its historical origins, scientific merits, and appeal to various groups, including the attraction it held for people advocating conser-vative and fascist ideologies. I started by reading all of Driesch's works and took diligent notes. My work took many twists and turns for a variety of reasons.

First, I had to pass the written and oral PhD exams. They were very difficult, especially the written ones. I took them in March 1973. Hayden White administered them. He handed me a set of questions on various intellectual history topics and gave me several hours to write down my answers and reflections. I struggled but I passed. The follow-ing oral exam I nearly failed. I was questioned in five fields: modern European intellectual history, my main field; the history of modern science; modern German literature; medieval/early modern history; and political science. The professor with whom I had taken medieval/early modern history (Claus Peter Clasen) did not want to give me a pass. Like me, he was a German immigrant and spoke with a German accent. And it was obvious that I had not prepared for his questions as much as I had for the other four's. Also, I believe he was trying to show the other professors that he was not going to pass me merely because we had similar backgrounds. For example, he asked me detailed questions on minute differences between theological positions held by various Lutheran factions, which I did not answer to his satisfaction. He knew I admired the (to him) "revolutionary" Hayden White and that I spent most of my time studying his material, reading too much Marx and Hegel, to the neglect of Luther, Melanchthon, and the Middle Ages. He made my passing contingent upon a long paper I had to write on a topic on which I had demonstrated a particular weakness. But I did pass. Not passing could have been traumatic.

I had a German friend in mind who had failed his PhD orals in Byzantine history and later worked as a manager at a McDonald's in my hometown of Düsseldorf. The story at UCLA was that only one out of six students in PhD programs would actually manage to earn a doctorate. Many would leave with a "terminal" MA, a sign of defeat. Plus, Hayden White was known for not accepting initial submissions of dissertations, demanding lengthy revisions or complete rewritings. More than twenty years later, when White and I spoke over the phone, he told me that one of the students in our group, Burkovici, had finally finished his dissertation. It took me "only" six years. But those six years were full of adventure.

THIRTEEN

Meeting Sue and Our Adventures Together: Mexico

In 1973, I not only passed my PhD exams but also met the true love of my life, Sue. At this point, I was thirty-five years old and still unmarried. And yes, I'd had affairs. Some longer, some shorter, but all associated with the usual drama of trying to make things fit when they don't or no longer do. And for a number of reasons, I was a difficult case for any woman. For as long as I can remember, I have been a restless spirit, always unsatisfied with what I had and angry with the rules of life that worked against me. Most people feel that way. But most people also eventually adjust to the circumstances they find themselves in, play the cards they have been dealt, and try to find contentment with what they have. I was no exception. But I kept the hope that I would find true love someday if only I could hang on a little longer.

My greatest gripe with life when I grew up in Germany was the feeling that other people were holding me down in my efforts to advance. Like most of Europe at the time, Germany was still very class conscious. One was born into a specific class at birth, and there were strong feelings that you could not escape your station. During my Boy

Scout years, I had friends from families that belonged to the "solid middle class" (gute Bürgerschicht), while I belonged to the "working class" (Arbeiterklasse). To us kids, it didn't seem to matter at first. But when the middle-class kids started high school (secondary school) while the working-class kids had to remain in primary school (Volksschule, today Hauptschule), I felt betrayed, especially because I felt that I was smarter than many of the kids going on to better schools and universities and greater positions in life.

Most of my working-class friends dealt with this injustice one way or another, and many did quite well, despite the obvious limitations. But I was not easily reconciled and I developed a bitter resentment against society as a whole. This resentment carried over into my relationships with women. For instance, when I was a decorator apprentice at Hertie in Düsseldorf, I had the opportunity to date some pretty girls who also worked there. It was no surprise that, by and large, they envisioned a partner hopefully above their station, a student or a son of a well-to-do family.

Parents told their daughters early on to "marry up." I could play that part to some degree. After all, I had early intentions of switching from decorating windows to building stage props. But I couldn't get into the required art academy because I had no high school diploma. But that's not what I told the girls. I built myself up, as all of my friends did. But the game was usually up when money came into play.

At that time, guys paid for entertainment, expecting amorous favors in return. We working-class guys were small on the first and big on the second. The resulting conflicts were predictable. And everyone was looking for true love despite the odds. Of course, it sometimes came true for someone else or in the movies. And hope never dies.

My struggles to make it as an immigrant in Canada took most of my energy. But there always seemed to be time for dating. My experience with Canadian women was that they had poor flirting skills. Even when they tried, they looked awkward. They generally dressed without style. They hid their legs in ugly-looking pants while presenting their boobs in licentious manners to "knock you out." On the positive side, I found Canadian women, and men for that matter, to be patient and nonjudgmental listeners, which was refreshing, given my German background full of opinionated hotheads. This was a great help, given that I knew little English and tried to keep conversations going by asking for the names of things, often by pointing or drawing sketches on napkins. In Canada, most women were eager to help. Many were also eager to learn more about Europeans, as they had heard that in Europe young people were more sexually liberated. Those were the days when it was an advantage to be French, or at least to look French, or fake being French. My stereotypical Nordic look made me appear more like the barbarian male they were seeing in the many Nazi movies Hollywood was producing at the time. Still, women gave me a second chance to prove otherwise. Many of my weekends were filled with coffeehouse dates and movie outings. None of these affairs were serious. Though when I was leaving Toronto for California, I could not convince the woman I was dating then that she could not come along. When she found out I was planning to go there with Edwin, she probably suspected I was coming out of the closet.

My relationship with women remained troubled by my suspicion that their interest in me would dissolve quickly when the man with the MD or the money bag showed up, no matter his age or looks. I couldn't win this game. I still saw myself as the disadvantaged working-class kid on a wild goose chase for a better life. The trappings of the good life became vividly apparent when Edwin and I arrived at the Santa Monica beach and decided never to leave.

Edwin, a six-foot-six hunk, soon went steady with a pretty stewardess he'd met around the pool. When they returned from one of their weekend trips to Las Vegas, they told me they were married. Things did not work so quickly for me. Yes, I dated. But times were rough when I started college and I had to survive on a starvation budget. A German friend (Peter the Beautiful) who was in the same situation had no qualms about taking money from women. If I couldn't at least pay my share on a date, I wouldn't go. As a result, my dates were mostly other poor students. We were all struggling and kept discussions about a possible future together under wraps. After all, by that time, we were part of the "sexual revolution," and marriage talk was so "old-fashioned." I, too, felt a sense of liberation as I noticed my earlier distrust of women slowly vanishing. I eventually lost my working-class inferiority complex and became more emotionally mature. I increasingly noticed that women found my presence more rewarding than before, and some even began to see me as a potential life partner. But I was still searching for true love. If I couldn't find it, I figured I could always settle for someone after I received my PhD and had a regular income on my own terms. In 1973, I seemed close. But true love was still to come.

After I passed my PhD exams in March 1973, I was going to visit my family in Germany. A week or so before leaving from Los Angeles, I was invited to attend a surprise birthday party for one of my fellow students, Ron Baar. His wife had all of the guests gather in the apartment next to theirs, and at one point, we were told to invade Ron's room and scream, "Happy birthday to youuuuuuu!" The apartment where we all gathered was Sue's. I arrived with my girlfriend at the time, and we tried to find a seat in that crowded place. I found a spot next to Sue, and we immediately started talking. She was strikingly beautiful and kept her focus on me. I assumed she was married (after all, we were in UCLA married student housing), and I later found out that she assumed I was too.

Nevertheless, we started flirting animatedly—too animatedly, it must have seemed to everyone watching. In fact, we were inseparable during the party. In the end, we promised to see each other again after my return from Europe three months later. The next day, she called me to let me know she couldn't wait three months. I said I felt the same, and we met the next day at a swanky dance bar in Marina del Rey. We told each other our life stories and spent the night, the next night, the next one, and so on, together until I had to catch my plane to Germany. I learned she had two small children, John (eight) and Jason (four); that Jason, whom I had seen at the party, was severely handicapped; and that this had contributed to the deterioration of her marriage to her husband, Michael. Michael, in fact, had recently moved out, and she had filed for divorce. She assumed full responsibility for the care of Jason to the point of total exhaustion. She had been a student but now was working as a waitress. Her wages were meager, and she could not support her family. Neither Michael nor anyone else in his or her family came to her aid. There seemed to be no way out for her. She spoke about this hopeless situation in a calm voice that bespoke great inner strength.

All that summer in Europe, I saw her face in front of me and figured that I, despite all that I had been through during early childhood, probably would crumble under that kind of pressure. As I tried to think of ways for her to get out from under the avalanche descending upon her, I fell deeper and deeper in love with her. You know true love when you meet it. And this was it.

After my return from Europe, I saw that Sue had been very busy trying to find solutions to her many problems. She had created some breathing space for herself, meaning a few hours of available time to tackle problems other than work and taking care of her kids, by finding occasional babysitters for Jason and by letting John stay temporarily with a friendly couple, the Dell family, who had small children too and lived at Deep Springs College, a small college in the White Mountains of California.

Sue told me that since no one would help her and Jason, who would need costly care all of his life, she had to find a way to earn top money somehow. Weighing all possible options, she figured that becoming a medical doctor was the most prudent way to go. She would make enough money to support Jason and help him with his medical problems too. But she had two immediate strikes against her. Going to medical school was expensive, and getting into one at her age (almost thirty) was nearly impossible. Also, she still needed to take a few courses to finish her BA in zoology, a major that might or might not be considered appropriate for entering medicine.

Nevertheless, she had already started applying to some medical schools. But she was not invited for a single interview. She learned that it was possible to train at a foreign school and transfer the medical degree to the US, a complicated but doable undertaking. We started applying to some German medical schools in the hope that some would have English-speaking programs. If not, would they accept her with the understanding that she would learn German quickly? But all of her applications were rejected. She knew Spanish and heard of a medical school in Mexico that admitted international students, Universidad Autónoma de Guadalajara (UAG). She applied there and was invited for an interview. All of this took some time.

As for myself, I started working on my dissertation, which initially consisted primarily of research. UCLA provided me with a desk at the Charles Young Research Library, something they did for all PhD candidates. Financially I survived on a small stipend, a work-study program, student loans, and the occasional stint as a waiter in fancy restaurants. Sue also worked as a waitress, mainly at the famous Lawry's in Beverly Hills. Jason was inside the hospital more than he was out. He was born at UCLA Medical Center, where they continued to do extensive research on the rare lung disease (hyaline membrane disease) that almost killed him at birth and about which little was known at the time.

Children with the disease die of respiratory distress shortly after delivery, and until recently, little could be done to save them. But when the First Lady, Jacqueline Kennedy, saw her son Patrick die of the disease in 1963, her husband, President John F. Kennedy, made it a priority of his to provide the medical profession with as much money as it took to conquer this scourge.

When Jason was born in 1969, doctors were able to keep him alive, if barely. For years he was on respirators, breathing mainly through a tube inserted into his trachea. Because his lungs could not absorb enough oxygen, his body did not develop normally. His left side suffered severe paralysis, and he experienced spastic symptoms and epilepsy. He is blind in his left eye. His brain functions are impaired. His immune system is compromised. The list goes on. Sue was often told that he might not make it through the night, the week, the month, the next year, but that regardless, he would die early.

Jason defied all the odds and, as of this writing, has made it into his fifties and lives relatively independently. Jason endured, among other things, because he learned to live with pain. When he was the subject of extensive research at UCLA, Sue was told many times that the medical results would benefit other children who would not have to endure the same fate. Later in life, when we told Jason how much he had helped other kids with his suffering, he felt very proud.

The medical staff at UCLA trained Sue to care for Jason at home. The work was overwhelming, and since her husband left, it seemed like an impossible task. Somehow, she managed. But how could she go to medical school with Jason requiring around-the-clock care? She figured she could try placing him in foster care until she received her degree. She went to the various agencies that dealt with such matters and was able to place Jason with a family in Fontana, outside Los Angeles.

Tony and Helen Lamers had four smaller children of their own and took in an equal number of cases that needed special care, like

Jason. They were a godsend. They treated Jason like one of their own, and later in life, he always considered them his real family. He became especially close to Tony, a Dutch immigrant who had been in an industrial accident that burned most of his body and who stayed home to help care for the kids. When Tony died years later, after Jason left the Lamers family, Jason mourned for a long time and probably will never get over the loss of what was probably the best friend of his life. Tony taught Jason some Dutch words, and Jason still uses these words to show how close he feels to Tony all the time.

There was another person who helped Sue right from the start, a nurse from the UCLA intensive care unit who cared for Jason, Lynn Montgomery. Lynn helped convince Sue to go to Guadalajara and even helped with some grocery bills when food was scarce.

In the midst of the struggle, Sue also tried to keep in touch with John, who lived with the Dell family at Deep Springs Valley. She was painfully aware that John must have felt shoved aside by the desperate attention given to Jason and the turmoil caused by the breakup of his parents. But she went up to Deep Springs as often as she could. It was a nearly six-hour drive through the ghastly Mojave Desert and Owens Valley to a place close to Death Valley. Deep Springs Valley is a small place of fertile ground amid a sea of rocky soil and cliffs. It once supported a farm with large cattle, but in 1917 it was turned into a small college by the industrialist L. L. Nunn, who had made a fortune building alternating current power plants across the western United States. His legacy was the college, where around twenty young men were trained to be rugged leaders of America in the image of Abraham Lincoln and Teddy Roosevelt.

The program rests on a foundation of academics, labor, and self-governance. Only students with the highest scores on college entrance exams were admitted (preferably National Merit Scholars). They had to work twenty hours a week, running a farm with around 300 cattle, and they had to administer certain aspects of their academic programs. There were five faculty teaching a variety of subjects. Roger Dell taught mathematics and physical sciences. His wife was a friend of Sue. And John stayed with the Dells. I went along on these trips and got to know everyone quite well. In fact, Randy Reid, the director of the college, asked me whether I could teach some history and philosophy courses during the fall of 1974. I gladly accepted, though Sue's situation was not yet settled. She had an interview in Guadalajara in early June 1974 and, if all went well, might enter medical school there in the fall.

We decided to take the trip to Guadalajara together, turning it into a real adventure on a shoestring budget. We booked train rides with sleeper compartments from Tijuana to Mérida, a nearly 3,000-mile stretch. It was a slow ride marked by clickety-clack sounds, swaying passenger cars, and travelers carrying produce to market, among other things. The heat was oppressive. We stayed at the cheapest hotels, costing between one and two dollars a night. The hotel in Guadalajara had running water, which was really no more than a trickle, for only an hour a day in the morning, and it was cold. Sue couldn't miss it to get ready for her interview. She had brought a sharp-looking dress to impress the interviewer, and she looked oddly out of place as we were leaving our flea trap looking for the dirty streetcar. Her beauty was striking; she turned most of the macho heads her way. She had her map along with the required documents under her arm, proving that she was an excellent candidate for the medical program of UAG. The interviewers agreed and told her the written confirmation of her acceptance was a mere formality. Afterward, we strolled through a luscious, Spanish-looking park full of tropical plants and sweet-smelling flowers. Her hair waved in the sun, and I knew I could never leave her. At the hotel, we changed back into our faded jeans and sweaty T-shirts and, a few days later, headed for the train to the Yucatán.

The summer of 1974 was also the summer of the World Cup, held in Germany. Mexico is a soccer-crazy country, and all the games were shown on TV. Germany was a contender for the title, and I tried to catch as many games as I could on the trip. The cheap hotels we stayed at had bars with TVs. In Mexico City, we visited the Chapultepec area, the cathedral, and, of course, the Teotihuacán pyramids, and we watched another soccer game. When we arrived in Mérida, Germany had managed to qualify for the final against the Netherlands, which was to be played at the Olympic Stadium in Munich on July 7. We watched the game in an overcrowded, noisy cantina, where we drank too much tequila with Mexicans who seemed to all be rooting for Germany. Germany won 2 to 1, and the winning goal scorer, Gerd Müller, became a household name in the soccer world.

Sue and I stayed another week in the Yucatán and explored the Mayan ruins of Chichén Itzá and Uxmal. It was difficult to find them in the thick jungle. There were no easy roads leading there and no helpful signs. Everything was overgrown, and even the bus driver, who let us off at a road near Chichén Itzá, seemed unsure of how to get there. But we followed a small path he suggested and eventually saw the ancient stone structures appearing before us. There were a handful of people there.

In Uxmal, there were only a few more. When we returned years later, Chichén Itzá looked more like Disneyland, with big tourist buses resting in a large parking lot, an air-conditioned restaurant serving expensive burgers, and a tourist shop offering everything from Mayan toy dolls to imitation stone knives used for sacrificial acts. There were people as far as the eye could see. We didn't stay long that time.

Back in Los Angeles, we prepared for the coming tasks ahead. Sue would drive her VW Bug to Guadalajara to start medical school, taking John with her. I would drive with my VW Bug to Deep Springs College to start teaching until Christmas, after which I would join them in Guadalajara. We had no money. Sue left her apartment and sold all of her furniture for a measly $200. That would at least get her and John to Guadalajara and allow them to stay in a cheap hotel until I could send some money from the wages I made by teaching. I ended up being able to send all of the money I earned since the college supplied food and housing.

Before Sue took off for Guadalajara with John, she and I went to Deep Springs to get him. From what I had seen, John suffered a lot from his parents' breakup but had adjusted to living with the Dells rather well. He'd become close friends with their children. He knew it was temporary, possibly hoping his parents would reunite. He missed his dad, a UCLA student as well, whose gregarious nature and good looks easily made him the center of attention of any group. Both of them liked to hang out at the beach together whenever they could. John must have looked at me as an irritating intruder who would soon disappear. But when Sue told him that we were all going to move to Mexico together, he reached the limits of what an eight-year-old boy can endure.

He became withdrawn and stoic around us but cried when he

thought no one was watching. I tried to tell myself that what we all had to do was secure the future for Jason and that someday John would come to understand that. Sue later told me that the long trip through Mexico, which lasted three days, with John silently sitting next to her in that rusty VW Bug, was one of the hardest things she had ever had to do. She was sure he felt the same way. And while the future was anything but certain, she also felt there was no turning back. Few people in this world have that kind of courage. I am glad Sue and John are among them. In Guadalajara, they both had to gain a footing somehow. It's a city that even then had over a million people and a noisy and, in many areas, chaotic street life.

Sue spoke Spanish, but it was rusty. Spanish had been Sue's foreign language in high school, and she spent a year with her husband in Madrid, where John was born. Sue and Michael had both been students at the University of Kansas, where Michael studied Spanish literature and Sue studied botany. They had plenty of reasons to fall in love. Both came from the small town of Neodesha in the southeastern corner of Kansas. Michael looked like the all-American boy from a well-to-do family, and Sue was a high school princess who'd found her prince. After Michael left for Madrid in the summer of 1965 on a year-abroad study program, Sue realized she was pregnant. She followed him with the good news, and they got married at Gibraltar. John was born in Madrid on March 16, 1966. At that time, Spain was still under the fascist Franco regime. Under the circumstances, Sue confined herself to playing the role of the good housewife. Her ability to practice her Spanish was limited. But she learned enough for daily use, which turned out to be a blessing. Still, Mexican Spanish differs much from the Castilian Spanish spoken in most of Spain. But she adjusted quickly. She had to be quick in many areas, having entered a culture dominated by a macho mentality suspicious of assertive women.

Fortunately, one of the other American medical students, whom Sue met through the university, offered her and John a spare room in his place until she was able to find her own. She quickly learned that there was an entire contingent of American medical students who socialized together and helped each other in many ways. This was also how she found a nice duplex outside town, in Ciudad Granja, with two bedrooms, a kitchen, a large living room, a study upstairs, and affordable rent. She also found a private English-speaking school for John that he could get to by public bus. The school later folded, and John ended up attending three more schools before his educational adventure in Guadalajara came to an end. This was certainly a moving experience for him, and he matured beyond the educational level he attained during those years. John was not able to enter public school because he was not a Mexican resident. Neither was Sue; nor was I. We were foreign visitors who lived in Mexico on a tourist visa that had to be reissued every three months outside Mexico, usually by Mexican border officials when we reentered the country. This required a lot of trips back and forth between Mexico and the US.

Private schools probably violated Mexican laws when they admitted tourists as regular students. But the students filled a demand and paid tuition, and no one seemed to ask questions. If people did, they could be convinced to look the other way with a bribe, a mordida. We learned from experience that a mordida was the solution for almost everything. Without money, one was completely lost. But it was difficult to bring money into the country. It was impossible to make currency transfers from private American bank accounts to private Mexican bank accounts or to deposit American checks in private Mexican bank accounts. Banks only accepted Mexican checks or cash, Mexican pesos or US dollars, for deposit. Everything had to be done in cash.

Sue opened an account under her name at a local bank and deposited the few dollars she had brought with her. The dollars were converted into pesos, usually at an unfavorable rate and with a hefty transaction fee. It was at least three months before Sue could return from the States with more cash to deposit. Any checks I sent her were worthless. So I had to send her dollar bills in the mail. Mail with cash often disappeared, so you had to be creative in finding ways to make envelopes or packages look worthless. For instance, thick birthday cards worked, but not always. One had to consider the averages. Sending $100 in five thick birthday cards with one $20 bill in each card might mean that $80 would reach the recipient. Lynn Montgomery also sent an occasional $20 bill, which kept Sue and John going. At the time, the purchasing power of one US dollar was about three to four times higher in Mexico than in the States. All the American students were in the same boat and would loan each other money to overcome temporary cash-flow problems.

All in all, Sue and John survived the first term intact, and we celebrated Christmas together at Deep Springs College. We managed to get Jason to join us, but John stayed with Michael until we headed back to Guadalajara.

At Deep Springs College, I got my first teaching experience. It was the kind of experience I would never have again. All twenty-two students were exceptionally bright and knowledgeable. Several were not even eighteen years old and had finished high school early. The youngest was fourteen. I offered the classes History of Ancient Philosophy, Medieval History, and The Reformation Period. A handful of students signed up for the first two classes but only one signed up for The Reformation Period. The focus of the first two classes was the study of the great works of such thinkers as Aristotle, Plato, Saint Augustine, Thomas Aquinas, and Dante. The one student I had in the Reformation class ended up reading most of Luther's relevant works. He came from a religious home and did not tire of discussing the pros and cons of Luther's doctrines right down to the real existence of the devil. I played devil's advocate and did not always end up on the winning side in our discussions.

Never in my life have I met such bright students. Even years later, when I did a short stint at the prestigious Middlebury College, I still found the students were not as promising as this first group. The unique aspect of Deep Springs College was its holistic approach to education, based on the premise that students become more productive and responsible citizens when their minds and bodies work together. They'd read Plato in the morning and feed the cows in the afternoon. Students grow their own produce, raise chickens, take care of around 300 head of cattle plus several horses, and do everything else required to make the place successful. Incoming students acquire the necessary skills from second-year students under the watchful eye of an experienced manager and a few ranch hands. I have participated in an old-fashioned cattle roundup, where the calves were branded with an iron heated up in a campfire. I felt like a real cowboy and sometimes rode a horse for hours across the mostly barren valley.

The ranch's kitchen and dining hall were run by an elderly couple who worked tirelessly. They asked Sue and me whether we would take their place over Christmas break so they could visit family. Though most people were gone during that time, we still worked hard because we had to take care of Jason, whose medical needs were still very extensive. But we managed and served up steaks every day, for which we got a lot of applause, especially on Christmas Day. In early January, we were on the road to Guadalajara again. Jason was back with the Lamers family, and John rejoined us after his time with Michael. I had not driven to Guadalajara before. Sue and John had done so six months earlier, and I started to realize what a feat it was.

Starting in Los Angeles, it was a 1,600-mile stretch, which went mostly through barren land, much of it desert. On the last leg, it turned into steep and windy mountain roads. Our little VW Bug was no match for them. Most were in disrepair, full of potholes and debris, and were sometimes used by animals. Mexicans, for the most part, let their animals roam free and hardly put up fences along roads. The likelihood of running into an unexpected cow was high, especially at night. There were hardly any traffic signs or lights. Many potholes were deep. To alert drivers, large boulders, usually painted white, were sometimes placed in front of the potholes, in the middle of the road.

After we arrived in Ciudad Granja, a small village outside Guadalajara where Sue had found a duplex, Sue and John continued with the tasks they had left behind a few weeks earlier when they went to spend Christmas in California. I had to start from scratch. They went to their respective schools, and I set up my writing corner in the upstairs room. It was a while before we all found a daily routine. John had the hardest time. Ciudad Granja was a dirty little place where few Americans lived, certainly no American children. Our duplex was, by local standards, a nice middle-class home, built with bricks and covered with plaster, circled by high walls and a wrought iron fence and gate. It was surrounded by mostly smaller houses built with mud bricks, cinder blocks, wood boards, and metal sheets, typically with one or two rooms, a kitchen corner, and a small toilet. Not all of the houses had running water or sewage pipes. Many doors and windows were covered with sackcloth. Most rooms were lit with dim light bulbs hanging from the ceiling. Though newer structures were slowly replacing older ones, it did not look very promising. Our house was located

Sue and I in front of our house in Ciudad Granja.

Sue, John, and I in the front yard of our house in Ciudad Granja.

along an unpaved road where, at one point, trenches were dug for pipes and cables. But that time never came. The roads attracted roaming dogs, ready to pounce if not fended off with yells and kicks, usually by kids who delighted in the dogs' barking.

John had to walk these streets for half a mile to catch a public bus that would take him to school. He was bullied by the local kids who were eager to give a gringo kid a lesson in territorial dominance. For them, he was an intruder who needed to be shown his place at the bottom of the pecking order. It would be quite a while until he could turn the tables and assume a dominant position. Sue drove the VW Bug to and from the university and had fewer problems getting around. She tried to ignore the befuddled looks of local men spotting an attractive gringa behind the wheel.

Most of the time, I sat at my table and worked away on my dissertation, unbothered by anything except the clucking of chickens and barking dogs. Soon I realized I needed more material from the UCLA library. I had to make the trip to and from LA at least every six weeks or so. I took the car a few times, and on other occasions I flew with Aeromexico.

After I returned from my first trip, Sue had a big surprise for me. On my birthday (Valentine's Day in 1975), she gave me a riding horse, a quarter horse mare named Gitana. She was beautiful, light brown with a white stripe adorning her forehead, and she ran even better than she looked. Sue had seen how much I loved riding horses at Deep Springs and knew how much joy I would get riding across the open fields behind Ciudad Granja. She had managed to keep a little money aside from what we brought over after Christmas, and it was enough to get Gitana, plus the English saddle that I preferred. I had had many surprises in my life, but that was the biggest to that point. Sue had even arranged for Gitana's keep. On one side of our house was a little farm, no bigger than an acre, that kept some chickens and a dairy cow and had room in the stall for a horse. I had to take care of her, of course, but I got a lot of help from the family who lived there, a middle-aged couple with a teenage son and an elderly father, Porfidio.

Porfidio looked ancient and swore he had ridden with the revolutionary leader Zapata. He loved horses and seemed to enjoy Gitana's presence. Soon, I was saddling up and exploring the vicinity of Ciudad Granja almost every day. Under the watchful eye of Porfidio, I learned how to clean Gitana properly as well as feed and groom her. Soon I developed a routine. I would write until 4:00 p.m., when Sue and John came home, and then ride for at least an hour, until dinner. There were other people in the village with horses. Two American students not far from us had one, and Sue occasionally borrowed their horse to join me.

We found hidden places to rest and let the horses drink water and eat grass for a while. On one occasion, the horses took off, and it took us almost a full day to locate them on foot.

Now that I had a horse, we considered finding a dog for John. We did, but not in Mexico. On our next trip to LA, we got one at a pound, a mutt that looked mostly like a German shepherd. John picked it out, called it Grover, and they immediately became good friends.

Driving back, our little Bug was packed with boxes, between which John and Grover had to struggle for space. In Ciudad Granja, Grover quickly adjusted to his new environment. John built him a doghouse, and the two became inseparable. Sometimes Grover would take off for a day or two, but he always came back. I would often take him with me on my rides on Gitana, and he could keep up even when I was going fast. We got two more pets: One was a white rabbit named Honeysuckle who would run figure eights around our legs, begging for food, and stand up under the table. The most amazing pet we had was a little mockingbird that followed us on foot, sat on our shoulders, watched over us, perched on curtain rods, and slept next to us on the couch. Coco Loco could fly but liked walking more. The bird would walk behind us into the shower, sit in the corner getting wet, and dry itself by flapping its wings. Coco Loco would sit on my shoulders for hours when I was reading under the lamp, nibbling on my earlobes and pulling the buttons off my shirt. Which is why we named it Loco.

Whenever we could, we would go on short trips exploring the surrounding countryside, the buzz of the city of Guadalajara, beautiful Puerto Vallarta by the sea, enchanting Lake Chapala, and the artist colony Tlaquepaque. Tlaquepaque is famous for, among other things, its handmade painted pottery and china. We could not afford any of the regular pieces but managed to collect a traditional table service by buying "seconds" (pieces with slight but usually invisible flaws) at a much lower price, one piece at a time. The set has made it intact through all of our moves, and we still use it as much as we can today. John in particular liked Tlaquepaque.

John learned Spanish quicker than we could manage. He attended a bilingual American school, and in the beginning, we tried to encourage him to play and visit with his schoolmates as much as possible. There were other American couples who had children in American schools, and with them we arranged joint outings and get-togethers. One Mexican American couple had a boy in John's school that John really liked, and he spent a lot of time at their place. But the drive was long, making a sustained friendship a real challenge. Unfortunately, the Ciudad Granja kids and adults continued picking on John.

At one point, during market time, John came home almost in tears, telling me some tough older kids had roped him around the neck. I told John we were going to go back there and beat them up together. We did not find the guys, but we looked for them for quite a while. Everybody was watching us, and it was clear what our intention was. This may have helped to give John a bit more breathing room. But what seemed to turn things around more than anything else was an incident involving me.

When I started my afternoon rides with Gitana, I always passed by a small grocery store that was located almost catty-corner from where we lived. It was a hangout for local men who sat along the curb in front of it and drank beer. Sometimes they would taunt me by calling "Gringo" or "Fuck you." I noticed one guy in particular who seemed to enjoy a leadership role. I always ignored the calls and rode on by.

But at one point, on the way back from my ride, I noticed the same guy yelling "Gringo" and decided I had had enough. Rather impulsively, I galloped toward the group of around eight men at high speed and jumped off Gitana right in front of them. I screamed at them in loud German that I was not a "gringo" but an "Aléman," that I was tired of their obscenities, that they could all go to hell, and a few more such things. Then I took Gitana and walked the 200 yards to her stable, where I unsaddled, dried, and fed her. The whole time, I was worried I had made a big mistake because things could only get worse in the neighborhood, especially for John. So I walked back to the store, where the group still stood in befuddlement, probably trying to figure out what language I had spoken. I walked straight into the store, went to the ice chest where the beer was kept, took two bottles, opened them, gave one to the loudmouth and told him to drink "bottoms up." He couldn't get it down in one swallow, but I could. This was something my military training in the Bundeswehr had prepared me for. I opened another two bottles. Same test. Same result. I could. He couldn't. We did this seven times. He never managed a single bottoms up. On the contrary, I managed all seven.

I used my twenty words of Spanish and told the storekeeper, who had watched open-mouthed the entire time, to distribute all the beer left in the chest to all the guys present. I could not have come up with a better way to become accepted in the neighborhood. Things turned around immediately. Of course, we were all pretty drunk soon, especially Carlos, the guy who couldn't keep up with my seven beers. Carlos eventually sat on the curb and was unable to get up. How I managed to remain standing, I don't know, but I told myself that this was how you

Gitana and I explored the surroundings of Ciudad Granja almost every day.

gained respect in this neck of the woods. And I was right. Everybody talked to me simultaneously in Spanish with some English words mixed in, of which I understood nothing. I just kept nodding and they kept talking. It helped that I was no gringo. To find some common ground, I mentioned the names of a few German soccer stars that I figured they might know, like Beckenbauer and Müller. And they did.

Germany had recently won the Copa de Mundo, and they had all watched the games. Things could not have turned out better, but I was slowly getting dizzy. To avoid the fate of the guy I had just beaten in the beer-drinking contest, I had to make it over to my place while walking was still an option. I managed and must have fallen into bed quickly. Sue and John told me later that they had watched a bit from a distance and were prepared for anything.

Things changed after that. When I rode by the corner store the next day, the guys waved and yelled, "Hello, Aléman!" Coming back from the ride, I stopped and bought everyone a beer again. Carlos invited Sue and me to a party at his house a few days later. He wrote the address down on a piece of paper and said to be there at six. Although his house was only a few blocks away, it took us a long time to find it. We asked many people in the village where the place was, and no one could tell us. We later found that hardly anyone knew addresses correctly. When we showed them our piece of paper with Carlos's address, they sent us to the strangest places a few blocks away. Eventually, one guy knew which Carlos we were looking for and told us how to get to his house. The house was a bit bigger than most, with a stone wall and wooden door leading into a small courtyard. We were greeted by a woman holding a pig's head under her left arm and a rusty razor blade in her right hand, which she was using to trim the hairs of the pig's head. The head, we soon found out, would be the main dish. By then, it was almost seven, and we thought we were late. But the reality was that no one else was there yet. Even Carlos was missing.

The woman told us to sit on a bench and proceeded with her work. She threw small pieces of pigskin, bones, and intestines into a huge kettle that hung over an open fire. She was cooking chitlins. By and by, neighbors started to show up, and we began drinking the beer that Sue and I had brought. It ran out quickly, but I made sure more was on the way by sending a small boy to the corner store several times that evening. We were sitting among very poor people, and they shared with us the little they had. Sue, unlike me, got a sense of what was being said by the other guests and learned that the chitlins were deep-frying in grease that had been in the kettle for a long time. They were served on boards with salt. They did not look appetizing; I could only get them down with massive amounts of beer. Sue couldn't eat them at all. She pretended to put them into her mouth but threw them on the ground behind her back when she thought no one was watching. Once on the ground, they blended in with other leftovers from previous meals.

We discovered that Carlos was an important man in the neighborhood because he was the village butcher. He slaughtered people's animals and was paid mainly in leftover bits of meat. He had just slaughtered a pig and brought home the skin, feet, and head, most of which was frying in the kettle.

Much of the meat people got from their animals was cut up and sold at the market. Carlos promised us that we would have the first pick of the most precious items from the slaughtered pigs, the loin fillets (lomo). And indeed, from then on, Carlos would come to our house and offer fresh loins every time he had slaughtered a pig. We always bought them from him.

As the evening progressed, more people from the village arrived, and Carlos introduced all of them to us. Among them there was a young couple who had lived in the States illegally and knew how to speak some English. They were leaving again for the States a few days later. They wouldn't say how, but they were trying to raise some money by selling the few pieces of furniture they had. They sold some pieces to us, which we never collected.

Eventually, a neighbor with a guitar showed up, playing heart-wrenching traditional Mexican songs with great skill. When we were asked to suggest songs he could play for us, all I could think of was "La Paloma," which I shouted out in my drunken voice several more times that night. Of course I spoke in German, trying to imitate Hans Albers. By that time, all the women had disappeared into the kitchen, and Sue joined them.

Increasingly it became a macho night, and I was holding my own. And I learned about some of the hardships the villagers had to face on a daily basis. For instance, in the village there was a brick factory that employed only children. They had to work with chemicals that burned their skin and left scars on their hands. Most youngsters and men were unemployed and bounced between ill-paying temporary jobs in construction or fieldwork, making too little to live and too much to die. Girls got married early and bore many children, many of whom died due mostly to epidemic diseases (such as dysentery and measles) and insufficient health care.

Some younger girls and women managed to find work as domestic helpers or in sales. A few had regular jobs in the city. But all were chronically underpaid and could barely afford enough food or clothes to wear. Still, all of them had a sense of pride in their ability to endure and not complain. When I connected with that emotionally, it made me cry into my beer. As a small child, I had been in the same shoes. And although I could not convey this to my drinking buddies because of the language barrier, they sensed that I understood and we all felt as one.

Sue was long gone by that point. Someone had taken her to get Gitana for me to ride home on. I did so in the early morning hours. Some of the guys propped me up on the horse, and Gitana somehow found the way home on her own. At home, I fell into Sue's lap and began to cry again until I regained my composure. We did not return to Carlos's house. Perhaps we did not have another opportunity. I guess it is easier to talk about people's tragic lives than to really share them, even if it is only for a few hours.

Word must have gone out that we were okay people. Things eventually took a turn for the better for John as well. He came to be accepted among the kids in the neighborhood and made friends. He hung out a lot with a kid his own age from across the street called Huero. John also quickly learned the Spanish spoken in the streets and soon sounded like a Mexican kid himself.

I thought it would boost his image in the village if he were seen riding around on Gitana. It would also be a good thing for him to learn how to handle horses. So I took him over to the neighbor's small field where Gitana hung out and explained to him the basics of horseback riding. We saddled up, and Porfidio, an old horseman himself, watched as I helped John mount Gitana. She was a bit nervous, sensing that she was dealing with an unfamiliar rider. I told John to stay calm and follow my instructions on handling the double reins I used for the English riding style. As I tried to show him that the lower reins were for turning and the upper ones for stop and go, he pulled a little too much on the upper reins. Gitana reared up some. I told him to stop pulling, but he was confused and pulled some more, causing Gitana to stand up on her hind legs while doing bicycle kicks with her front legs.

Fearful of falling off, John desperately hung on to the reins, making Gitana fall backward on top of him. It took me a while to get Gitana up again, and I wasn't sure whether John had survived the crash. He didn't move or make a sound. Sue had pulled up with the Bug and ran toward us, a horrified look on her face. I picked up John's limp body, and we ran to the car. Sue sat in the back, holding John on her lap while I raced to the nearest hospital. We were relieved to see he was breathing, though he was unconscious.

As we numbly watched, the doctors immediately gave him emergency treatment. He was bruised all over, but miraculously, nothing was broken. His testicles had been pushed into his stomach area, but there were no cuts or tears. He was in great pain but medicated enough to handle it. The doctors took X-rays and showed them to us. All he needed, the doctors said, was rest and painkillers. Our relief could not be put into words. I don't remember how long John stayed at the hospital, but a few weeks later, he was back on his feet without lasting damage. I was raised a Catholic but had fallen to the agnostic side long ago. Still, whenever I entered a Catholic church after the incident, I gave an appreciative nod to the boss upstairs for having spared John. Sue was more of a believer and gave many heartfelt prayers to the Lord and Savior. As far as we know, John never got on a horse again.

I noticed that John handled this potentially fatal incident in a style I had observed many times in Mexican youngsters and Mexican society in general. He was stoic and did not show pain. I would witness this again in a case involving John's friend Huero. He came home one day, his right thumbnail having been pulled off by a public bus door. His mother sent him over to see Sue. But Sue was about to leave the house for the university and told me to take Huero to a pharmacy to get a brace and medications like iodine and to apply them immediately.

John worked hard on Porfidio's property next door.

Huero's pain must have been considerable, but he did not move a muscle. Tears kept silently running down his cheeks. I put him in the car and raced to the pharmacy about thirty minutes away. A police car stopped me for speeding.

As was the norm in Mexico, I carried five-dollar bills with me to get a pass. But giving it away would have only left a few pesos for Huero's medication. I tried to impress upon the officer the urgency of the situation, but he pretended not to understand English. I had Huero show him his injured thumb and stressed the need for immediate help. I left the car running, certain he would understand or even assist us on our quest. Instead, the officer had us both exit the car. He looked at Huero's thumb again and must have seen his tears. Then he asked me for the car papers, my driver's license, and eventually the passport I didn't have. He began examining the car very slowly. I figured he was waiting for a bribe, which I didn't have. After a while, he told me, in English, that he had to impound the car. He ignored me when I asked why. Then he abruptly jerked the license plates off my car, told me I could get them back at the city's motor vehicle office, and drove off. The whole affair took about twenty minutes, and Huero's thumb kept swelling. I had to speed again to get to the pharmacy, this time without license plates. We made it, and I treated Huero's thumb as best I could. Sue followed up the next day with more painkillers.

Huero's nail eventually grew back. To get my license plates returned, I went to the German consul in the area, a violinist from Munich who owned a music shop in the center of Guadalajara. He was an honorary consul and supported his consular work by selling instruments. He gave me a letter for the motor vehicle department and told me to present it with "extreme politeness."

At the department, I was ushered off to a plush-looking office, where I had to wait quite a while until an elegant-looking señor entered and introduced himself formally, told me to sit down, and lectured me on the rules of Mexican society. I hoped he would give me back my plates and let me go. But instead he gave me a form to fill out, and I had to stand in a long line to pay a $100 fine for speeding, equivalent to an average worker's weekly paycheck.

Later I was told I got off easily, considering everything. And we were glad to see Huero's thumbnail growing back. Huero showed a thankful demeanor when he came over to play with John and his dog. He helped John take care of Grover, President of the Dogs. John and Grover had a special relationship. Grover would take John to the bus in the morning and then run alongside the bus until he couldn't keep up any longer. He did the same with our Bug, chasing it until he knew he had lost the race. He also would follow me on Gitana and try to keep up when we galloped fast. Sometimes other dogs would join and even attack Grover. I took a Chinese slingshot and hit them from above when I needed to fend them off. Grover, of course, slept in his doghouse in the courtyard. But he learned how to jump over the gate at night and roam around the neighborhood. John did not want to put him on a leash. Dogs on leashes are unhappy creatures and bark a lot. Sometimes Grover stayed out for two or more days, and we started to worry. There were mean dogs in the neighborhood.

Around the corner, someone kept a Great Dane that looked like a lion. It was known for vicious attacks, and all the other dogs were afraid of it. Its owner called it Hitler. Grover often came home limping after a night out, once with a gunshot wound. But he loved hanging around the courtyard during the day, waiting for John to come home to play with him.

But one day, he didn't come home. For weeks we hoped he would show up again, wag his happy tail, and fall all over his food bowl as usual. But it didn't happen this time. After nearly two years of close companionship, it was a hard blow for John. And I had to ride alone now and sensed that Gitana, too, missed Grover.

Gitana and I experienced a few other mishaps, of which the following are noteworthy. I often rode on the median of a divided highway amid moderate traffic. Rather than going around a sign about seven feet above the ground, with two posts about six feet apart holding it up, I decided to let Gitana go under it with me leaning back in the saddle. When I got stuck, with the sign pressing on my chest, Gitana did not stop but started running, throwing me down on her left side, my boot stuck in her left stirrup. She galloped on the hard cobblestone highway, dragging me under her belly while her front hooves kicked me. After about a minute, my boot got loose from the stirrup, and I fell to the ground. I probably looked like a dead piece of meat. I remember a woman close by watching and not moving. After another minute, I tried to get up, and somehow, I managed. I hurt all over, but nothing was broken.

Soon I developed an intense pain in the back of my head and right elbow. I also turned black and blue. But I could walk, and I had to search for Gitana. After walking about two-thirds of a mile along the road leading into Ciudad Granja, I saw her tied to a vendor's sales truck, happily munching on some greens the vendor was feeding her. The vendor noticed my limp and tattered clothing and laughingly handed me the reins with a few remarks about liking horses that had spunk. I managed to ride home but was incapacitated for several days afterward. My second mishap was even worse.

In the vicinity of Ciudad Granja was a waterfall where Gitana liked to drink while I rested, listening to the splashing of the falling water. To get to this place, I had to ride through a village in a small ravine that had, like most Mexican villages at the time, an open sewage system. All liquid waste, including toilet waste, would run down sloped pipes into the streets, where rainwater would eventually flush it along to lower-lying places or holes dug out leading to a cesspool. Over the years, the village had accumulated a small pond of sewage about forty feet across and four feet deep. It was filled with green-looking slime that smelled horrible.

Whenever I wanted to see the waterfall by using this shortcut, we had to make it through the sludge. Gitana would get clean in the brook when we finally arrived, and we went back the long way around the village. But one day Gitana stepped on something sharp in the sewage pond and threw me off. I went under and Gitana ran off. As I exited the smelly mess, all the villagers came out to laugh at the green monster. I was able to fetch Gitana again and rode off. Sue was home. I yelled for her to stay away while I undressed completely and hosed myself off. All I kept from that episode was my wide-brimmed cowboy hat. I burned everything else except the memories.

The third mishap did not happen to me, but I felt responsible for it. One day I rode along a street where I saw a boy with paralyzed legs sitting in a chair beside a modest hut. He walked on crutches, and some of his friends ran after me, telling me the boy's greatest dream was to someday ride a horse like Gitana, and could I fulfill his dream. After some hesitation, I did. I propped him up on the saddle, his thin legs dangling down, and showed him how to hold the reins, just as I had with John. Then I showed him how to grab the mane and told him to hold tight if Gitana started galloping, which I was sure she would not do, and with me holding her bridle, we walked.

After we'd walked for a couple of minutes, the boy beaming and his friends clapping hands, I dared to let go of Gitana's bit, step in front of her, and give the boy the feeling that he was in total control. That was a mistake. Gitana took a jerky step to the side. The boy flew off and hit his head on the hard cobblestones. I picked him up and placed him in his seat by the roadside. His mother ran out of the house and carried him inside, not letting me in, though they indicated he was okay. A couple of days later, an official from the city came over, telling me that the boy was in the hospital and I might be charged with something.

We visited the boy and to our relief found him in good spirits. But hospital administrators told us that surgery might be necessary, and we might have to carry the costs. Days later, the boy was home, and we never heard anything official about the accident again. As far as I could tell, the boy had had a bad fall but had sustained no lasting damage. But we were all on pins and needles for a while because earlier an American missionary, whom we knew, had killed a pedestrian in the village with his car and then disappeared, making it back across the border into the US to escape the consequences. We had indicated that we would take responsibility for the possible medical bills for the boy, but we were never asked. Soon, the boy was again spending most of his time in his chair by the road. But he had been the cowboy of his dreams, even if only for a few minutes.

FOURTEEN

The Hard Way Back to the US

The American medical students at UAG eventually had two ways to practice medicine in the US. They could obtain a medical degree, a Mexican doctorate, at UAG and then take a series of tests in the US given to foreign graduates who wanted to practice medicine in the US. Or they could try to transfer to a US medical school if an opening became available. US medical schools liked to graduate as many students as they admitted. But some students always left the rigorous four-year program for various reasons, and the school administrators tried to fill their spots with students who had had medical training elsewhere, including foreign schools. American medical students abroad regularly checked with US medical schools for such spots. Not many were successful, but Sue was.

By 1976, our life had taken on a certain routine. Sue knew Spanish well and passed all of her classes with high grades. I was making real progress on my dissertation, though it was a more difficult project than I initially thought it would be. John had found his way, despite the many school switches, difficult trips to LA, and our rustic living conditions. He had mastered many challenges and grew more confident by the week. We all knew that our stay in Mexico was temporary.

Sooner or later, we would return to the US and stay there permanently. But one day, it looked like "soon" meant "immediately."

Sue came home early from the university and said drily, "I think it's over." She had had a run-in with the head of security that she felt was leading to her dismissal from the school. The university had a strict security system since its founding in the early 1930s. As in much of the world at that time, communist and fascist forces and their political allies were vying for control of their respective states. The seriousness of that global struggle had been on everyone's minds as they watched the rise of the Bolsheviks in Russia and the Nazi regime in Germany. Mexico was engulfed in the struggle between "left" and "right," out of which two university systems emerged. One was state-sponsored and largely left leaning, and one was much smaller, autocratically capitalist, and largely right leaning. It tried to remain autonomous and independent of state power.

UAG was a result of the latter. In the 1930s, there were armed street fights between the left and right. UAG enlisted armed guards to protect its campus. When we saw the campus for the first time from the outside, it looked a bit like a prison: high walls, closed gates, armed guards, controlled admission, and ID tags for everyone, even visitors.

Like everyone else on campus, students were then, and probably still are today, required to wear ID tags that must be visible on the upper left side of one's clothing. On the day in question, Sue had her tag correctly attached to her jacket while she was sitting on a porch and taking a short lunch break between lectures. She got up and went to the nearby food service area, leaving the jacket hanging over the back of her chair. While she was in the food line, an armed guard approached her and asked for her ID. "It's on my jacket on the chair over there," she replied. "Go and get it," he said, which she did.

He confiscated her ID and told her to pick it up at the head of security's office. She had to do so immediately because students could not enter lecture halls without an ID tag, and arriving late to a lecture would be recorded and would have a negative effect on her grade. She also had to pay a fine for not wearing her ID. Students called the chief security officer overseeing this restrictive system "head of the Gestapo," or within his earshot simply Jefe. Sue had to get her ID back from him. She was led into his office and told to wait. When he eventually showed up, she pleaded her case. She was a straight-A student with no absences or tardies on her record.

Students who had an unsatisfactory record were not allowed to take the regular exam at the end of the semester but instead had to wait an entire week to take the second round of exams, and they were also charged an extra fee. Sue explained to Jefe that she always had to plan her trips to and from LA very carefully because of her handicapped son, Jason. There were things she had to do with him during the short time over the upcoming Christmas break. She explained that not letting her take the examination at the regularly scheduled time would prevent her from taking care of her son. All because her ID had not been on her blouse but was instead on the jacket draped over a chair a few feet away. But Jefe saw it differently. However innocently, Sue had not abided by the ID rule and needed to be punished.

Sue thought he did not understand the seriousness of her situation and explained the entire story again. And again, he told her she needed to appreciate the importance of strict rules on campus, and she would not be allowed to take the first exams. Leaning back in his large executive chair, trying to exude an aura of authority, he gave Sue a long lecture on the importance of discipline for medical professionals. Again Sue appealed to his sense of justice and compassion. As he sat there stone-faced, without a shred of empathy, Sue noticed that he himself was not wearing an ID tag. And as he had just explained, campus rules did not allow for any exceptions. So Sue asked him why he criticized her when he was violating the same rule. He nervously opened his desk drawer, found his ID, and tried to pin it on his jacket. Sue reached over the desk and snatched the ID out of his hand. She held it up and yelled, "Do you know what this is? This is a piece of shit and should go where it belongs!" Then she ran to the office toilet and flushed his ID tag down the drain. He ran behind her and tried to fetch his tag as it spiraled out of sight. Sue ran to her car, drove straight home, and told me it was time to pull up stakes and get out of Dodge.

We were standing in the courtyard discussing what had just happened when another student who lived in our building unit heard us and came out to see what was happening. His name was Jose, and he was a Chicano from Houston who was one year ahead of Sue's class. He was also the middleweight boxing champion at the university. He calmly listened to Sue's story and our decision to call it quits in Mexico and move back to LA. "Not so fast," he said. "I know people at the university and will see what I can do." He immediately drove off. We later learned that Jefe liked Jose for macho reasons and that he was willing to listen to Jose regarding Sue's situation.

Hours later, Jose came back with good news. He had managed to get the university president to handle Sue's case himself. She was expected to be in his office the next morning at eight o'clock sharp. She arrived looking as neat and professional as possible. The president's secretary coolly told Sue to wait. Sue sat and waited until the office closed at 5:00 p.m. and was told to return the following day, again at 8:00 a.m. She did, and again she waited until she was finally let into the president's office in the afternoon. In front of him, he had Jefe's report. He read some passages to her. The report was very long, and the president did not seem interested in reading much of it. Instead, he let Sue explain her version of the events. Then, he told Sue he was going to look at some horses at a stable outside the city. He invited her to come along.

When they arrived, some specific breeds of horses had been prepared for his visit. He rode several horses around the course to see which one he liked the best. Eventually he narrowed it down to two horses and had Sue ride both of them, in her skirt. He wanted to know what she thought of them. She said that they were both excellent horses but that one of them seemed to have more grit than the other. "You are right," he said. "It has spunk." Then he looked at Sue with a calm smile and added, "Plus, it has 'brilliance.'" (Like the beautiful woman he was parading around.) "I will buy it."

They drove back to his office, where he tore up the Jefe report and told Sue that there would be no entry in her records, that she could pick up her ID badge at the main gate, and that she could take the regular exam as scheduled.

I was waiting on pins and needles for her to come home. When she entered the house, I immediately saw that things had turned around. We did not have to pack after all. Things might have turned out differently had Jose not intervened on Sue's behalf. We visited him later in Houston, where he lived with his family, and thanked him from the bottom of our hearts.

We continued with our usual routines, and when it came time for summer break in 1976, I think Sue thought it was time for me to get to know her family in Arkansas. I agreed. We discussed the idea with John, who told us he would like to spend the summer with his dad on a California beach. Michael had moved to Venice, and we arranged for John to travel to LA and back by air. Sue and I crossed the high interior mountains in our little Bug and sometimes had trouble making it up steep and rocky roads before crossing into Texas at the Laredo border.

After three days, we arrived in Benton, a small town outside Little Rock, where Sue's parents, Milton and Aurelia Caple, lived. All I knew was that Milton worked as an electrician at the nearby Alcoa aluminum plant and Aurelia was a homemaker. Bruce, whom they had adopted when he was a small child, was grown up and lived nearby. Sue's parents looked just like the pictures I had seen of them.

Sue and I were exhausted from the trip, and I was glad when Aurelia finally started supper. We exchanged the usual pleasantries, but the conversation was impaired a bit because I had some problems understanding the deep Southern drawl that Sue's parents spoke with. They also had problems with my German accent. But the food was good, and I was looking forward to sleeping with Sue in the extra bedroom of their otherwise small house.

But that is not how things went. Despite the sweltering heat, Milton told me I was to sleep outside in his enclosed pickup truck. I was a guest and did not ask why, but Sue explained that this was because we were not married. Milton and Aurelia were deeply religious and would not allow sin to be committed under their roof. The heat and humidity in the truck were so intense that I could not sleep at all, not even for a minute. Instead, I walked around town for hours and managed a few winks here and there under some bushes. In the morning, Milton asked me how I had slept, and I told him I hadn't because the heat in the truck had made sleeping impossible. "Too bad," he said, "but you will have to sleep there again." After I had spent three nights in the truck, Sue and I decided it was time to move on, and we continued westward to Los Angeles. Again, it was a three-day trip, and we had lots of time to mull things over and digest everything.

We had been together for three years and had not exchanged much information about our parents. That was partly because we had both lived with many family tensions while growing up, and we did not want to revisit the stories associated with them. As we talked, we realized that our parents were similar in many respects. Both of our fathers were skilled workers (an electrician and a typesetter), and both of our mothers were housewives dominated by their husbands. Both sets of parents lived typical social, economic, and political lifestyles that we, "children of the sixties," summarily dismissed as neurotic and hypocritical, or "ticky-tacky," as one song at the time put it.

On that long drive through the Southwest, Sue and I opened up more about our respective pasts, the pains they had caused us and still did, and what it all meant in general and for our future in particular.

Now it's time for Sue to introduce herself and her own past up to the point where we met in LA at her apartment in May 1973.

SUE

FIFTEEN

Childhood: Family, Religion, and Moving in with Aunt Connie and Uncle Sam

I was born on August 15, 1944, in a small doctor's office (one waiting room, one consultation room) in the small mining town of Bauxite, Arkansas, to Aurelia (born Jones) and Milton Caple. My parents were also born in Bauxite, my mother in 1923 and my father in 1921. They both attended the Bauxite school until seventh grade when they, like most kids in town, left school to try to find employment, which was very difficult to come by at the time.

Bauxite got its name from the mineral it sat on, which was mined in the area by the three largest aluminum companies in the US: Alcoa, Reynolds, and Kaiser. Bauxite was the company town for Alcoa. It housed the Alcoa workforce, from which Alcoa squeezed as much labor and profit as possible. Most of the town's roads were unpaved, and the dirt from the roads penetrated everything from clothing to kitchen cupboards. The company owned everything except the school and post office. Rent for company-furnished housing and supplies obtained from the company-owned general store were deducted from paychecks (Tennessee Ernie Ford's "Sixteen Tons" comes to mind). There was shaft mining and strip mining, and work was difficult everywhere.

My dad's first job with Alcoa was as a "monkey," a guy who drills holes deep into the rock being mined, then shoves lit dynamite sticks into them. Then he'd run fast enough to escape the flying debris. The explosion loosens the rock, which is then hauled off to extract the bauxite.

Bauxite-rich ore is also extracted from shafts, some of which reach deep underground. One of my mother's brothers, Uncle J. P., worked in the shafts. One day he and his work crew experienced a large explosion and were buried for three days underground, where they did not expect to ever see daylight again. But luckily, they were rescued.

When J. P. emerged from that dark shaft and saw the sun, he threw down his pick and shovel and yelled, "I ain't going down in no hole no more as long as I live!" Instead, he became a company painter and union organizer, fighting for decent working conditions and fair pay. He engaged in such activities as smuggling union pamphlets into the workplace in his lunch box and taking on strikebreakers who wanted to cross picket lines. Paw Paw, my grandfather Jones, had one of the most desirable jobs. He drove a EUC, a huge hauling truck. It gave Paw Paw a certain status among the other workers, which he wore with pride. I shared that pride, knowing the company wouldn't give that expensive truck to just anybody. Paw Paw was special. My proudest moment as a little girl was when our picture was taken together in front of his EUC, the wheels taller than me. That proud moment has stuck in my mind ever since.

When my parents tried to find work in this small company town, the economy had tanked to a slow sputter. The Great Depression started in 1929 and devastated much of American production, and it was followed by unprecedented job loss. The aluminum business was hit especially hard. Alcoa's orders had dropped to a trickle. But rather than laying off workers and keeping only enough to fill existing orders, the company adopted the Henry Ford model, that is, keeping the entire workforce and reducing everyone's hours equally as needed during the height of the Depression. This sometimes resulted in one day of work per week per worker. The Depression had global repercussions, and the hardships it caused left indelible marks on the collective memories of many nations.

In Europe, the Depression contributed to the strengthening of extremist political parties and eventually to such dictatorships as those of Mussolini and Hitler. In the US, it led to the creation of President Roosevelt's New Deal, with its large public works programs. My dad and millions of others benefited by being admitted into the Civilian Conservation Corps (CCC), working on reforestation projects in such places as Yellowstone and Yosemite National Parks. After the Japanese attack on Pearl Harbor in December 1941, FDR appealed particularly to young men to join the armed forces and help defend the country. My dad heeded the call and immediately went to the army recruitment center in Bauxite. He was a small, slim man (his friends called him "Bird Legs"), and he was not accepted. So he went to the navy recruitment center, where they agreed to take him.

Before he joined up, my father went to see his sweetheart, Aurelia Jones, and asked for her hand. Like many other young couples at the time, they married quickly. Milton then went to basic training and was shipped out to duty in the Panama Canal Zone. He was trained as an electrician to work on small navy planes. He came to see Aurelia several times on leave, and during one of those trips, probably during Christmas of 1943, I was conceived. My mom had found work in a local ammunition factory as the war finally overcame the crippling unemployment that had caused so much hardship for so many people for so long.

Following the end of the war in 1945, enlisted soldiers were allowed to have their families join them in housing provided on or off base. Mom and I joined Dad at his base in the Canal Zone in early 1946 when I was barely eighteen months old. My memory of this time is very hazy. I know we lived in a small tropical house built on stilts with large glassless windows and flaps that could be lowered during heavy rain. One of my earliest memories is running barefoot outside in a diaper, then climbing the steep stairs to our flat on the third floor on my hands and knees. There I sat and looked at all the people below. I recall someone shouting: "Susie, don't move!" We had a maid who babysat me and reportedly loved me very dearly. Unfortunately, I have no recollection of her.

After about two years in Panama, Dad was reassigned to a naval base in Dahlgren, Virginia. There, too, I have only vague memories of that time period. We lived in enlisted men's housing, where the walls were so thin you could overhear the conversations next door. I remember a pretty lady next door with three children. She was lively and energetic. Her husband built a flatbed trailer, and she painted it bright green. She smiled a lot—her face was like sunshine—and I wished my mom was like that.

One day, we all went together to visit nearby Washington, DC. I remember the cherry blossoms on the trees that the Japanese government had given as a gift. They were beautiful, like a white cloud. It was a nice day and we had a picnic. I also remember Captain Sayers, someone my parents knew and who had come along. He looked like Santa Claus and enjoyed talking to me. When I laughed, his whole face lit up. He tried diligently to adopt me. He argued as a captain he could provide me with more than my father could. Of course, my dad said no, and my mother said nothing.

After Virginia, we were transferred to French Morocco. We did not live on the naval base but had a little concrete house on the beach of Port Lyautey. There was a wall around the house with a metal gate. The house was cramped and dark and brutally hot. The kitchen stove ran on kerosene. The bottle that contained the fuel was on top of the stove, right next to the burner. The bottle was upside down, and gravity and a valve determined the height of the cooking flame, which was often right next to me. Even I realized how dangerous that was. There were other dangers as well.

One day I admired the fragrant mint that grew in the shady corner of our tiny yard. As I brushed the plants back and forth to release the lovely smell, I noticed something shiny, black, purple, and silver, and for a moment, I did not know what it was. Then I moved the plants a bit more and realized it was a large snake. Fear struck my heart, and I ran inside the house. It was so dark, I couldn't even see my mother, who could sit in that dark for hours. I told her about the snake, but she did nothing. So I went back outside, hoping the snake had left.

One night, excited voices and cracking sounds woke me up. They came from the other side of our wall. Close by, someone's house was burning down. I asked to see it, but my father said no. He told me the loud cracking came from burning dry wood but that no one was hurt.

Close to our village was a tuna factory that gave off a horrible stench. Men on boats put chains around the tails of lifeless tunas and moved them with large cranes into the nearby factory, where they were processed. That's when I realized that some jobs are horrible.

One day I was at the beach by myself when I saw two young guys coming ashore holding a third one between them. His leg had been bitten off at mid-thigh, probably by a shark. We knew he would die. Blood was pouring out of his leg, with big clots hanging down. He was groaning in agony, rolling his head from side to side. I felt sorry for him and his friends, who had to look on helplessly. I was only four or five years old, but I realized that Port Lyautey was not a safe place.

Public places were in constant turmoil. People moved around erratically, and cars mixed with donkeys and camels. There were seemingly no traffic rules. Camels were everywhere, usually sitting down with heavy loads on their backs. Camels are not nice. They will bite you or spit on you if you get too close, and you will stink for days. Donkeys were not quite as bad, but they, too, would kick. And everything came together in the open marketplace, the legendary bazaar. Everything and anything was for sale, and everybody was hawking something, vying for your attention in any way possible. It all looked very chaotic to an outsider, but there was a method to the madness.

I observed that Arabs knew how to bicker and barter with imagination, and for a long time, until a reasonable price was agreed upon. Bazaars were full of men wearing traditional long gowns and fezzes on their heads. Women were fully covered except for their eyes. Unmarried women could show both eyes, and married women only one. I remember the bazaar to be very dirty and full of slippery objects, and I wondered how women using one eye could negotiate the place. It looked like punishment to me, and I thought it wasn't good to be a woman. In many respects, it was not good to be a man either.

With the defeat of the Germans (who had ruled in the former French colony during WWII) in 1945, the French had reassumed their former colonial powers in Morocco and were eager to demonstrate this to the local population. I frequently saw French soldiers riding around in open jeeps, about four at a time, looking for something. Sometimes they would jump suddenly from their jeep and attack small groups of men with billy clubs. I thought it was strange that the men being attacked did not defend themselves. I later learned that fighting back would have made things much worse for them. The soldiers brutally beat the Arabs while shouting at them. They would usually pick one or two for questioning and more savage punishment. The French had total control and exercised it frequently, indiscriminately, and publicly. Even as a little girl, I knew that was wrong.

We had a maid called Fatima. Like most Moroccan women, she wore a robe, headscarf, and veil. Quiet and retiring, she moved around silently. She and her husband lived in a small tent pitched on the sandy ground near our house. Fatima showed me how to wash cooking pans with sand. Her husband, Mohammed Bin Sedu, befriended my dad by inviting him to a tea-drinking ceremony in the open area behind the tent. This was quite an honor, and Fatima set everything up with a big shiny silver tray on which she placed a sparkling tea service set that looked like it belonged in a palace. This traditional ceremony was a men-only affair. But my dad asked Mohammed to accept my presence, which he did as a compliment to my dad.

With me present, the two men sat there for quite a while, talking and sipping tea, bonding in a mutually respectful way. Mohammed, surely, was also trying to secure his worth. My parents helped him and his family survive under the harsh Moroccan conditions by giving them leftover food. Mom would peel potatoes so that the peelings were really thick and add other small cutoffs.

Though my mom's food was nothing to look forward to, at least we had food, even if it often consisted of little more than Spam and powdered milk. I had problems downing the powdered milk, and Dad invented a game that made me drink it. He knew I admired the sunset, and he made me look into the glass in the direction of the sun as it went down. Just before it dipped into the horizon, I had to swallow the last bit of milk to see the full splendor of the sun's disappearance through the bottom of the glass. It worked.

To me, the highlights of our stay in Port Lyautey were the trips in Dad's car. Dad had bought a little blue Crosley, with a convertible top attached with snaps. A cluster of boys would surround the car whenever we went somewhere, calling out that they wanted to guard it while we were gone shopping. So when you parked your car, you had to pick one of the boys, who suddenly became "boss," telling all the others what to do or not to do.

I remember one of the nicest things about Africa being the evening call to prayer. The call is made five times a day from praying towers, called minarets. The calls made during the day just seemed like another part of an all-pervasive hectic life. But the evening call at sunset brought everything to rest. The hectic pace of life slowed down. Traffic slowed to a trickle. The dusty roads came to life with the reflections of the golden-red sunlight on the horizon. People walked from all directions to the mosques. They listened devoutly to the muezzin's call to prayer, and his chant brought their humming day to a peaceful close. Men walked alone or in small groups. Children were no longer lively and loud. Women walked together. There were no family groups, as in Western churchgoing, although some men held their sons' hands. It created a feeling completely unfamiliar to me, and I liked it and looked forward to it.

London followed Morocco, which was Dad's preference. He found a nice house off base (the only house I recall in my childhood). It was well-built and quiet. But it was almost always cold. We had an electric heater in the living room. At one point, I reached inside it, touched the live wires, and experienced a calm, painless undulating paralysis that I could not pull away from. My father knocked me loose.

I was of school age, and Dad enrolled me in first grade at the elementary school in our district. The British children would not befriend or play with me because I was an American. During recess, I was shunned and could not join the games being played. To bear this severe ostracism, I would hide in the coal bin and watch through the cracks in the door while the other girls played together. When recess was over, and we had to line up to return to class, the teacher would come over to me, knock the coal dust off my clothes, and admonish me: "Susie, you will have to stay out of the coal bin." It seemed the teachers did not care about the shunning.

After a few months, I got expelled because I was not a British subject. British law allowed only British subjects to enroll in public schools. The law further stated that once a child was expelled, for whatever reason, he or she could not enroll in another school for six months, even if a school was willing to admit the child. This meant I would effectively lose my whole first year of school. My classroom teacher, Mrs. Rutherford, felt so bad about this that she offered to tutor me privately at my home after school. My dad paid her with groceries and things that were rationed at the time. She treasured the canned goods, butter, and sugar greatly, and once, she got a pair of stockings that seemed like pure gold to her.

I used to play by myself and with my doll. I don't remember any interaction with my mother, who was home all day long like me. But that was just the way it was. On my birthday, my dad took me on his bicycle to a toy store and said I could pick out anything I wanted. I spotted a Steiff bear on the highest shelf and said that I wanted it. Dad asked how much it cost. When the saleslady told him, he looked like he had been punched in the gut. He then asked me whether there was anything else I would like, and I said, "No, I want the bear." He bought it. But looking back on it, I don't think that was a very happy birthday for my parents. It must have cost a fortune for them. I only found out later that the German company Steiff was to toy bears what the Swiss company Rolex is to wristwatches.

One day I was playing doctor with my rubber doll. I got Dad's pocketknife and "operated" on her leg. The blade was sharp, and I made a smooth incision about one inch long. I pretended to "fix" whatever was wrong and placed a very nice bandage on the leg. I knew it would take a while to heal, so I waited three days and removed the bandage. I can still feel the horror I experienced when I saw the incision was the same and had not healed. It was overwhelming; I felt as if I had killed my patient—the ultimate physician's nightmare. I was inconsolable for a long time.

After two years in London, a time during which I received little formal schooling, Dad got redeployed back to the US, "stateside" in military jargon. But first, we went to our old home in Bauxite, Arkansas, to see our family: my grandparents Mama Jones (Pauline) and Papa Jones (Big Doc) and their children, Little Doc, Phil, J. P., and Ronnie, as well as my grandmother Mama Caple. My dad had two brothers, but they had moved away. I quickly got used to how someone in the family would put me on the kitchen counter and ask me to say something. Then they would laugh out loud. I didn't know what was funny. I spoke with a British accent, which was hilarious to my family in rural Arkansas.

After the visit to Bauxite, we moved to Orange Park in Florida, into a trailer park near the naval base in Jacksonville, to which Dad had been transferred. I was eight or nine years old, and my mother took me to the local school and enrolled me. She had washed my hair and put it up in curlers. The principal took my mother and me into the classroom and introduced me to the teacher and the other children. I remember feeling embarrassed about my appearance. The other kids looked at me, too appalled to snicker. The teacher said something about the curlers and my hair, to which my mother replied angrily, "At least it's clean." Then I took my seat in the back row. Nobody talked to me. I don't remember the teacher's name or any of the many teachers I had after that. But I remember that we children had to stand at attention whenever the principal entered the classroom and that I never understood what the teacher and the other kids said. I also remember riding the bus to school and looking at my reflection in the bus window. That was the only interaction I had on the bus, me with my mirror image. I didn't know any of the kids. The bus went by the colored kids' school. This was still during the time of segregation.

The colored school was down by the St. Johns River. It was an unpainted one-room building on pilings about four feet high. It had no glass windows, just flaps that could be lowered when it rained. The yard around the building didn't have a single blade of grass. The kids ran all over the place, many of them barefoot. They always looked excited—playing, laughing, yelling, and chasing each other. Some crawled under the building. Many, mostly the girls, crouched around an old wire fence. Others, mostly older boys, were down by the river, setting up fish traps to take home fish after school. I remember thinking that they did not have a very good school, but they did have much more fun than us white kids. I felt sorry for them, though, because of the run-down school and the general neglect of their environment. And I knew it wasn't right that they were separate. After the bus let me off at our house, I tried to play a little outside, but no other kids were around.

After a while, Mother called me into the trailer to give me my daily whipping. She would call out, "Suuusieee, what have you been up to again?" Then she grabbed one of my arms and spun me around while whipping me all the time with the other hand. She usually beat me shortly before my dad came home from work. I did not dare to ask for the reason for this daily ritual. It would have only made things worse. Instead, I accepted it as the natural lot of being a kid, something I would be free from in adulthood. Besides, I had other things to worry about.

For instance, early one morning, a tremendous explosion in a nearby trailer woke me up. Mr. and Mrs. Lachemacher lived there. He had already gone to the shower room outside to wash up and shave as he did every morning. She had started making coffee and the stove exploded when she lit it, setting the whole trailer ablaze. He ran to get her out, but she was already burned badly. Someone wrapped her in a blanket and laid her on the ground. Everyone in the trailer park watched the fire, their backs to her. So I went over to sit on the ground with her. She moaned quietly; she was unable to move or speak. The prickly army blanket revealed her face, nose, and lips, which were almost completely gone. I thought an adult should be with her. It was still dark when the firemen came, and the trailer had burned completely. The ambulance came and its crew carried Mrs. Lachemacher away without even looking at her. Many months later, she would return, disfigured, her formerly pretty face scarred.

After Orange Park in Florida, Dad was transferred to Norman, just outside Oklahoma City, where we moved into another trailer park. Our little trailer had a small concrete patio. We had no furniture for it, and it had no awning, but I thought we were living "upscale." The trailer was twenty-eight feet long and eight feet wide. Because it had only one bedroom, I slept on the couch.

I had a hard time learning things. One day, my parents gave me a coin and sent me to a roadside stand a ways from the trailer to buy some lettuce. I felt very important because my parents had trusted me with money. But I did not know the difference between lettuce and cabbage and bought the wrong thing. Mom and Dad were upset and explained the difference to me. Sometime later, they sent me again, and I made the same mistake. I never got sent to the roadside stand again after that.

There were a few other kids in the park, and at last, I had playmates.

I don't remember any of the kids' names anymore, but we all played almost every day after school in a log pile that was a result of bulldozing trees down to extend the trailer park. The pile was full of snakes, which we saw almost daily. Whenever one of us kids and a snake wanted the same space, a wordless negotiation took place. No one ever got bitten. All of our parents knew what was going on. Today's helicopter parents would be near heart attacks knowing about situations like that.

Our school was about twenty miles away, and the bus drove all the kids from grades one through twelve there and back. I compared myself to the older girls on the bus. They were always clean looking while I noticed the dirt lines in my elbows.

I remember very little about the school. There were extracurricular sports and sometimes a school dance or "sock hop" where kids would dance on the gymnasium floor in their socks. I couldn't go to these because, according to my parents, dancing was sinful. My parents belonged to the Church of Christ and lived according to a very fundamentalist reading of the Bible. Neither could I participate in or watch any sports activities because the school was too far away.

I don't remember my teacher's name anymore. All I recall is that she had dark hair and long painted fingernails. She used to inspect all of her pupils' hands every day. We had to lay our hands on our desks, palms down, and she would walk around and inspect each of us. I always had dirty fingernails, and she would tap hard on the backs of my hands with a ruler and tell me to keep them clean. Equally embarrassing was the discovery that I had a giant tapeworm (it came out by itself) and my learning that I was full of other types of worms too, which were removed by swallowing a Ping-Pong-ball-sized pill that nearly choked me to death. Dad shoved it down my throat, insisting that the doctor had told him the whole thing had to go down in one piece. And eventually it did, to the relief of everyone.

It was in Norman that I had my first and only childhood birthday party. I got a bicycle, which Dad bought for me. The gift was given to me with Mother's bitter admonition to "take care of that bicycle; it's the only one you're gonna get," which took the joy right out of it. Anyway, I was thrilled, and my birthday party consisted of Dad turning the jump rope for as long as we kids wanted to jump. It was great. All the kids loved it better than balloons and crepe paper. There was no cake, though. But I never had a cake anyway. Afterward, Dad complained about his shoulder hurting from so much work, which hurt me a little, thinking that he regretted doing what he'd done for me.

It was also in Norman when, at the end of the school year, my teacher called Dad to school and told him that I would fail the fourth grade because I could not read. I don't know why she waited to break the news beyond the point when corrective action could have been taken. Dad was horrified and said I would not fail because he would try to teach me how to read at home. It wasn't easy.

Because of our many moves, I had never learned how to use the alphabet to construct words and sentences properly and was completely lost when it came to phonetics. So Dad started reading with me. He soon realized that I could remember a text but not read it; that is, I couldn't make out individual letter combinations and their corresponding sounds. Then he had me read backward while explaining the reading process to me. I could not memorize sentences read backward, and so I had to focus on individual syllables, words, and word combinations. Eventually, I learned how to read and passed fourth grade just in the nick of time. It was a very humiliating experience, and I promised myself never to fail a grade again. To this day, I am an extremely slow reader and was always the last student to hand in exams all through college and medical school. But I still managed to pass exams with high grades.

Ever since I was a kid, we went to the Church of Christ three times during the week and twice on Sunday. We went to every prayer meeting and revival service, Sunday school, and Wednesday night Bible study. My mother was the driving force behind all of this. The church influenced me deeply and has left its marks on my psyche. It is a strict, fundamentalist church, taking the text of the Bible to mean exactly what it says. It appeals particularly to more literal-minded people.

The congregations are typically between a handful and a few dozen congregants at most and composed mostly of farmers and blue-collar workers. They did not always own their meeting places and often met in storefronts, pole barns, or other such sites. I remember there was no air-conditioning, so to cool down, women used paper fans mounted on sticks. Men just sweated, sometimes profusely, in their suits. Under such stressful conditions, I would start to wiggle a

Me as a fourth grader in Norman, Oklahoma.

bit. My mother would cross her arms and, with the hand closest to me, pinch me very hard, long, and often. The preachers' sermons were full of human condemnation, calling for sinners to repent. They used images that frightened me into sleepless nights, conjuring up pictures of poor souls dangling by a thread over the fiery pits of hell. The preacher was the only one to raise his voice. We, the poor sinners, had to second his proclamations with statements like "Praise the Lord," "Amen, Brother," and "I know that's right."

What we knew was right, as our preacher said, is that members of the Church of Christ were the purest of all Christians. Among other things, this was because we could resist temptation where others could not. We could, for instance, resist the temptation to laugh at a joke, however innocent. Except for rejoicing in the Gospel's truth, joy and fun were sinful. We didn't even have potluck suppers. Instead, we had to listen to the preacher as he condemned all kinds of sins with intense fervor. He got especially riled up when he condemned "fornication." As his volume increased, his face would turn lobster red, his veins would swell out of his neck, ready to burst, and sweat would run down his face in heavy streams. Even the hard of hearing got the message. The emotional climax consisted of congregants confessing personal sins to the entire congregation.

Fornication with other members of the congregation was a favorite. When it got to that point, the temperature in the room was searingly hot, with a real feel of 100-plus degrees. Then the preacher started the highlight of his show. Public forgiveness in the name of the Lord Jesus Christ, who died for our sins on the cross. I liked baptism more. It was a calmer event. At the end of every service, the preacher requested that anyone who wanted to be saved and had not been baptized follow "the call" and ask for baptism at that time. This usually initiated a busy moment since baptism would be immediately carried out in the baptismal pool of the church, or tub, or a nearby river, pond, or lake. There was no scheduling or announcement. It was all very spontaneous.

When the Spirit calls you, you follow immediately. I, too, followed the call one day. As a result, I felt I had a deeper sense of right and wrong, particularly a profound understanding of how to follow Christ's teachings in his Sermon on the Mount. Still, I always thought that of all the Christians in the world, the Catholics were the luckiest. They had pretty churches with stained glass windows and music during mass. Kids got pretty cards with pictures of saints and other notables when they went to Sunday school. And when they confessed their sins, they could hide in a black box and whisper through a screen to a priest who couldn't see them.

My mother came alive in church. She liked to sing high soprano on all hymns. Unfortunately, her voice lacked quality. It was thin and sounded metallic. And she loved the high notes, always ensuring her voice was preeminent. She placed her right hand, fingers spread, on her chest for such performances. When church was over, she would "visit," which meant talking to other church members for one to two hours while I stood impatiently to the side. Despite this experience, I maintained rigorous church attendance until I entered college. Later, at the University of Kansas, I met principled Christians who drank beer, played cards, went to dances, and engaged in many other worldly things I had learned to condemn. It started a critical thinking process I found liberating.

Regarding my school life in Norman, I had barely passed fourth grade with my dad's help. At least I could read. I don't recall much of what happened in fifth or sixth grade, except that I remained a poor reader. I had problems following the class discussions and was terrified of reading aloud. I couldn't "sound out" the letters properly and was the worst reader in my class. This was reflected in my standing among my fellow students.

For instance, when we played team sports, I was always the last one picked for the team. I lost all confidence in achieving anything, which led to corresponding results. Things changed a bit when I took algebra, a subject I liked and excelled in. That was my first positive experience at school.

My dad had become a navy expert in electronics, was good at algebra, and helped me understand the subject's powerful logic and its beauty. When I entered ninth grade, he was transferred to a navy station in Quantico on the coast of Virginia. I was the best student in my class and became a bit of a star. This was furthered by the fact that I had become a noticeably pretty girl and began to receive attention from boys. In many respects, this was a mixed blessing.

Junior high had many extracurricular activities that I wanted to participate in. My schoolmates all went, but my parents wouldn't let me go. They continued to argue that sock hops, movies, card games, etc. were all sinful. In fact, as time went by, they became increasingly strict in controlling my behavior and faulted me for every slight infraction of their demanding standards. I tried to comply diligently but never seemed to please them. My dad told me numerous times, "I'm gonna send you to reform school." My mother wholeheartedly agreed.

I could not date, barring one exception. My father had found someone considerably older than me to take me out one evening. We were supposed to be back at my house by 10:00 p.m. Not much happened, and we were back by 9:30, sitting on the porch talking and waiting for the cuckoo clock to strike 10:00. When it did, I walked into the house, where my father received me red-faced, breathing heavily, and holding a hairbrush threateningly. When I asked, "What's wrong?" he said, "I told you to be back before ten, not after ten."

It was at that moment that I realized things would not turn out well for me in the long run if I stayed in that house much longer. As hard as I tried, I could not achieve the perfection my parents demanded. I needed to get out. There was also always the fear of being moved to another base, another school with different teachers, and new friends to whom I would have to prove myself all over again.

Later that summer, I asked my Aunt Polly to let me live with her and her family at their place in Arkansas. She had always been my favorite aunt. But she said, "Well, my goodness, Susie, what would happen if you were to rip your rompers?" implying the shameful consequences and my parents' anger if I were to get pregnant. I was shocked that she thought I might be sexually active. Her view of me was a bitter disappointment. It showed that she had little trust in me.

Next, I asked my Aunt Connie in Kansas if I could live with her and Uncle Sam. Being my mother's twin sister, she said, "Well, of course." I was pleased and relieved, knowing my life would change for the better. My parents did not object, and I moved to Neodesha in the summer of 1959.

SIXTEEN

Life in Kansas:
Neodesha

Aunt Connie, my mother's twin sister, lived with her husband, Sam Curt, and their two children—my girl cousin Sammie, who was a few years younger than me, and Larry, still a small boy—in a modest house near the center of town. They were a loving and stable family and welcomed me with open arms. Uncle Sam and Aunt Connie were extremely hardworking people. Sam had two jobs, working the night shift at a local oil refinery, where he monitored operating machines, and selling cars at a secondhand dealer during the day. He was tired a lot because we kids disturbed his daytime sleep hours. Despite all the pressures he had to endure, he had a friendly personality, and I don't remember any conflict at home. Connie, although not the manager, "ran" Neodesha's Plymouth car dealership. She was indispensable to its operations and had a very secure position.

From the start, I began doing chores around the house and tried to make myself as useful as possible. I helped without being asked, washed dishes, took out the trash, did laundry, cleaned the house, etc. I made sure not to be a burden, which required that I never get into conflict with Sammie. I sensed that she objected to sharing her bed and bedroom with me. I also did better in school and overshadowed her in other fields as well, leading to provocations on her part almost daily.

I had to bite my tongue for three years out of respect for Connie and Sam. They were both lax on discipline, the opposite of my mother and dad, and they tolerated much of Sammie's behavior. But both my aunt and uncle supported me wherever they could, including buying me clothes, paying school fees, and providing me with meals. I tried to be as independent as possible under the circumstances.

I got a job as an assistant to the local dentist. This was rural Kansas, and during those days, no one thought about formal job training. I learned on the fly, cleaned teeth, made bridges, assisted with dental surgery, cleaned the office, sterilized reusable equipment, sharpened needles, polished floors, handled the billing—in short, I did everything. Come rain or shine, I had to be available at all hours. For instance, one Saturday morning, Doc Gausman ordered me to the office to help pull an abscessed molar from the swollen jaw of a heavy farmer sick with a fever who could barely talk. It was a difficult extraction.

The tooth was rotten and broke into several pieces as Doc Gausman worked his magic. It was a hot summer day, and there was no air-conditioning. Doc rolled his toothpick from side to side, as he usually did during procedures, and started cussing loudly, which was uncommon. As the tooth cracked and broke, I got dizzy and fainted. When I came to, I was nose to nose with the farmer, who had also fainted. Doc had fully reclined the dental chair, which in the end allowed the heavy patient to slide to the floor. Doc was angry because I had fainted. I could not hold the patient up, and Doc told me to "never do anything like that again." I tried not to. I earned $1 an hour, which was the best job for a girl in town.

I did well in high school, almost forgetting my earlier days of dismal struggle. In the summer of 1959, I enrolled in the tenth grade at Neodesha High and stayed there until graduation three years later. Dreams I didn't even know I had came true once I was out of the oppressive environment of my parents' house. I quickly became popular and became a cheerleader, which was considered a pretty big deal in those days. I was able to participate in all the school activities I wanted. I also got around on my own. Uncle Sam taught me how to drive on the dirt roads around town and showed me how to change a tire. He loaned me his 1949 Ford, which was built like a tank. One time, I knocked the entire garage right off its cinder blocks, and the car barely had a scratch.

I still remember an incident that could only happen in a small town like Neodesha. Two farmers in pickup trucks going in opposite directions met on Main Street, stopped, and had a conversation through their open windows. I was behind one of them and patiently waited for the conversation to be over, but they were in no mood to end it anytime soon. So I tried to get around the truck in front of me, knocking the fender of the truck. There was no dent on either the Ford or the truck, but I had knocked off the dried mud from under the truck, showing the outline of the truck in the middle of Main Street. The chief of police took me to the station, filled out papers, and called Aunt Connie. All of this was just to "teach me a lesson." At dinner that night, Connie said, "I heard you were speeding down Main Street today." I got the message that if farmers want to block traffic with their trucks to talk about the weather, you better let them.

Shortly after I knocked the mud off the farmer's truck, I had a chance to really do some speeding, so much so that the car went airborne. The nearby town of Independence held its Bathing Suit Beauty Contest, and some people in Neodesha thought I might be a hot candidate to win first place. To represent our town appropriately, our Ford dealership loaned me a brand-new Ford Sunliner. It had a red bottom, white top, and sharp fins and was adorned with lots of chrome. The dealer specifically told me not to drive it over 55 mph because it wasn't "broken in yet." I had a job at the dentist's office that day, and when I left work and got to the dealer to pick up the car, I was running a little late for the contest. I dashed over the rolling hills of Kansas and started to get a fluttering feeling, like the car was made of tissue paper. I looked down at the dashboard and saw that the car was going 115 mph and thought, "Oh my God, I have ruined the car already."

I reached the swimming pool with plenty of time to spare. I briefly met the competitors. Soon, we were ushered into the locker room to change into our bathing suits. We were told that we could not "enhance" our figures with extra material, but we did it anyway. Then, we filed out, were each given a number, and lined up. The all-male jury awaiting us was scattered around the swimming pool. They called out numbers, and individually the contestants before me walked the periphery of the pool and paused in front of the judges, who sized them up slowly from top to bottom. Something inside me said, "I have got this made." My turn came and I walked the rim of the pool like I owned it. I paused at the last set of judges, facing the pool. Gazing over my right shoulder in a sultry Betty Grable manner, I noticed the men leaning forward. Their looks told me that I should never do such a thing again. At the same time, I knew I had nailed it. When I was announced the winner, I acted like I was surprised, and I collected the flowers, the little tiara, and the three-piece set of Samsonite luggage, as well as a lifetime pass to the pool. I never went to the pool, but I did use the luggage a lot. Moreover, I had learned something about the leering fascination with the show. After that, I never looked at the Miss America contest with the same thrill as I had before. Years later, when a makeover artist told me I needed to learn how to "use my eyes" more, I had a flashback to the swimsuit competition and let my eyes roll any way I felt.

Of course there were boys, many of whom wanted to date me. But I fell in love with Dick Umbarger, a smart, athletic type, and he fell in love with me. We shared many romantic hours and dreaded our eventual separation. He was a couple of years older and went off to the Air Force Academy in Colorado. However, we stayed in touch, and soon he invited me to a grand Academy ball in Colorado Springs. As a sixteen-year-old, I was dazzled by the whole affair, the school's impressive architecture, the dapper young men in uniform, and the pageantry as I entered the ballroom, wearing a white ball gown, on the arm of Dick in his full dress uniform. We walked with other couples under an archway of sabers held by the Academy's cadets. It swept me off my feet. During that romantic night, Dick gave me his pin. The next morning, he was shaken that I wasn't wearing it. I did not understand that the pin implied my betrothal to him and that the next step was formal engagement. The love was certainly there. But I was only sixteen, and my youthful ignorance and the distance from Dick eventually took their toll.

After a while, back in Neodesha, I started to date another boy, Michael. But he also left Neodesha to go to the University of Kansas (KU). I didn't know it at the time, but that's where I would meet him again later. However, when he left, I didn't think I would go to college at all. No one in my family ever had, and there were no expectations that I should go. The fact that I was doing well in school seemed of little consequence. I had received high grades in difficult subjects and excelled in extracurricular activities. I was even the salutatorian. But back then, the general expectation was that girls, smart or not, should prepare for family and motherhood first, and perhaps take a low-skill job between graduation and marriage. I remember thinking, "What am I going to do after high school? Hairdresser? No, I can't do hair. Secretary? No, I can't type well." I felt lost.

My high school counselor, Duke Donnelly, must have read my mind. He recognized that I was a bright girl with some potential but no backing or money. He called me to his office one day and gave me a stack of applications for every college in Kansas. There were over twenty applications, as I recall, along with request forms for financial aid. All he said was "Fill them out and bring them back to me." I remember being encouraged at the thought of going to college, and I went to work diligently. I filled out the forms and he mailed them for me, knowing I had no money for the applications. Then, it was a waiting game.

Soon, the responses trickled in. I kept a list of all the schools I had applied to, and all of the letters started with something like "We regret to inform you . . ." Eventually the last letter came and I opened it at lunch. (At that time students could go home for lunch.) It was from KU, the most prestigious school in Kansas. My heart sank. I figured if the minor schools would not take me, certainly KU wouldn't either. I put my brave and cheerful face on, waved the envelope in the air at the kitchen table, and said, "Well, here is the last rejection." I opened it and read, "We are happy to inform you . . ." I couldn't finish the sentence as my eyes watered and my heart climbed into my throat. All I could do was wave the letter around and jump up and down to everyone's bewilderment. What a wonderful, life-changing moment it was. Thank you, Mr. Donnelly, wherever you are. Knowing that someone put their trust in you and helped you succeed against all odds to achieve something extraordinary is a very empowering and overwhelming feeling. KU admitted any resident with a high school diploma, but mine came with a scholarship. There were only a few of those. Without it, I would not have been able to pursue higher studies.

SEVENTEEN

The University of Kansas

I eagerly awaited my enrollment at KU, and Aunt Connie took me and Sammie up to the Lawrence campus in the fall of 1962. KU had given me a small stipend, and I was assigned to stay at Watkins Hall, one of the scholarship halls for smart girls from modest backgrounds. Watkins was the most prestigious one. It was located next to the chancellor's mansion. There was also Miller Hall for girls and two halls for boys. It was quite an honor to be selected.

When we got there, the welcoming committee rushed to greet Sammie. She was two years younger than me but looked older. Eventually, they got me moved in and explained the scholarship hall program to me. It required cleaning the hall, cooking the meals, observing house rules, and much more. I loved being in the program and felt like I belonged. I also appreciated the system honoring girls like me who came from a less privileged background.

I shared a room with another girl and slept on the top bunk of our bunk bed. When I got to choose my desk in the study room, I felt extremely excited and happy. The hall had kitchens in the basement, sitting rooms on the first floor, study rooms on the second floor, and "sleeping porches" on the third. The hall program included acquiring

As a University of Kansas student at Watkins Hall: etiquette über alles.

proper etiquette, especially table manners. The assumption at the time was that students who grew up on a farm needed sufficient social graces to do well at university functions, as possible members of sororities, or to simply be more successful later in life.

The program had its humorous sides. New girls, for instance, were asked to pick one kitchen utensil and were then forced to eat with it alone for an entire week. I remember one girl picking an egg beater and struggling to get her food from her plate to her mouth. After one week, we were given a fork and could only eat with that. Nonetheless, it was an improvement over what we had chosen before. As the weeks went by, we were given knives and spoons and learned all about their proper use, formal place settings, and the like. It was a great way to learn because it didn't single out particular girls for good or bad manners. Thank you, Mrs. Watkins, who designed the program.

Like most college freshmen, I had no firm idea about a suitable field of study and did what most students do; I enrolled in many different kinds of classes to find out what interested me the most. I decided to take one class from each major discipline. For instance, the PE department offered fencing and I signed up, soon finding that I had talent. KU had an inviting philosophy. It was a land grant college, created after the Civil War, admitting all Kansas residents with a high school diploma. But most high schools did not prepare students for the rigorous academic work needed to succeed at KU. Neodesha High School certainly didn't. I became painfully aware of this as I studied my butt off to make the grades. I was totally lost in Western Civilization. I didn't even know who came first, the Greeks or the Romans. The only students who seemed to be prepared came from Kansas City schools, especially from those of the Shawnee Mission district, and there was no way to keep up with them.

Moreover, students in the scholarship hall were under added pressure since remaining there was contingent on grade point averages. Still, I liked my courses and did well, even though I must have been one of the poorest students on campus. I lacked everything, especially clothes, which was a particular problem during the cold winter months. I couldn't even afford enough underwear, so I stole some from my roommate, who had plenty. She must have noticed but never said

KU fencing team. I am the captain (the person to the right).

anything. I have felt bad about it for many years. This is not a part of one's life one can easily shake off.

There were some highlights, however. I did well in fencing. I had initially enrolled because I had seen some fencing pictures in the encyclopedia my dad had bought for me many years earlier, never dreaming that someday I could be doing it. Because my fencing coach, Mr. Giele, realized I had no money to buy the required equipment, he got it for me. He realized my talent and enthusiasm for the sport. I participated in several tournaments and ranked high enough to participate in the 1963 national fencing championship in Atlantic City. I was in my element. Several coaches from around the US gave me lessons, and I was seen as a rising star. I received special attention from the coach of the University of Illinois team and his son. It was a very enjoyable time. I did not place, but it was my first championship, and that was to be expected. But I did become the captain of the KU women's fencing team, an achievement I cherished a lot and carried with pride for years to come.

Another highlight was my election to KU Princess for the Kansas Relays of spring 1963. Watkins Hall nominated me for the contest and I won. I remember that I, together with the Relay Queen, had to parade around with a sash and flowers and drape the victory medals around the necks of the winning athletes, one of whom was the soon-to-be world-famous middle-distance runner Jim Ryun from Wichita.

There were two not-so-pleasant events that stand out as part of my lasting KU memories. Because my fencing practices coincided with dinner, the girls at Watkins Hall would leave a plate of food for me in the oven. One day, I went to get it and started to light the oven, which exploded and enveloped me in a ball of fire. I was rushed to urgent care on campus, where they cleaned my face and slathered it with ointment. I was in the hospital for three days. Bandages encircled my whole head and face. However, my biggest concern was my eyesight. When they removed the bandages, I was greatly relieved that I could see normally, but all of my hair had been singed away, including my eyelashes and eyebrows. I had to wear a headscarf for several months.

The second incident was equally scary. My fencing practices were mostly held in the afternoons. One day, when it was already late in the evening, I went to the basement locker room after practice to shower and get ready to go home. As I stepped out of the shower, a man put a towel over my head and started dragging me toward a couch. I screamed as hard and as loudly as I could. Suddenly, the sounds of the men's fencing team practicing upstairs stopped and the sound of men rushing downstairs toward the locker room took over. The man trying to tie me down to the couch let go of me and quickly disappeared. I ran halfway up the stairs and sat down, covering myself as the men streamed past me to search for him. They found a window open, but the man was gone. One of the fellows draped his jacket over me on his way down the stairs. I never knew who he was, but I thought he must have had a sister because he was so kind. I am grateful to him to this day.

And yes, I did some dating. There was the Chancellor's Scholar, an incredibly bright student from Pakistan, who had an apartment in the chancellor's mansion, right next to Watkins Hall. He made chicken curry every weekend and would always invite me over. He taught me how to make it and told me he wanted to "make out" with me. But I wasn't romantically interested in him, and we slowly drifted apart.

A Swiss student of international law was very delighted with me. He was several years older and looked like the perfect European gentleman: well-raised and with lots of old money in his family. He invited me to cultural events in Kansas City, including ballroom dances. He taught me the Viennese waltz, and I was very impressed. He treated me with the utmost respect, but I felt like a decoration on his arm. He talked to his family in Switzerland about me. His mother sent me a beautifully laced handkerchief, and he told me he wanted to marry me and take me to live with him in Europe. As much as I liked him, I could not see myself as a high-society lady in Switzerland. I was a poor girl from the plains of Kansas and Bauxite, Arkansas, and I could not imagine myself fitting in over there. I was still very young and uncertain of myself. In the end, the handsome young gentleman from Switzerland went back home without me.

I also ran into Michael, who was still attending KU. He was further along in his studies and had picked Spanish literature as his major. He, too, was tall and handsome and very sociable. I fell for him again.

In many ways, my first year at KU was one of the happier years of my life. I was desperately poor and always tried to hide that fact from my fellow students, which produced some awkward moments, but I managed. I was doing well academically and liked fencing, a sport in which I increasingly excelled. I had made friends and liked living at Watkins Hall. But something happened that put an end to all of that.

The first semester at KU always saw a huge thinning out of students. But I worked hard and felt I had very little to worry about. My academic advisor put me in an English composition class that met on Tuesdays, Thursdays, and Saturdays at 7:00 a.m. It was held in an old wooden building with creaky stairs, drafty single-pane windows, and insufficient heating, which became a problem, especially in the cold winter months. We all huddled there wearing coats, hats, and gloves, struggling through English lessons with a textbook that had the answers to all the questions listed in the back. One day I told the teacher, a graduate student teaching assistant, that I expected something more from him than reading the lessons in the book and looking up the answers in the back. We were all freezing our butts off in the early morning hours and could do that at home. He stared at me and clutched the back of the chair in front of him. His nose was red and his face pale. He didn't say a single word. Neither did any of the other students, whom I knew felt the same way I did.

During Christmas break back in Neodesha, Connie opened one of my letters from KU and told me, "You got an F in English." I said it had to be a mistake because I hadn't failed anything. Back at KU, I went to appeal my grade and brought all my papers and tests, showing the lowest grade I had received on anything was a C. The administrator said he would talk to the TA and then call me back. When I returned, he told me that he agreed that my classwork was, while not at the A level, definitely not failing, but that the TA said he had the "academic freedom" to give me any grade he wanted to. I told the administrator that this meant I would lose my spot in the scholarship hall at the end of the academic year and that I had no way to pay for school. He said he was very sorry, but the TA would not change the grade. A great shadow fell over my experience at KU.

From delight and elation, I entered into the grind. What a difference a TA, or any teacher, can make in the life of an aspiring student if the administration lets them. I didn't know what I was going to do. I could not turn to my mom and dad or Connie and Sam. Going into that summer break after my first year at KU, I had a feeling of dread. Then, my parents told me they needed their house painted, and they were willing to pay me something to do it. So that is what I did. It was a very boring and uneventful summer. However, I was determined to get back to KU, even without the scholarship.

I found a room off campus that was free in exchange for babysitting. The room was a corner of the garage with a single bed and a small shower. There wasn't any furniture, not even a desk. There was a small electric heater that could only be turned on when I was there. The garage was miserably cold, and I slept in my coat, hat, and gloves. I rode my bicycle to campus and ate supper at a drugstore that had a soda fountain. I paid $1.25 for a plate of food that was never enough to satisfy my hunger. One day while babysitting, the mother of the children was cleaning up after supper, and there was a pork chop left over. She fed it to the dog. I would have loved to have it. It was the most luscious pork chop I had ever seen.

EIGHTEEN

Living in Madrid with Michael: The Birth of John

My days at KU ended quite abruptly in the summer of 1965. I was dating Michael but knew things might come to an end between us when he received a scholarship to study abroad in Madrid for a year. I remember taking him to the Kansas City airport, watching the plane take off until it went out of sight, and feeling an unbearable weight on my shoulders, knowing that I had been left behind pregnant. The first person I told was my fencing coach, Mr. Giele. He was really angry because he had put a lot of money and work into me, hoping to groom me to become an Olympic contender. He was also mad at Michael for leaving me and demanded that he should return to the US and assume his responsibilities as a father. There was no chance of that. I had him drive me to Neodesha, where I told Aunt Connie of my dilemma. She knew Michael's parents, who owned the local funeral parlor and counted themselves among the members of Neodesha's upper crust. They got in touch with Michael and bought me a suit to get married in and a plane ticket to Madrid. I had the feeling they wanted to get rid of me quick.

I informed my parents about all of it. They, too, did not want to get involved. I assumed they thought that I (not Michael) had sinned and had to face the music by myself. I had to withdraw from KU.

I boarded the plane to Madrid with mixed feelings. Michael picked me up at the Madrid airport, and we had a long talk about ourselves and how we would manage things in Spain. Michael had a tiny apartment near the center of town, close to the university, where he studied every day. I would take on the housewife role, making things as comfortable as possible with a less-than-shoestring budget, while expecting a baby. We did not have the money to buy enough food and had to stretch everything. Michael, at least, could eat at the university. But we both lost weight.

Michael's grandparents came to the rescue at some crucial moments, thank God. They paid for my doctor, who repeatedly told me that I was very anemic and should "Eat, eat, eat liver!" We didn't have money for liver, nor for the oranges that I craved.

Madrid had a number of US military bases with post exchange stores where I was able to get groceries with the PX card that I still had as a veteran's dependent. But my dad did not want to risk the military finding out that I was a married woman and no longer his dependent.

The circumstances of our marriage were bizarre. I tried to get us married by the local judge, as was the custom in Spain. He told me that we were required to post banns of marriage in our own church. When I told him that we had not posted banns, he slid our paperwork off his desk and said, "You will not be married in Spain." And that was the end of it. I felt the culture shock, as I would many more times.

Michael learned that we could get married in Gibraltar, a protectorate of Great Britain at the Strait of Gibraltar, more than 300 miles away. So we took a train and were married by a justice of the peace. Our "honeymoon trip" was a ride around Gibraltar in a taxicab. Someone took a picture of us—Michael, me, and the taxi driver. Looking at it much later, it seems more like Michael was the taxi driver, his face suggesting he had been stiffed.

At the time, Spain was still a fascist dictatorship run by Generalissimo Franco, propped up militarily by the US. Hitler and Mussolini had helped Franco to assume power earlier, but they had since perished. However, Franco would hang on until 1975. The signs of dictatorship could be seen everywhere, especially in the way the police ruled the streets, both overtly and covertly.

One example of this was that Spain had a general draft. The country was too poor to outfit its recruits, so, as a rule, the young recruits had to bring their own uniforms. Families bought uniforms that would fit any member and were handed down to the younger men when their turn came. The uniforms were made of thick wool, looked coarse and worn, were often dirty, and were held on the body with a large, tight belt. These soldiers did not look "smart."

I remember a couple of American girls on a bus, obviously exchange students, laughing at two young soldiers, commenting in English on their "dirty and itchy" appearance. The soldiers got off the bus, and two members of the uniformed Guardia Civil (Grises) got on. They escorted the girls off the bus and arranged for their immediate return to the US. The Grises struck terror into most hearts at the time. They usually walked in pairs. Their uniforms, unlike those of the military grunts, were nothing to laugh at; they wore well-fitted gray suits and gloves; hard gray folded hats; flashy high boots; and large, imposing, swaying capes. They were given great leeway and they ruled the streets. They looked intimidating, and I was wary of them and the ruler they served.

Franco was the only political figure who made me hold my tongue. On the positive side, crime and civil disturbance were at a historic low. But the price for it, the loss of civil liberties, was high. For instance, we had British neighbors and occasionally we visited with them. One night, well after midnight, we heard a car pull up by our building and the footsteps of several people approaching the door. The Brit jumped up and ran to the open balcony, trying to see what was happening. Then he jumped onto a ledge of the building and hid. Pounding on the door followed. The wife opened the door and three men entered the apartment, searching all the rooms. They went out on the balcony, pulled the neighbor in and muscled him away without saying a word. Later, I found out that he had been bringing stolen cars into Spain and selling them. His wife had to go to prison every weekend with a basket of food, since the guards hardly fed him or any of the other prisoners. She had two little boys, two and four years old. I never saw their father again.

As my pregnancy developed, I hardly left the house. The baby was due in mid-April, and I tried to stay healthy and fit on our meager food rations. But contractions started early, on March 16, in the middle of the night, which prompted a crazy rush to the hospital. First, there was the transportation problem; the streets of Madrid at that hour were empty. Buses and streetcars had ceased running hours before. No one in the house had a phone to call a taxi. Michael woke up the only guy in the house who had a car, the maintenance man. He owned an old Citroën Duck, which was on its last legs and had to be revived in the basement garage. Soon, all the people in the house woke up and started running up and down the stairs, shouting over each other. All I could do was think, "I am going to have this baby right here, and everyone is just running around and yelling."

There were two American exchange students in the house, girls who helped to introduce some order into the chaos. Michael and the Duck owner had managed to get the vehicle running. Michael and the two girls squeezed into the back seat of the tiny car while I was in the passenger seat up front. It didn't work well, and I held myself up as best I could. The driver had problems shifting gears with this overloaded car. We made it to the hospital on time but found the front door dark and locked. I was crowning and my water was close to breaking as everyone ran around the building trying to find an open door while yelling for nurses.

Eventually, a nurse appeared, looking sleepy and moving slowly. She understood our problem, though, and disappeared to the back to get another nurse with keys. We were finally let in and I was helped onto the delivery table. The nurses got caught up in our excitement, and one yelled into the telephone on the wall: "Contracciones, contracciones!" I felt completely helpless. Finally, my doctor appeared, full of excitement himself, scrubbing his hands and yelling in Spanish, "Empuje! Sí, empuje!" (Push! Yes, push!). I thought my face was about to explode as I pushed, stopped, pushed, stopped, again and again, until eventually a warm, red little boy came out. What a joy! I held him for a while and felt indescribably happy.

I remember that I was put in a comfortable hospital bed and that Ami Beski, one of the American students, stayed with me. Michael had left. I'll love Ami forever for that. Ami was a Hungarian princess. As a small child, she had to leave Hungary and came to the States with her parents when the revolution of 1956 failed.

The hospital was quite grandly built, more like a villa of a grandee. But many of the usual hospital trappings were missing. There was not even a hint of sterility. It was Catholic and staffed with nuns in full religious attire.

My room was flooded with light and beautifully adorned with high arched ceilings. It had a balcony that faced the yard and another room for a maid that was helping me. The baby was brought to me in a white wicker bassinet, twice a day. The food was excellent. Michael and I tried to think of a proper name for the baby, and I suggested John, in memory of an uncle of mine (John Winfred Jones), whom I remember fondly from my early days in Arkansas. He had been a lieutenant during World War II, fighting in the Pacific. Tragically, he died in a plane crash on his way home, years after the war was over.

Six weeks later, Michael's paternal grandparents visited us and were thrilled to see their great-grandson. They were warm and kind and very accepting of me. They bought us a VW bus, and we all traveled around Spain together. I think they really enjoyed traveling with us and having Michael as their tour guide. I have fond memories of them and the trip we took. It is interesting how people in one family can vary so much.

NINETEEN

Back to the US: Life in LA

Soon we had to arrange our trip back to the US. We were now the proud owners of a VW bus that we planned to take with us. We found a small freighter, the *Grote Beer*, the smallest ship allowed to cross the ocean with a few passengers. In the summer of 1966, we set out to cross the Atlantic with the goal of arriving in New York. It turned out to be one of the scariest trips of my life. After a few days in rough weather, the small vessel collided with a Russian fishing trawler, which ripped the starboard hull open just above the waterline. The Russian boat did not stop and moved on. The *Grote Beer* sat there with a gaping hole that made the continuation of the trip impossible. So it turned back to the nearest harbor for repairs.

After several days, the ship started out again on its journey across the Atlantic. The weather had gotten worse and we bounced around like nutshells, listening to the howling winds and waves that engulfed the ship for days. When we finally set foot on New York soil, a great sense of relief came over us as we realized that we and our VW bus had made it back intact. John had done especially well, sleeping all the way through one of the scariest trips of his life.

The drive to Kansas was nice and full of anticipation. A new phase in our life was to begin, and we had to sort things out. Michael had been accepted into the graduate program for Spanish literature at the prestigious UCLA. After we stayed a few days with Michael's parents in Neodesha, we took off for Los Angeles.

UCLA provided us with a small apartment in the married student housing complex, about five miles from campus. It was a bit run down and located in a noisy section of West Los Angeles, right next to the busy San Diego Freeway. Married student housing had been located on campus a few years before, but complaints about too many clothes-lines and kids playing prompted the school to move the complex. Our apartment was old, in poor shape, and riddled with cockroaches. Most students living there were poor, just like us. There were co-ops, includ-ing babysitting, which we used for John. Michael got a scholarship for the Spanish PhD program, but it wasn't enough to support the three of us. Therefore, I had to get a job.

My first job was scooping ice cream and giving out Blue Chip stamps at the drugstore across the street. The pay was low, so I got a better job working as a secretary for a surgeon. I still didn't earn enough to meet the needs of my family. I asked around and found out that the best-paying job for unskilled women was waitressing at ex-pensive restaurants, which LA had a lot of. But only a few of those had waitresses. Most of them had waiters. I searched for days until I was hired by one of the premier places in this glitzy town: Lawry's The Prime Rib.

I learned that most of the waitresses were aspiring movie actresses, and it helped that I was a pretty woman. There were very strict dress codes that were rigorously enforced. We had to hold out our hands for inspection before the doors opened to make sure they looked immaculate.

Tables were set with heavily starched tablecloths and sterling sil-ver service. One evening, a woman put the salt and pepper shakers into her purse. I informed the manager and she said, "Oh, our guests can have anything they want as long as they pay for it." So at the end of the dinner, I presented the check. A short time later, the silver was back on the table, and I "corrected" the check.

After a while, I was getting along well at Lawry's and making enough money to keep the family afloat. John liked the nursery school at our housing complex. It had a large collection of sanded-down pieces of construction wood with which he built cities. Most of the time he was not ready to leave at closing time. We waited for him as he proudly explained the projects he had worked on, usually big cities connected by roads.

We all liked the Santa Monica beach and would go there four or five times a week. John would dig deep holes for hours and Michael would "boogie board." I felt especially happy when I was able to resume fencing, in Beverly Hills of all places, at the Joseph Vince Fencing Studio. Joe had been an Olympic coach. His clients were mainly a mix of actors who needed fencing skills on their résumés or wealthy people who found the sport extravagant. There were also a couple of real fencers. One woman had even been an Olympic champion. Joe was Hungarian and loved classical music, which was always played in the salle. When Verdi's "Celeste Aida" played, he stopped fencing, removed his mask, elevated both arms in a grand fashion, and sang in full voice with his eyes shut. Then, he would calmly resume teaching and strike a dramatic point against you. Joe was impressed with me and allowed me to take lessons in exchange for training some of his clients.

As usual, I had to do everything on a shoestring budget, and on many days I could not even afford the money for the parking meters. At one point, Joe told me he wanted to train one more champion. He offered to send me to train in Europe on a rigorous program. John was one and a half years old at that time, and I told Joe I could go only if I could take my little boy with me. But that was a no. Michael was not in favor of me going either. I sensed that he disapproved of some of my dreams when they interfered with our established routines. And everything centered around his PhD studies.

However, I did try to set aside some time for myself whenever I could. I enrolled at UCLA as a part-time student to complete my BA. Since I liked flowers and plants a lot, I decided on botany as my major. I made a little desk for myself in the living room closet and worked on my calculus, physics, and chemistry. But Michael reminded me not to neglect my "housewife" duties, which involved prioritizing his desires. For instance, he played the piano, sometimes for hours, and often yelled, "Susie, get me a beer!" while I was studying. If he wanted a sandwich, I had to get busy in the kitchen right away. We had a few ugly encounters over that, but I thought that was part of being married.

On the other hand, I thought that Michael didn't take his own studies too seriously. More often than not, he hung out with his "intellectual" friends and resumed drinking heavily, a habit he had acquired many years ago. Meanwhile, I had problems getting enough money to buy groceries.

I also participated in some political demonstrations that became increasingly common during the late sixties. UCLA was a center of the anti–Vietnam War movement. A neighbor, Marilyn Dell, and I got involved, but our husbands did not come along.

In June 1967, I went to a major protest at Century City to urge President Lyndon Johnson, who had given a fundraising speech to the Democratic Party there, to end the Vietnam War. More than 10,000 people assembled before the Century Plaza Hotel, demanding to talk to the president about his war policies. He never came out to talk. Instead, the LA police came out in force and started to beat up on the protesters. Many demonstrators were arrested, some even beaten to a bloody pulp, and they ended up in nearby hospitals. I escaped police brutality only because the officer who chased me with his billy club showed mercy when he saw I was carrying little John with me.

A much larger anti–Vietnam War rally that we attended a few months earlier in San Francisco by comparison was more peaceful. Again, our husbands did not get involved. Life plotted along on many, not always converging, levels until I got pregnant again in late 1968.

TWENTY

Jason: "And whoso shall receive one such little child in my name receiveth me."

On May 23, 1969, about six weeks before my due date, my water broke and I had to go to the doctor at the UCLA Medical Center. Michael wouldn't take me, so I used the shuttle bus. The doctors admitted me right away, and soon after that, I had the baby boy, whom we named Jason. He weighed only five pounds. They told me that everything was okay. I wanted to hold him, but they said that they wanted to keep him in the nursery. The doctors were clustered around him. A couple of hours later, one of them told me that Jason was having some trouble breathing. When I went to see him behind the glass window, one of the doctors pulled the window shade down.

The feeling I had was one I will never forget. The doctors explained that Jason had hyaline membrane disease (HMD), which retards the development of the lungs. This condition, I learned, had always been fatal in the past, but new research showed that there was hope for survival, although at great cost to quality of life. After I digested this information, it was like an atomic bomb went off inside me. I knew from then on that things would never be the same. They kept Jason in the hospital, where he stayed for five and a half months. I stayed with him as much as I could, trying to learn as much as possible about his condition and prospects for life. And I started a journal.

I learned that a few months before his assassination in November 1963, President Kennedy's son Patrick was born with HMD and lived for only two days. Kennedy was told that not much was known about HMD, and he immediately appropriated large funds for medical research in this area. Jason benefited greatly from this, as a team of UCLA researchers studied his HMD and kept him alive.

However, Jason went from one life-threatening crisis to another. UCLA did not have a pediatric ICU. They had to create one in a corner of the nursery, hire round-the-clock critical care nurses, and convert a linen closet to a bunk for a doctor. There were no critical care instruments for premature babies. The existing instruments were too big but had to be used anyway. There were only two ventilators for infants. They once told me that there was another baby who needed the one Jason was on because it had a better chance of survival and asked if they could use it. I agreed. But the next morning, Jason was back on that ventilator. The other baby had died.

I watched the struggles Jason endured again and again. There were many bleeding disorders needing whole blood transfusions, chronic heart failures needing cardiopulmonary resuscitation, multiple organ failures, hepatitis, gram-negative rod sepsis, constant seizures, and much, much more. He received endless drips and injections. At one point, I counted 125 needle marks on him. All the while, his mouth tried to hang on to a funny pacifier. It was more than I could stand. So I asked God why he would let little children suffer like this. The answer to me was obvious. He was either powerless or evil. Either way, I did not want to be part of his world any longer. I longed to be grass on the ground, a tree in the forest, or a bird in the sky.

Yet, life went on. I had to take my waitress shifts at Lawry's, do the shopping and cooking at home, take care of the house, show up for co-op duties, study for my classes, and be a good all-around housewife and mother. I still managed to see Jason once or twice a day. Michael's visits were rare; at most he came twice a month. John must have felt

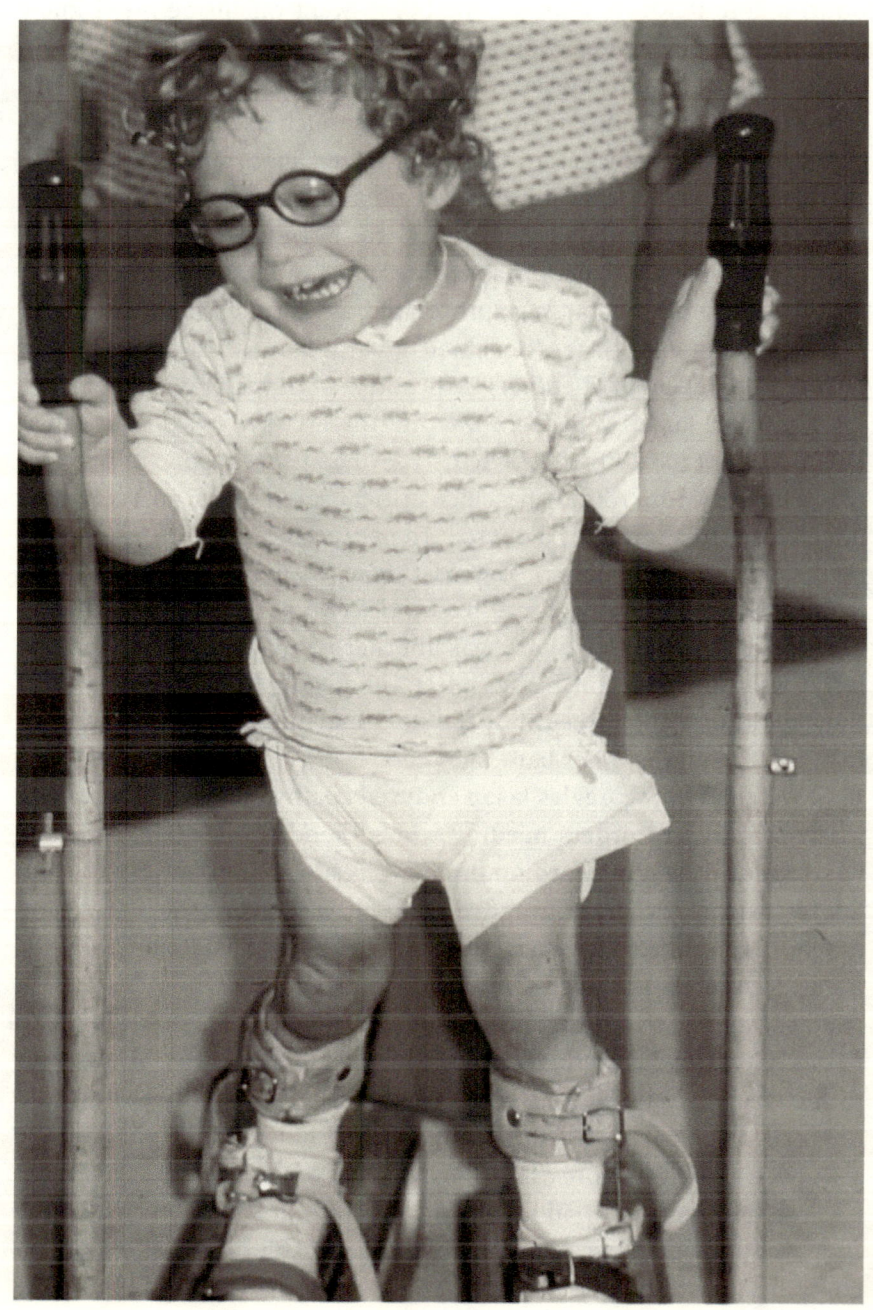

Jason, two years old, defying the odds.

neglected all that time but obviously understood the despairing dilemma causing it.

Things grew more challenging when, after almost six months of gruesome clinical treatment, much of it experimental, Jason was released into our care. This was an around-the-clock job, and I had to learn how to take care of his many complicated medical needs. He still weighed just five pounds. The doctors had performed a tracheostomy that had destroyed Jason's vocal cords and left a gaping hole in his throat through which he had to breathe with the help of a removable tube. The mucus of the trachea came out of that tube and needed to be cleaned constantly. Plugging could be fatal. If mucus didn't come out sufficiently, it had to be removed by suction. The suction machine had to be handled skillfully. It could not be taken outside the home. There were mechanical mucus removers we had to take with us everywhere. Handling the mucus and equipment was a messy job. Handling the many other problems Jason had was similarly complicated.

To help parents deal with these issues, UCLA created a nursery where they could take their handicapped children and share knowledge. Couples were given group therapy by medical professionals who provided desperately needed psychological support. All children, except Jason, were taken there by two parents. Michael would not come along. During group therapy, I had no one to comfort me. I realized that not only did I have a life-altering, medically complex child but I was on my own. We were also financially strapped and I had to work harder than ever to make ends meet.

Somehow, we managed and I watched Jason grow. We were holding it together, and I was hopeful that things would work out in the end if Michael stuck to his guns, graduated soon, and found a teaching position somewhere. But the grind got to me. As much as I urged him, Michael did not try to get a part-time job to help pay for the continually scarce groceries. He always said he had to focus on writing his dissertation. But after a while, I had the feeling he wasn't moving along as planned. He found many diversions and often didn't seem motivated.

Eventually, I got tired of working to feed everyone by myself and told Michael that unless he found some employment, I was going to take the kids to stay with my parents in Arkansas. I took my share of our bank account and in early 1972 bought plane tickets for John,

Jason, and myself. My parents finally realized the extent of our desperation and agreed to help. After I had left them to live with Aunt
Connie in 1959, they adopted a ten-year-old boy, Bruce, from a troubled home in Florida. He had given my parents a lot of grief, but at that
time, he was living in Benton on his own.

My parents had a small place but managed to house the three of us
the best they could. My dad was still working as an electrician at the
nearby Alcoa plant, and my mom was still a stay-at-home housewife.
She took care of the boys but required a lot of instructions regarding Jason's special needs. I took two waitress jobs in Little Rock and
thought about ways to become independent with my kids. The stress in
the house increased quickly as my parents had problems adjusting to
the dramatic changes our arrival caused. My dad especially was very
concerned with keeping orderly routines and giving the appearance to
the neighborhood, and especially their church community, that everything in the family was prim and proper.

When I came home late from night shifts, my father suspected
possible affairs with restaurant customers, which was the furthest
thing from my mind. Nevertheless, he threatened severe consequences
if his suspicions turned out to be correct. My parents had been my last
place of refuge, but I knew that I could not stay under those conditions. I was still married to Michael, and John and Jason were his sons.
I had to give it one more try.

We returned to Los Angeles and found that Michael had made the
most of our absence, enjoying the Santa Monica beach. He still had
no job, had taken in a roommate to pay the rent, and had no plans
regarding Jason, let alone the future of our family. I realized he really
had to go. When I told him, he replied that he couldn't leave because
he had nowhere to go. So I found him an apartment and gave him the
keys. Then he said he couldn't go because he didn't have any furniture. So I called up one of his friends who had a truck and told him he
needed to come and help Michael move. He showed up, and by evening, Michael and all the furniture he wanted were gone, including his
beloved piano. When he left, I told him that he had one year to learn
how to be a responsible father. After that, I would file for divorce. His
parting remark was "Can we date?"

Now I had to sit down and make some hard choices. I probably could not count on Michael to help take care of the family. Given Jason's needs, relying on my waitressing jobs to support the family would soon drive us into the poorhouse. Despite the implementation of President Johnson's Great Society programs passed by Congress a few years before (such as food stamps, housing assistance, and affordable education), America was still a cold, capitalist country where nothing counted as much as money. Given my own situation, the only way I could envision getting sufficient amounts of money was by becoming a highly paid professional. Also, Jason's future needs would most certainly require extensive and very expensive medical services. I felt the personal responsibility to understand every aspect of his medical conditions and treatments.

The conclusion seemed obvious. I had to become a medical doctor, preferably in a field that could be of service to Jason. I had toyed with such ideas before but had always subordinated my own visions to Michael's career choices. If and when he would receive a PhD in Spanish literature and whether he would find lucrative employment with it was uncertain. Plus there was his unwillingness to deal with Jason's impairment. The choice was clear. I was going to become a medical doctor or die trying. I had to sort out my priorities and keep my undivided attention on them.

The first priority was to support the kids with as much effort as it would take. Second, I had to enroll full-time in the UCLA premed program and succeed. I kept my focus on these two goals. During the day, John went to school and Jason had a babysitter whenever I could find one. There was a well-to-do lady who would watch Jason at her Beverly Hills poolside as a Good Samaritan deed. There were times when I had to take Jason to class with me and sit with him in the back row. At other times, I, and hundreds of other students, had to make it to and from class facing riot police.

Waves of protests against the Vietnam War and in favor of extending human rights to minorities swept the country, often turning college campuses into battle zones. In 1970, National Guardsmen shot demonstrators at Kent State University, killing four students and wounding many others. One day, I stepped outside the chemistry building and found a helicopter spraying tear gas over students. This, despite the fact that the protests were peaceful. Students had merely disobeyed orders to disband. This kind of behavior would eventually lead to deep and widespread distrust of government for many years to come.

Through it all, I stayed focused on my required classes. They were very difficult, and I didn't have as much time to study as other students did. My grades were okay, if not always tops. But I made progress and stayed on track. I tried to work fewer waitress shifts and study more.

Eventually, I swallowed my pride and went to the welfare office. We got enough to eat but not enough to pay the rent. John had to drink powdered milk flavored with chocolate until he was seven years old. On the positive side, I took the MCAT and did okay, scoring very high on vocabulary, which at that time was a key factor in selecting students for med school. All in all, things started to look up a bit.

Michael's situation did not change, however, and after a year of separation, I filed for divorce. The separation agreement was such that John would be with Michael from Friday through Sunday. But Michael would not stick to it. He rarely showed up to pick up John, and I, overwhelmed with my other duties, developed an almost uncontrollable sense of resentment. In the ensuing conflicts, John became an unwilling pawn between Michael and me. When Michael would not pick up John, I would take John over to his apartment and show my anger. One day, I broke the glass window in Michael's door so I could open it and leave John by himself, not knowing when Michael would come back. John's large eyes watched me helplessly through the window as I walked away. That image will haunt me forever. I have done many things in my life that I should not have done but that I felt I could earn forgiveness for. That is the one thing I cannot forgive myself for, although John has told me that he has forgiven me.

Through it all, I managed to juggle school, work, waitress shifts, car trouble, the welfare office, housework, and never-ending emergency care for Jason. I tried to keep my eyes on the prize. For instance, I saved all the quarters I got as tips working at Lawry's for going to medical school. At one point, I had $2,000 in quarters. Every so often, I would take them out and let John play Uncle Scrooge McDuck on the bed. He would swim in the quarters and let them rain all over him. He really liked that, and I enjoyed his laughing face. Then we would put the quarters back in the sock drawer where they were secure.

Still, I knew that quarters would not hack it. I needed serious money to get into med school. $2,000 would be just enough to make it to some interviews. Here, a good friend tried to help me. Her father was the head of the UCLA med school admissions committee. When I interviewed with him, he looked at my application and shook his head but said, "I can get you into our newly constituted dental school with a four-year scholarship." I turned it down. I wanted to be a "real" doctor and not a dentist. In hindsight, this may have been a big mistake. But at the time I knew what my "prize" was. So I wrote more applications to different med schools across the country. Unfortunately, all I got were rejections, not a single invitation for an interview. I wasn't surprised. I was a nearly thirty-year-old single mother with two small children and a B student to boot. But I had a fallback option: attending a medical school in Mexico. Word among premed students was that UAG was the best shot if you spoke Spanish. I spoke some Spanish and could brush up and improve. There was another big problem, though. For the duration of my time in med school, someone had to take care of Jason.

The UCLA Neuro-Psychiatric Institute, where Jason had been treated, gave me a booklet that listed foster homes and suggested I interview as many as possible and pick the best one. This task was complicated by the fact that my car was destroyed in a rear-end crash and I had to rent a car, which I could barely afford. Also, searching for a foster home was a depressing experience. You knew you were getting close to one when the neighborhood became run down. Inside, you would typically encounter a dark living room with eight to ten kids on the floor and a TV on. In many cases, I'd look in and make my decision without even having a discussion. Frequently the women at the homes would assure me that they "just love them." By the third day of searching, I was ready to give up because I would not put Jason into any of those homes.

Finally, I found a home that was a very nice brick split-level in a good neighborhood. I thought I had the address wrong, so I drove around three times before I dared to knock on the door. A woman holding an infant answered. The house was bright, clean, and full of nice furniture. She had a license for taking care of only two children but had five of her own. Her name was Helen Lamers. Her husband,

Tony, had been in an industrial accident at a plant where he worked, burning much of his body, and he had just come home after eighteen months in the hospital. A large settlement afforded them a nice middle-class life.

Helen was already taking care of two impaired children. But after meeting Jason on subsequent visits, she determined that one of the two needed more institutionalized care, and she took in Jason in his place. He immediately became a member of the family. He grew very close to Tony, a Dutch immigrant, who eventually taught Jason some Dutch phrases to use in conversation. To this day, Jason refers to the Lamerses' children as his brothers and sisters. Leaving him there was a most painful experience. But the Lamerses were wonderful people and turned out to be a great blessing. As my early upbringing had taught me, "For all things be grateful."

Still, overcoming so many hurdles on my way to becoming a doctor showed me how isolated I had become from my own family. There was John, of course, who had to struggle with his own loss of his father's presence. As much as I tried to comfort him, he probably put much of the blame for the loss on me. Additionally, everything was uncertain, and the risk of failure lurked around every corner. And then, when I least expected it, I found love again.

Jason (up front with tracheal tube) with the Lamers family.

TWENTY-ONE

Meeting Horst

I still lived in married student housing with John and Jason when my neighbor Ron Baar's birthday approached in May 1973. His wife planned a surprise party. All of his friends would meet at my place, and at a predetermined moment, she would open their door, and everyone would rush in screaming, "Happy birthday, Ron!"

One of Ron's friends from his Hayden White group was a good-looking German guy (a Beach Boy type), who immediately started flirting with me in front of the woman he was with. He was very interested in me and asked a lot of questions about Jason, who was also there. I was a bit floored but responded courteously. He kept flirting until the party ended. Then he and the woman left as they had come, very amicably.

The party had been a smash success, and the next morning, I asked Ron who the guy was who had flirted with me so obviously in front of his wife. "Horst?" Ron asked. "He is not married. He just brought his girlfriend along."

"Is that so?" I said. "Can you give me his phone number?" So I called Horst and let him know how much I had appreciated his unabashed advances.

"Okay," he said, "we can continue tonight." And so we did, until the next morning. Horst was a PhD student in intellectual history and would soon be on his way to spend the summer with his family in Germany. We had a week or so before he left, and we made the most of it. The affair invigorated me in many ways.

A neighboring couple at married student housing, Marilyn and Roger Dell, had moved with their two children to Deep Springs College, a small college in the White Mountains on the border between California and Nevada. What was once an isolated ranch had been turned into an elite two-year college where about twenty male students were groomed to be leaders of the nation. They fed cattle in the morning and discussed Voltaire in the afternoon. The college was affiliated with Cornell University, where most students continued their education to obtain advanced degrees. Roger taught mathematics there. The life at the college ranch/farm was extremely pastoral and in many respects was ideal for children. So Marilyn and Roger, who knew all about our struggles and the pain John and Jason were enduring, invited John to live with them for a while until things were sorted out.

I received an invitation for an interview from the Universidad Autónoma Guadalajara. Horst had come back from Germany, and we continued where we had left off. He started working furiously on his dissertation, letting me know that his doctoral advisor, Hayden White, was known for his high rejection rate, putting many students' careers in limbo.

As I took my premed courses, I would often walk over to see Horst at his work desk in the research library. We would have lunch together, and for a short time the world would look like a happy place again. Horst accompanied me several times to see John at Deep Springs College, where he impressed its director, Randy Reid, with his vast knowledge of European history. When the time came for me to travel to Guadalajara for my interview in the early summer of 1974, Horst decided to come along. In fact, we planned a four-week trip and even watched the World Cup soccer final, which Germany won, in a noisy bar in Mérida, Yucatán. Horst wrote about this episode in an earlier chapter, and I don't want to repeat too much of it again here, except for one thing. It is true that in Guadalajara, we stayed in the cheapest hotel we could find. It was $1 a night. I had to prepare for my interview with practically no running water. It came on once a day for less than an hour and amounted to little more than a trickle from the shower-head. Horst said that, despite everything, I looked like a queen and the university had no choice but to accept me on looks alone. I was accepted, but purely on academic grounds. Horst decided to move with me to Mexico and write his dissertation there. After our return to Los Angeles, we prepared for our trip to Guadalajara.

John, of course, was going to come along, but Horst was asked to teach the fall semester at Deep Springs College. This was quite an honor and also allowed us to have a bit more money than we otherwise would.

In the months before our departure, I sublet my apartment and stayed with Horst, saving some money. Days before leaving, I had a one-day yard sale of all my furniture and belongings on the sidewalk of married student housing. It was painful to sell some treasured and personal items. The appliances were all in good working condition, and I had to let them go for just a few dollars because I couldn't take anything with me. I ended up with just enough money to stay afloat in Mexico for a couple of months. The rest would have to come from the little I had saved and Michael's monthly alimony for John.

Unfortunately, Michael never would pay me this alimony money, and I never challenged it in court. How could I while living in Mexico? Part of this shortfall would be covered by a nurse who had taken care of Jason at UCLA, Lynn Montgomery, who loaned me a few hundred dollars over the course of the coming year. Her wealthy stockbroker brother-in-law also loaned me a few thousand dollars for the initial tuition and to set up a house in Guadalajara. I thank them all. The ultimate guarantee, as it turned out, that I could sustain my student life with John in Mexico, was Horst's commitment to helping. He maxed out all the student loans he could get while writing his dissertation, and we put the funds into our common survival pot. Otherwise, it wouldn't have worked.

By mid-August 1974, our adventure began in earnest. As Horst headed north for his fall teaching assignment at Deep Springs College, John and I headed south for Guadalajara in my old beaten-up VW Bug. He would join us after Christmas.

HORST

TWENTY-TWO

A Tale of Two Cities:
Los Angeles and Guadalajara

When we arrived in Los Angeles from Guadalajara by way of Arkansas, we had no place to stay. John usually went to stay with Michael, who had an apartment in Venice close to the beach. Sue and I sometimes stayed with Jon and Alice Amsden, friends from my days with SWAC (Students and Workers Action Committee) at UCLA. They lived in an apartment in Santa Monica and always had a room for fellow "revolutionaries." They both held assistant professorships at UCLA, he in modern Spanish history and she in Third World economics. Their Trotskyite convictions were noted with dismay by the university administrators, resulting in his eventual dismissal and her move to teach at Barnard College in New York.

Their relationship had been stormy from the beginning. Alice came from a conservative Jewish family and Jon from a tightly knit Irish immigrant family. They met at Cornell University, fell in love, and got married. Not a single member from either family attended their wedding. They understood the roots of petty thinking very well and dedicated themselves to liberating the world from it. Without their help, we certainly would not have been able to do the many things we needed to in Los Angeles.

One of Jason's nurses whom Sue had befriended, Lynn Montgomery, had a large place in Westwood, close to UCLA, and we stayed there a few times. We also found short-term rentals in places like Glendale and Hermosa Beach. We managed remarkably well, considering our time constraints and chronic lack of money.

Once in Los Angeles, we had much to do. First, there were the visits with Jason. The Lamerses were always very accommodating, and we took Jason on trips. There were constant bureaucratic struggles with many government offices to make sure Jason would continue to receive good benefits. Then there were Sue's visits to banks and private individuals to ask for small loans to cover her costs at UAG.

Whenever she could, Sue would pick up some quick waitress shifts at a restaurant. Once, when we were visiting her parents in Arkansas over Christmas, she worked the entire holiday at Pizza Hut. She was never paid because management learned she was going back to Mexico and could not claim her paycheck from there. The claims made later were denied since management had no records of her work. We promised never to eat at Pizza Hut again.

Once, we got a job with wealthy friends of Lynn Montgomery, Peter and Carol Scow, to do projects on their fabulous estate in a secluded area of Pacific Palisades. We worked all summer and made enough money to sustain us through a full semester in Guadalajara.

One morning, Carol Scow told me to "do the trim" of the house's expensive redwood siding before she left with her husband for a couple of days. Sue also had to go somewhere for the day, and I was left alone to paint the trim. Instead, I painted all of the professionally treated, impossible to replace redwood siding in record time. When Sue came home, and I told her of my proud deed, she nearly fainted.

"Trim," she explained to me, meant the small wood pieces running above the redwood siding right under the gutters. I said that I thought "trim" meant the entire redwood covering, but that made no sense to her. She attributed my confusion to my supposed inability to get my mind off Carol's scantily clad Playmate body as she gave me instructions. An entire book could be written about what followed next. We tried to repair the damage as best we could with all of the wages we got working for the Scows. Not only did we work like dogs all summer long, but we worked for nothing and had a hard time buying food once back in Mexico.

What made living with scarce dollars especially hard was the fact that tuition and fees had to be paid in cash with pesos at fixed dollar rates. And the peso was continually devalued. For instance, in 1974, one dollar was worth approximately four pesos. Putting ten dollars into a Mexican bank account would show a deposit of forty pesos. Banks held no dollars. Withdrawals had to be made in pesos. In 1975, the peso lost half its value vis-à-vis the dollar, making the new rate one dollar to eight pesos, which meant that the deposited forty pesos were worth only five dollars, not ten. The $10,000 tuition of UAG had to be paid in pesos, 80,000 of them instead of the previously required 40,000. Students had to come up with an extra 40,000 pesos.

Devaluations happened on short notice, giving students, or anyone else for that matter, little time to guard against them. Also, banks would change dollars for pesos only for customers holding accounts, usually in limited amounts. Often students had no choice but to pay exorbitant fees trading their dollars at local currency exchanges to be able to pay their tuition on time.

Devaluation surprised us twice, and both times we lost a considerable amount of money that we needed to keep ourselves afloat. Devaluations also hurt many businesses in Mexico, especially small ones that had to import goods, usually from the US, for their operations. These goods became much more expensive, virtually overnight. Among those businesses were private schools that catered to children of American families. The tuition at these schools went up considerably if they managed to survive at all. John had to change schools twice. The last one, the bilingual JFK School of Guadalajara, remained financially sound, adhered to high educational standards, and was a blessing for John.

Some of our trips between LA and Guadalajara were noteworthy for several reasons. As I mentioned earlier, we had to travel around 1,600 miles over mostly abysmally bad roads, crossing the scorching Sonoran Desert and negotiating treacherous passes through the Baranqua Mountains in our beat-up VW Bug. We usually crossed into Mexico at the border town of Mexicali. We learned the hard way that customs officials had the right to ask for travelers' papers and search their belongings within a seventeen-mile strip on both sides of the border.

One time, I was driving by a small guardhouse seventeen miles inside the Mexicali border when I heard the shrill whistle of a Mexican patrol and vaguely made out angry hand signals through the dust in the rearview mirror. I turned around and knew I was in deep trouble when I saw the officer's face. He told us our entry papers were not in order, and we had to return the seventeen miles back to the border to get new ones. We should have offered him a bribe, but at that time, we didn't know how this game was played. Instead, we faced more irate officials at the border, who eventually told us to "leave the territory of Mexico and never try to enter it again."

We decided to cross at a different border station and drove along the American-Mexican border from Mexicali eastward, but we were refused every time. We assumed there had been an alert for us. Eventually, after driving for about 350 miles, we got to the town of Nogales, where we were let into Mexico after paying a huge bribe to the paper-checking official. It was then that we learned about the pervasive nature of mordida, and from then on, we were always prepared to pay the right amount in the right way (never obvious) for the right "service."

On another trip, we tried to do the nearly thirty-hour drive in two days. We had reached the halfway point after crossing the Sonoran Desert and were looking for a cheap hotel along the highway running next to the Gulf of California. It was 10:00 p.m. and very dark, and we were dead tired. But for some reason, no hotels had a vacancy. So we drove on and decided to get some sleep in the next town, Los Mochis. Sure enough, none of the approximately ten hotels on the main drag had any vacancies.

There was one that said there might be a vacancy if we checked back in an hour. So we did, and we were given a standard room for two. I felt sweaty from the long trip and immediately headed for the shower. As I felt the water running down my back, I noticed fresh blood splotches all over the tiles of the shower walls. I ran out to tell Sue, who had spotted a large patch of recently cleaned-up blood on the carpet next to the bed. Upon closer inspection, we noticed more blood spots that had been cleaned up very recently and went down to the reception to complain. We were told there had been an "incident," but that the room had been cleaned up and that we did not have to take it if we didn't like it. We took it but slept with one eye open and furniture shoved up against the door. Later we learned that the Los Mochis area was the preferred territory for gangs making drug deals. We had scarier trips than that.

One summer, Sue, John, and I were returning to the US. We decided to visit Sue's folks in Arkansas before moving on to LA. Our old VW had recently developed engine trouble and was losing too much oil. We had repairs done for our long haul back at a VW dealer in Guadalajara. After we left Guadalajara in the direction of Zacatecas, we soon entered the treacherous parts of the Baranquas, full of narrow, winding roads in desperate need of repair. Suddenly, it happened. Struggling up a steep hill, the Bug started stalling and smoking before giving up the ghost. There we were, high up in the mountains, on a small and little-traveled road, far from any settlement, in a rather wild part of the country.

After ten to fifteen minutes, a car came by, and we decided that I would go with it to the next village and arrange for a tow, if possible. Sue would stay with John by the car, a dangerous undertaking in itself. The next village was more than ten miles away. It was very small and had no repair shop. But the friendly driver helped me find someone in town who offered to tow us down the mountain with a pickup. He would pull our Bug on the flat and uphill roads, and I put on the brakes when going downhill. That worked for a while until the brakes gave out on me. Because the roads were so narrow and steep, the whole operation looked like a suicide mission from the start. But things had clearly got worse.

Our options were to either push the Bug over the edge of the small road into the deep ravine or get it to the village somehow without brakes. The pickup driver agreed to continue "pulling" us while stopping our VW from rolling downhill by holding it back with his rear bumper. Because the two bumpers did not line up, we concocted a buffer using a spare tire, a blanket, and a pillow. Since there was a chance that the VW could end up in the ravine after all, I insisted that Sue and John ride with the driver in the pickup. Sue refused. John sat in the back of the pickup and signaled to the driver how things were going, with the cars bumping into each other going downhill. The driver adjusted his speed accordingly. It was the scariest ride of our lives.

We finally made it. The pickup driver agreed to store our car at his place and drove us to the station of the bus line that would take us back to Guadalajara that evening. The next morning we went to our car insurance agent and reported the incident. He called a lawyer, who came right over and went with us to the VW dealer that had repaired the car. He gave the manager there an angry lecture on fleecing Americans by charging outrageous prices for shoddy work. It gave Mexico a bad name. The dealer agreed to tow our car back and install a new engine at no cost. That's what he did, but we could not wait for the car to be finished. So we traveled on a Tres Estrellas bus to the Mexican border and then on Greyhound to Little Rock. I remember carrying a big box with a handmade Mexican lamp we had promised to bring Aunt Polly. John sat up front with the Mexican bus driver for the long ride and later told us that he wanted to become a bus driver for Tres Estrellas someday.

The dumbest ride we ever made was not in Mexico but in the US. I think it was in 1977 when the three of us made a trip from Arkansas to California. Moving along Interstate 40, we eventually hit Flagstaff, got a hotel, and decided to peek into the Grand Canyon the next morning.

It was a Sunday morning, and we had a long breakfast. I got *The New York Times* and started reading. Sue reminded me we had to press on. So we drove to Grand Canyon Village and walked along the canyon's edge. We saw a sign that read BRIGHT ANGEL TRAIL and decided to follow it a bit. It was about 10:00 a.m., and the temperature was around 60 degrees Fahrenheit. We wore jackets. I carried the fat *New York Times*, in case I saw a bench. We did not have food or water with us. The trail looked inviting, and we walked farther down into the canyon.

There were occasional signs pointing to this or that lookout point. After a couple of hours, we saw a green valley in the far distance and a sign saying it had a campground. We thought we could make it and continued down the trail. It got hot. We took off our jackets. I unloaded my *NYT* between two rocks. We got very thirsty and figured getting water at the campground below would be quicker than the restaurant up at the canyon's edge.

We got there hours later and ran for a small creek next to a hostel called Pipe Creek Resthouse. Some people told us that the Colorado River was just a short distance away. It was late afternoon, probably around 4:00 p.m., and we had to think about our climb back out. But we figured this was the chance of a lifetime, and we had to put our feet into the famous Colorado River. We were absolutely elated wading through the dirty brown water of the shallow river. John even took a small swim.

We had a camera and took pictures of what would turn out to be one of the most dangerous family outings on record, for we had to make it back up to the rim again. Returning to the Pipe Creek camp, we were glad to find a ranger on duty. We asked whether we could stay at the Resthouse. But it was all booked. And we could not sleep at the campground because we had no camping gear with us. All he could do for us, he said, was give us a water bottle and a flashlight and wish us good luck on the arduous climb up.

It was around 6:00 p.m. when we left him. "I'll call the people up there and tell them that you're coming," I remember him yelling as we walked away. The shadows started to grow longer, and soon we walked in a sort of twilight that lasted for a long time.

Initially, we had little problem keeping up a steady pace, knowing that we could waste no time. But after a while, we felt the strain of the day in our muscles, and fatigue set in, especially for John. He was only eleven years old and had walked to the bottom of the Grand Canyon without food or enough water. Sue felt very bad as well, though she made every effort not to show her discomfort. Her main problem was that she was wearing cowboy boots without socks, which was all the rage among the cool girls at the time, but she had developed bloody blisters on her feet.

I had to face the bitter truth that despite my blue-collar background and assumed tough guy image, deep down, I really was a *New York Times*–reading intellectual who often lost touch with the real world around him. I was the one who had suggested going just one more turn down into the canyon and then another until we hit bottom under the worst possible conditions. I had to ensure we would not get

At the bottom of the Grand Canyon, next to the Colorado River.

stuck and perish. I tried to exude confidence, played down the perils ahead, pointed to the distance already traveled, pretended to see the edge of the canyon above, and the like.

We took many breaks, and I noticed an increasing reluctance, especially in John, to get up again. And then we found a piece of wire, about eight feet long. It was a godsend. I fastened one end to the back of my belt and the other to the front of John's. Then I pulled him up the narrow trail, counting thirty steps and taking a one-minute break sitting down. We continued in this way until we had to take a longer break. We did this without much talking, knowing we had no choice. Eventually, after a very long time, we thought we heard the faint sound of a car engine through the starry and by then cold night. After a while, it also seemed that we could see faint light way up above, though we could not yet make out the edge of the canyon. But we were energized, knowing that civilization was within reach again, conjuring up visions of hamburgers, fries, and Cokes.

Still, it took us a couple of more hours to reach the top, with ever longer breaks along the way. Our exhaustion had become palpable. John stumbled a lot, and Sue's blisters caused silent tears to run down her cheeks. When we finally reached the top, the lights of a nearby restaurant almost blinded us. It was around midnight, and the restaurant was empty. We entered and told the staff where we had just come from. "Oh, it's you," they said. "The ranger down at Pipe Creek called and said he would send out a search party if you didn't show up soon. He'll be glad to hear you made it. And he wants his flashlight back." We must have looked like a miserable bunch, and they agreed to stay open past closing time and feed us. It was one of the best meals any of us have ever had. I am also certain that we broke some kind of record that deserves a place in the famous Guinness book, probably under "dumbest trip ever taken" or "luckiest people to be alive." Whenever I tell the story, I see faces that seem to say, "This guy is making all of this up."

Back in Guadalajara, life had assumed its own, not always predictable, routine. Sue went to the university, usually taking the Bug. John went to school by bus. I stayed home and wrote. As much as possible, we had regular meals together. Our social life revolved around meeting with other Americans, taking trips to nearby places, going hiking and swimming, and eating out when we didn't feel like cooking and when we had a couple of extra pesos to spare. We took care of our pets: Gitana, Grover, Honeysuckle, and Coco Loco.

Of course, we were in a different country and had to make adjustments. Many new things left indelible impressions, for they highlighted the cultural differences we experienced on a daily basis until they, too, became routine. For instance, on my daily rides on Gitana, I saw how the local farmers fertilized their fields with the organic waste they collected in gullies behind their houses. Increasingly, the waste contained manufactured trash like Coke bottles, plastic bags, empty cigarette cartons, and such, which mixed in with the natural compost that covered the fields as fertilizer. It damaged the seeds, in some cases preventing any growth at all.

One would think that the farmers would learn their lesson, but no. I had heard and could see for myself that the amount of manufactured trash ending up in the organic waste, which for centuries had been used to fertilize crops, had increased over the years. The sight of

broken glass and shredded plastic covering the spring fields also became routine. After a while, I didn't notice it anymore.

Seeing people in extreme distress also became routine. I remember a driver whose midsized truck had broken down in the middle of
a busy intersection close to where we lived. The axle had broken, and
the truck sat flat on the pavement. The driver tried to repair the damage himself without proper tools, amid passing traffic. He worked on
the truck for almost a week, a few hours each day. Every morning, he
brought his water bottle and tortillas wrapped in a newspaper until
one day, he and the truck were both gone.

Sue frequently saw people in great distress at the clinics where
she did service as a medical student, and she became painfully aware
of how patiently Mexican people endured their pain while hoping for
relief, waiting to see someone in a white coat. Often women in their
thirties who looked like they were in their fifties came in large groups,
sometimes carrying small children with potentially fatal conditions,
from dysentery to measles. When presenting their medical history,
they would usually give two figures for the number of children they
had, those who lived and those who had died.

Mexicans of indigenous, non-Spanish heritage fared particularly
badly. They have been exploited by landed and controlling upper
classes since times preceding European colonization, and they still
provide the labor necessary to keep society going, often against all
odds. Ultimately, they had nothing to show for it but misery and death.

Sue gained much more direct knowledge about this than I ever
could. In September 1977, she had the opportunity to work as a medical assistant in a remote village of Huichol Indians. UAG medical students had to do social service as part of their medical education, and
Sue had volunteered to do it at that village. She had applied several
times before being chosen to go.

SUE

TWENTY-THREE

My Time with the
Huichol Indians

The Huichol Indians live in parts of the Sierra Madre that are close to Guadalajara. They sustain themselves mainly with a rudimentary agricultural system centered on corn, and they organize their lives around the dictates of many deities that all descend from the sun god. Huicholes have had little direct contact with the Spanish colonists and generally know no Spanish. I knew very little about the village I would visit except that most people there worked for a silver mining company. But I was full of anticipation.

The only instructions I got for my assignment was that on a certain day, I should be at the Guadalajara airport at 6:00 a.m., and I should look for a small plane "way at the end." When I found it, I was shocked at how tiny it was. It looked more like a VW Bug with wings than an airplane. I saw only one seat, while the interior was full of tools and cement bags.

Eventually, the pilot appeared. He looked like a sixteen-year-old schoolboy. He nodded and climbed into the pilot's seat. He was all business as he motioned for me to climb in behind him, where I discovered a tiny fold-out seat. The plane had a rearview mirror, and the windows rolled up and down with a hand crank. We taxied along the runway and soon were airborne. The hot wind blowing, the small engine racing, and the single propeller clanging together made quite a racket. Soon we were bouncing through air currents following the peaks of the mountains. There were no towns or roads below.

This had lasted quite a while when the pilot suddenly took a nosedive into a green valley. He flew close to the ground over a green meadow and went up steeply again at the end of the field, making a loop for a second descent. I asked him why he did this, and he told me he would land on the field but had to make sure there were no rocks first. We landed smoothly in the middle of the field. I crawled out of the tin can and saw that there was nothing there. The pilot pointed to the end of the field, where I saw a small three-sided lean-to and a man on horseback with a mule in tow: the airport of the Huichol village.

The man on horseback approached us and indicated that I should get on the mule. The pilot flew off again without saying a word. I followed the man on the horse into rough mountain territory. There was no trail that I could see. After a couple of hours, we reached the mountaintop. We came to a very small town consisting of about twenty huts, the dwellings where the Indians lived, and four or five houses where the Spanish-descended Mexicans lived. I was reminded again of the difference. There were no paved roads, just a barren area around which the buildings were scattered. At the end was a dreary-looking, faded, whitewashed building, about thirty by thirty-five feet, adorned with a red cross. Ah, the goal was within sight.

The guide took me inside and spoke to the doctor's assistant, a man, then left without saying a word to me. The assistant told me the doctor was in consultation but would be out in a few minutes. I stood waiting. Suddenly, in burst a handsome man in his mid-thirties, full of energy and with a sense of purpose. He gave me the once-over and said, "Go in there and tell me what's wrong with the patient and how to treat it." Then he went directly to the side table, which had a radio on it, picked up the microphone, and ordered, "Come and get her again." I went into the exam room and found an Indiano, who did not speak Spanish. He was standing in a reserved way while sweating slightly and obviously uncomfortable.

Since we couldn't communicate verbally, I started a physical exam using sign language. When he opened his mouth, I saw he had a peritonsillar abscess and was quite ill. I went and gave the doctor my diagnosis and told him that the abscess needed to be drained and treated with penicillin. The doctor went back to the table, grabbed the microphone, and shouted, "Never mind about getting her again." I guess I passed the test. But the doctor still had a stern, unsmiling face.

The doctor spoke to his assistant, and before long, there was a gathering of several men, including a priest, at the doctor's house, which was right next door. I was not invited. The house looked nice enough. It was a small bungalow with trees, a fence around it, and a cool, shady garden. It looked comfortable and peaceful.

Once the meeting broke up, the doctor returned to the clinic, and the doctor's assistant informed me that I would sleep in the clinic and eat with the miners in their mess hall. Without knowing it, I had thrown a monkey wrench into the workings of that little town. The doctor was a single man, and it would have been unseemly for me to stay at his home. There was no restaurant where I could eat, and none of the men asked for their wives or housekeepers to send a tray of food over for me daily.

I slept on an exam table for six weeks and ate with the miners twice a day, breakfast and dinner, an unvarying diet of scrambled eggs, rice, beans, tortillas, and Nescafé. Meals were remarkable for their silence. The men did not talk among themselves and hunched silently over their plates, their eyes fixed on me. No one tried to bridge the gap with any kind of greeting, and I think I may have been the first gringa they had ever seen.

To clean myself, I had to use public showers. An inventive young guy had diverted a little stream and pumped the water into an arroyo, a shielded area providing some privacy.

The young man charged a few centavos for using one of the four stalls. They were separated by shower curtains but open to the sky and with slippery, mossy floors. He handed out slivers of soap but no towels. For drying, one had to use one's own clothes. The shower was a cold trickle and did not encourage long stays. Fortunately, whenever I went, there was no one else there. I don't know if ladies went there or only men. I was pretty much on my own the whole time I was there.

My communication with others was restricted mainly to discussing medical issues with the doctor regarding the patients we saw and related matters. He was very dedicated to serving the village as a proud professional. His main problem was that he could not help as much as he wanted to. When the Huicholes had problems with their health, they preferred going to their own "medicine men" rather than to the clinic. They saw the doctor only when all else had failed and they were desperate. It was really sad when they brought in their sick infants, as it was often too late for us to be of much help. Under those circumstances, we didn't seem much more capable than their medicine men. However, for trauma and surgical problems, we clearly had the edge.

Most villagers worked for the mining company, and some features of their lives reminded me of my childhood in Bauxite. In a conversation with one worker, I mentioned that there were miners in my family too and wondered whether I could see the mines. He agreed to set something up for me.

On a specified day in the predawn hours, I met him in the center of town and walked with him to the mine headquarters. As we walked, I noticed women and children watching quietly. Their number increased as we approached the mining company buildings. I began to realize that this was an *event* for the town. Several mine operators were there waiting. They invited me into their office and showed me maps. They talked about the qualities of the silver ore they mined and showed me some samples.

The demeanor of the men was like that of the men in my family when they talked about the qualities of the "Bird's Eye" bauxite ore that they dug up in the shafts of Arkansas. They spoke with a similar sense of pride in their accomplishments.

I was told I would be escorted to the mine entrance, and they pointed to it, off at some distance. I was confused because I could not make it out, and I wondered where we were going. Then I noticed about six men gathered around a tripod mounted over a hole. A five-gallon white plastic bucket hung over it, which was attached to a rope from a reel connected to a gas motor. This was the entrance to the mine, through which these Huichol miners descended and by which the ore reached the surface.

I was appalled and frightened. Looking down the shaft, I saw spots of dim light but no bottom. The sisal rope attached to the bucket looked worn. Every eye was fixed on me, including those of small children hugging their mothers' legs.

None of the children were playing. This was serious business. I thought, "If these people can build their lives doing this, I can at least visit. I may die in this shaft, and Horst and John may never know what happened. But the Huicholes face this daily, and I will not be a coward chickening out of this." I stepped into the bucket, hung on to the rope, held my elbows together so I would not get stuck in the shaft, and was lowered down.

As I was lowered, I passed by horizontal shafts with a bit of an open area up front, where the miners would get off and into the bucket. The shafts quickly turned small in the distance. This is where the Huichol men had all clustered to get a glimpse of "la Doctora" passing by. I was humbled. I will never forget the eager expressions and the curiosity in their eyes below their sweaty brows. They worked in semidarkness, with dim, battery-operated lights mounted on their hats. There were no overhead electric lights. The shafts were only four or five feet high.

Everyone leaned forward and had to work in a bent-over position. Eventually, the bucket stopped at what looked like a newly built shaft. The men there helped me out of the bucket and showed me to the end of this particular vein of silver ore. They pried the ore loose with a pick and shovel, placed it into baskets strapped to their backs, and carried the ore to the bucket I had just come down in. They emptied the ore into the bucket and gave a sign to the top that the basket was ready to be pulled to the surface. All of this was done in relative silence.

There was no cheering or noisemaking of the kind I associated with American workers. I sensed that the Huicholes had a different worldview about the mountains and their place in them.

On my way back to the clinic, my knees wobbled, and I thought about people who would dismiss the ore the miners toiled so hard to get and the many products made out of it as "cheap Mexican silver." The internship with the Huichol Indians taught me a lot about Mexico and its native culture, including about the conditions many natives still had to endure due to the Western, mainly Spanish, influence.

I continued my medical education at UAG successfully. I was prepared to finish it with a doctorate before applying to practice medicine in the US as a "foreign graduate." It was a long and arduous haul, and most American students tried to avoid it by attempting to get into a US medical school during their time at UAG and finishing with an American MD.

Few succeeded. I, too, tried the coveted way of "transferring out," as we called it, and figured I had the best chance of applying to the University of Arkansas medical school. There were too many Californians at UAG trying to get into the few spaces available in California schools each year. So on various trips to the medical school in Little Rock, I presented myself as an Arkansas girl ready to come home. I was born there and had roots there. And in the end, it worked.

Since every medical school tries to graduate as many students as it admits, occasional dropouts are usually replaced with qualified transfers like me. In early 1978, I was offered the opportunity to start at UAMC (University of Arkansas Medical Center) as a third-year medical student. I had already done three years at UAG, for which I was given two years of credit. I had to do the last two clinical years in the US and would receive an American MD. We were overjoyed when I got the admission letter, and we started planning our departure from Mexico.

HORST

TWENTY-FOUR

Leaving Mexico and Living in Arkansas

One of our immediate problems was money, not so much for getting out of Mexico but for setting up a household in Little Rock. We returned to an idea we had talked about for a while. We would buy some young macaws for around $50 apiece, tame them, and sell them for around $1,000 in the States. Trading those huge, colorful, endangered birds was illegal, but owning and traveling with them across the Mexico-US border was not. The limit was two birds per person. So we bought four, which I had to tame relatively quickly. I bought a book on the subject and learned that the nearly three-foot macaws could bite my fingers off if I didn't care about taming them.

Finding strong iron cages for travel was another problem. Somehow we managed. As our departure day drew closer, we sold most of our furniture and gave away the rest. We kept a few pieces as souvenirs, especially the standing lamp made out of a uniquely twisted tree trunk. I had written much of my dissertation sitting under its warm lampshade. Gitana found a new home. The daughter of an English (and slightly shady) businessman promised to take good care of her. I remember with Wehmut (I wished there was an English term for it) my last ride through the fields of Ciudad Granja with her, and I sensed that she was just as sad as I was.

Finally, we had to load up our pickup truck, which we had brought from Little Rock in anticipation of our departure. We had so much stuff that we wanted to take back with us that we overloaded it. We even had a few things strapped to the top. The massive iron cages with the screaming macaws had to be tightly secured before we could close up everything. And off we went.

John had left a few days earlier. Michael and his new wife, Anne, had come to pick him up to spend the summer with them in California before he would join us in Little Rock. That worked out fine. Of course, John looked very sad as we were all preparing to leave Mexico for good. He had made close friends and, in the end, had come to stand his ground with all the tough kids in the rough neighborhood. No mean task for a gringo kid. But he also seemed very glad knowing that, finally, he would be back in the States, even if we were not going to live in his favorite place, California.

The trip to Little Rock took four days, and crossing the high Baranquas with our overloaded truck was no easy task. When we finally reached Laredo, the border town in Texas, we felt a sense of relief. But little did we know what was in store for us. The border guards must have pegged us for criminal characters for some reason. Maybe Sue's miniskirt was a bit too mini and my hippie hairstyle too wild. But they searched every square inch of our truck. It took all day. We had to unload everything. They opened every box, using box cutters and scissors where necessary. They got the sniffing dogs out several times and even locked them in the cab of the truck, hoping to find drugs.

The fact that they found nothing seemed to make them even more determined, and they searched harder. The guard who had taken the lead occasionally disappeared and came back with what he clearly hoped was disturbing news for us. Our macaws had to be quarantined because of suspicion of mites.

He found that my German passport was almost expired, putting my Mexican tourist visa in question. Then, suddenly, around 6:00 p.m., he informed us that his shift was over and we could pack up again, which took several hours, with no help from the guards. Also, they kept the birds, telling us we had to pick them up in person several weeks later. Your tax dollars at work. But we were back in the States, and the next morning, we continued on to Little Rock.

In Little Rock, we had to find a place to stay and get jobs quickly, as we were flat broke. We found a small, run-down but fixable house on Kanis Road near the Baptist Medical Center. Sue found part-time work as a medical assistant at a doctor's office in Morrilton, about thirty miles from Little Rock. Sue's uncle J. P. got me a job as a laborer with a company (Austin Bridge) that was building a long highway on pillars over a swampy area between the city and its growing airport at the outskirts. I could start immediately. But I had no idea what was expected of me.

The work crew I joined was composed of about ten rough-looking hard laborers, all Black. I was the only white guy. They set the cement pillars for the highway, which required extremely demanding physical work. They worked ten-hour shifts, from 6:00 a.m. to 4:00 p.m., with two short breaks, most of it in sweltering heat under a blazing sun.

The summer of 1978 set many heat records, with stretches of days never dropping below 100 degrees. The news was full of stories about people dying of heat exhaustion in apartments and trailers, many without air-conditioning. Working in a swampy area increased the temperature and made the humidity almost unbearable. But the real problem turned out to be insects, some of which I had never heard of, chiggers and ticks, for example. They quickly became my worst enemies. Chiggers, too small to see, bore themselves into human skin and proliferate. The resulting itching becomes unbearable.

Scratching increases the agony. Insects, especially chiggers, invaded our boots every morning, no matter how much you sprayed them with insecticide, and wreaked havoc on our feet and legs. When I came home from work in the late afternoon, I was usually too tired to eat or do anything but sink into the bathtub and scrub my skin with soap for an hour in search of relief. Sleeping at night became a challenge. To manage life under those conditions, one had to become a stoic. My dinners consisted mainly of high-protein licuados, which Sue made for me and which I drank lying in the tub. But there were other problems.

One problem was that my hands grew in size as a result of using

Leaving Mexico. Minutes later we were on the road to Little Rock.

them all day long swinging hammers and handling wood planks. I asked myself why anyone would do such heavy work for relatively low pay. The answer was and still is that good-paying, skilled labor jobs are hard to come by and often controlled by trade organizations and guilds. Most require extensive training and certifications. In the South, a heavy racial component kept Blacks out of the better-paying labor market.

I knew that, eventually, I would find something else more lucrative. But for the moment, I had work that paid our bills. And the longer I worked at Austin Bridge, the more I felt I was privy to a world I normally would not have access to beyond scholarly articles and news reports. I could see firsthand the working life of Black people who felt trapped. Of course, these men were mostly from the lower income areas of North Little Rock, and they were interested in this strange blond guy with an exotic accent. They were curious what had brought me to Arkansas and why I worked with them in the swamps.

As much as I looked the part, I certainly did not fit the picture of the "redneck type" they were familiar with. So we shared a mutual curiosity. What a learning experience it was for me. I saw firsthand how Black people still lived with the legacy of Jim Crow. For the most part, skilled jobs were still out of their reach. And they had problems trying to figure out how to change that.

I saw a lack of the most basic education necessary for coping with daily life. When I told them I was from Germany, they wondered whether that was in Russia and whether I had come to America by train. The Central High School integration crisis that put Little Rock on the map was only twenty years in the past, and the Civil War had ended just a bit more than a century before. I came to realize how trapped Black people still felt.

One of the fellows did not like me very much, and I confronted him about it. He told me frankly that he had a girlfriend in the office of Austin Bridge, and from her, he knew that I was doing the same work he was doing but was being paid more because I was white. At first, I dismissed this as a rumor, but further inquiry confirmed his story. It was the moment when I realized I could not continue working there. I could have made this an issue with Austin Bridge, but I got the job through J. P. and therefore did not want to make this an issue. And indeed, I found a better job quickly. But a few other things happened as well.

TWENTY-FIVE

Work, Marriage, and Family Life

When the back-to-school time came, John joined us from LA, after his summer with Michael and Anne at Venice Beach, which he missed very much. He was forced to live with us in a crappy house that, despite our best efforts, never completely lost its white trash image. John knew nobody. And at the local school, Sue had to register him as living with a single parent. In Guadalajara, it hadn't mattered much that Sue and I were not married. We were always treated by the school authorities as a couple that shared responsibility for John, even though I had a different last name.

But in Little Rock, things were different. School authorities always wanted to deal with the mother and not her partner. One reason was that John was entitled to government benefits if a single mother was raising him in a low-income home. His school lunches were free, for instance. Still, Sue and I felt that our time of living in a "wild marriage" was ending, and we had to join "the establishment." We also planned on having more children and did not want to burden them with the mark of "illegitimacy," as it was still called at the time. So we planned an official church wedding as soon as possible, which would be followed by my formal adoption of John and Jason.

Philosophically we were both free spirits, with Sue entertaining more pantheistic notions of deities and I more Hegelian/Marxian ideas of human relationships and progress. But taking our vows in the Church would bring our dispersed families together and, most importantly, make things easier with Sue's folks if we were ever to settle in Arkansas. Though Sue was raised in the Church of Christ, she ultimately rejected its strict Calvinist interpretation of biblical scripture as condemning man's noble nature. And though I was raised Catholic, I came to see Catholicism as an integral part of the history of global culture rather than a manifestation of a divine plan in the world.

I felt I could still claim my Catholic roots without accepting Catholic dogma, but Sue could not claim her roots in the Church of Christ without also accepting its dogma. And she did not want to be a hypocrite. Therefore, we decided to get married in the Catholic Church. It was not an easy route to take. I had no standing in the Church, which is necessary to go through the required lengthy counseling sessions before receiving the matrimonial sacrament. So we started to go to mass on Sundays.

I also had to provide a requested letter from my Catholic diocese in Germany, stating that I had been in good standing until leaving the country in 1962. Also, Sue was a Protestant, and marriages of Catholics to non-Catholics had to be approved by the Catholic bishop in Arkansas.

In addition, Sue had been married before, meaning her former marriage had to be annulled in the eyes of the Church. All of this took time, but we eventually set the wedding date for December 26, 1978, the day after Christmas. It made many things easier. The holidays would allow people to attend the event more easily. However, Sue's parents indicated that since we were going to get married in a Catholic church, they might not come. We told them we hoped everyone involved would have an open mind about this. And like most things in our life, we had to get hitched on the cheap.

We cleared things up with the Catholic Church. Wedding expenses were nominal. A colleague of Sue's played the church organ. A fellow worker of mine served as the photographer. The community

Our wedding, Christmas 1978, Little Rock.

hall of North Little Rock that we booked for the wedding celebra-
tion was practically free. Through her work at the hospital, Sue knew
very reasonable caterers who prepared and served all the food inexpensively. We had no bridesmaids or groomsmen. Sue wore the wedding dress that her Aunt Connie had worn on her wedding to Uncle
Sam in 1943. It had not been worn since then and looked beautiful
on Sue. I wore my regular black suit and looked the part too. Connie
and Sam's son, Larry, a country-and-western singer, brought his band
from Neodesha to entertain the wedding party of forty-plus following the ceremony. He dedicated Merle Haggard's "Silver Wings" to Sue
and me in memory of the many times we had to say goodbye to each

other when boarding planes between Mexico and California, leaving the other one behind in sadness.

The ceremony included passages from scripture read by my two brothers, Erwin and Udo, who flew in from Germany with my mother. Erwin was thirty-six and Udo sixteen. Their flight had been a harrowing experience because they got lost at JFK airport and almost missed their connecting flight to Little Rock. Udo's school English apparently was not of much help. My father could not attend because of health reasons. My mother and brothers had never seen such a large family gathering or one with such a heartfelt display of joy for being with each other, and they looked pretty happy themselves. Udo later asked me whether he could come over from Germany to live with us. In the end, Sue and I fell into bed, full of champagne and, for the first time, legally married.

After the wedding, life went on as before. But we did begin making more detailed plans for the future. I started the adoption procedure for John and had to get Michael's consent. I wrote a long letter to him, explaining my sincere intentions to be an exemplary father to John while not competing with him for John's loyalty. Michael did not consent, letting me know that he would always be there for John himself. I did not dare mention that, in the past, John would have benefited greatly had he complied with the court-ordered childcare payments. And I was right in the assumption that no such payments were forthcoming in the future either.

I am sure, in his mind, Michael felt that the neglect of his paternal obligations was justified by such circumstances as the inability to see John regularly or his poor financial situation. Sue and I did not take issue with this, as my inability to legally adopt John for practical purposes did not change anything. We definitely did not involve John in any of our discussions. There would be plenty of opportunities for John to reflect on all of this later in life. And at the time, a familiar problem started to overshadow everything else again. Lack of money. I had left my job at Austin Bridge and had to find another.

At the hospital, Sue somehow got involved in a conversation with the manager of a large paint store about my situation, and he referred me to a large painting contractor in Little Rock. I didn't know much about painting but had done some wallpapering here and there. So I introduced myself as a wallpaper hanger. The contractor had enough work at the time to take me on. But I had to join the local painters' union as a full-fledged journeyman, meaning a fully trained painter. This required proof of past tests and years of experience in the trade. I told the union official many lies about work I had done in Germany, and I was admitted with the statement that there couldn't be anything wrong with "a German wallpaper hanger." Americans always thought Hitler was German, not Austrian.

I certainly did join a bunch of rednecks, but the pay was more than double what I'd made at Austin Bridge. And work was less strenuous. I was assigned to a crew of hangers who did a big building, and my foreman, Al, quickly realized I didn't know what I was doing. But he watched me and figured I was a quick learner, and most importantly, he immediately took a liking to me. Later I learned he was a full-blooded Native American and had heard somewhere that Germans liked Indians.

Perhaps he had Karl May's characters Winnetou and Old Shatterhand in mind, but I never challenged him on that. He overlooked my mistakes, showed me how to avoid them, and eventually got me up to speed. Speed mattered in this business, as in many other businesses, because it was how the contractors made their profits. Of course, they all knew each other and tried not to underbid each other too much on big contracts. And they all tried to keep the fastest workers on their crews by promising steady work and firing the slower ones quickly.

I wouldn't have lasted long had it not been for the early protection of Al. It took months until I could hold my own as a wallpaper hanger and a painter. Al was a real efficient worker, but having grown up on a reservation had left him without much formal education. Otherwise, he told me, he would have become a successful contractor himself. He was weak at calculating costs, and I tried to show him how to do it. Eventually, we went into business together, and I would do the paperwork, usually at night after work, and he would function as the boss at the worksite. It worked, up to a point. But before we launched our own company (Al's Wallcovering, "Experience Is Our Asset") in late 1979, we did a few other things together, at least one of which deserves some mention.

The contractor we worked for, McCormick, had a huge state contract painting the buildings of the Cummins Unit, a state prison about sixty miles south of Little Rock. The Cummins Unit housed nearly 2,000 prisoners. At the time, it also contained Arkansas's only execution chamber and death row. It also had become notorious because of its culture of violence and alleged torture stories. In the late 1960s, federal authorities moved in to investigate. They found several unmarked graves of prisoners whose remains showed marks of physical abuse and, eventually, a hidden mass grave of over 200 inmates.

Prisoners were worked to complete exhaustion, mostly doing fieldwork under the blazing sun and largely without shoes. Torture instruments included electrical wires. These findings led to a famous movie, *Brubaker*, released in 1980 with Robert Redford in the lead role. Johnny Cash, an Arkansas boy himself, had performed there in 1969. Reforms eventually dictated the enforcement of humane prison codes, which included updating all facilities. Our job was to paint the inside walls of all the buildings, including the cells, mostly with spray guns.

Al and I carpooled for the drive. He had a large pickup truck, which we mostly used. On the first day, we passed security and were instructed how to behave in prison territory. The cellblock where we worked had been emptied and completely sealed off from the rest of the prison. We got right to work spraying the walls. At lunchtime, I realized that I had left my lunch box in Al's truck, which was parked in a lot outside the prison walls. I got his key and backtracked the way we had entered. I went through two doors that were unlocked and stood outside the prison walls.

I made a beeline for Al's truck. Suddenly I heard a bullhorn behind me. "You, walking in the parking lot, freeze, raise your hands, turn around!" I did as I was told, facing a gun aimed at me from a nearby watchtower. The man with the bullhorn, also on the watchtower, said, "Don't move. Keep your hands up!" A guard, pistol drawn, came and frisked me. With my hands still up, I had to explain what I was doing. Then there were questions about how I got in and out of the prison block, communicated to the guards by some officials inside the prison via a walkie-talkie system.

They checked the doors and found that they had indeed been unlocked. The painting crew inside was informed that one of them had, against all advice, gone to the parking lot to get his lunch. I was quickly told why this was very dangerous. Painters, like inmates, wore white clothing and, at first glance, could be mistaken for escapees. There was one big difference. Inmates had real short hair, whereas mine came down almost to my shoulders. Inmates also had no paint splotches on their clothes. Those differences, I was told later, half jokingly, may have saved my life. Also, the doors I found open were never open again, and no one ever asked why they were open when I went to get my lunch.

There was another incident that could have turned out badly for me. After Al and I had driven to Cummins a few times, he told me I should know something. One of his brothers was an inmate there. He had been on death row for shooting a police officer. His sentence had been converted to life without parole when his case was reviewed. Al smuggled things into Cummins in his lunch box for his brother. He showed me his lunch box, and I saw a bottle of whiskey and *Playboy* magazines.

Al insisted that nothing would happen to me if I claimed I knew nothing. But he felt he had to let me know. I asked if he ever planned to smuggle in guns. He denied it, and I never asked anything about it again. However, the more I learned about Al's life, the more I knew I had to stay on guard. Al, too, had killed someone with a gun in a bar fight in Texas and had been indicted for murder. Because the evidence was inconclusive, the sheriff in charge worked out a verbal deal in which the DA would let Al walk, provided he would never return to Texas again. Those were the days when deals like this could be made.

Al and I worked at Cummins for about two months. For the last two weeks, my work had become easy. Our foreman asked the crew whether anyone could write letters and numbers on surfaces with brushes without using patterns, just freehand. I had done this as a decorator in Germany and raised my hand. I got the job. I wasn't good at it at first. But no one else could do it either. After a couple of days, my skills improved, and I was given extensive instructions on where to put text like Exit or No Entry. But mostly, I had to put numbers over cell doors. I walked around cellblocks on my own, carrying a ladder, paint cans, and brushes. This is how I saw Old Sparky, the electric chair used for all executions in Arkansas. I was told that a newer, more efficient model would soon replace it.

Al and I worked on a few more jobs together before trying our luck as independent contractors. We had to learn how to calculate bids for contracts we could do, meaning small ones at first. And although the bids were secret and submitted in sealed envelopes, we knew that the established contractors had a way of signaling to each other who was supposed to bid high or low to spread the contracts around evenly at profitable margins for everyone. As former employees of theirs, we were not accepted into their clique. But we got a number of small contracts that kept us busy right from the start.

In fact, we had so much work that we had to hire a painter from the union full-time. Aside from the usual things about small businesses (such as tax laws and insurance coverage), I had to learn about the rights and obligations of employees and how to pay into their Social Security and provide holiday pay, sick leave, and work breaks, much of it regulated by the painters' union. I had agreed to go in with Al because it allowed me some flexibility to teach a few history courses at the University of Arkansas in between jobs hanging wallpaper. I even enrolled in courses to obtain an MA in American history. This and my upcoming PhD in European history made me a welcome candidate for any kind of history teaching position in Arkansas.

I was still working on my dissertation, as was another Hayden White student, Gordon Patterson, an extremely bright mind who struggled with nervous breakdowns because White had refused several of his drafts as inefficient. White was known for high standards and shattering student careers. If Gordon couldn't get through, I certainly couldn't, I thought, unless I turned in a perfect first draft. So I kept rewriting, revising, and reworking ad nauseam.

I promised Sue I would have it done on our wedding day. But I didn't. I was close, and I sent the finished manuscript off to White at UCSC and the other three doctoral committee members in early 1979. I didn't hear anything for months. When I finally got ahold of White at UC Santa Cruz, where he had created the History of Consciousness Department, he told me that the draft was "quite good" and suggested a few minor, basically cosmetic changes. It was a short phone conversation, and I felt like fainting at the end

I remember Sue giving me a strange look as we sat at her Aunt Louise's kitchen counter in Benton, Arkansas, but I felt too numb to give her the good news. I had entered UCLA graduate school nearly ten years before, had busted my brains in White's high-flying seminars, delved into history of science courses that often seemed way over my head, struggled with the English language at the most sophisticated level in ways that only non-native speakers understand, and had always told myself that I might not make it but would die trying, all while having the hardest time keeping body and soul together. And this doesn't even take my early experiences at community college into account.

And now things had ended unceremoniously with a short "It's quite good" over the phone? Until I made the call, I had lived with an underlying tension about everything, which I began to feel slowly slipping away. I wasn't sure whether anybody noticed. Other people at the kitchen counter just nodded. "Good news, good news?" Sue understood, but I felt I didn't quite believe it. Recently she had had a serious conversation with Joy, Gordon's wife, who was planning on killing Hayden White if he didn't accept Gordon's dissertation the most recent time.

For some reason, I trusted White. But when the time came, a few months later, to do the necessary legwork at the UCLA campus to get my PhD officially certified, he suggested that it could all be done by mail. Instead, in between painting jobs in Little Rock, I flew to LA, got a rental car, and did everything myself. The last signature I needed was that of Hayden White in Santa Cruz. The drive there from LA by myself, along the beautiful Pacific Coast Highway, was one of the most exhilarating and memorable drives I have ever taken. I knew I had earned this drive and that, at heart, I would always remain a Californian.

Hayden White was very pleasant, congratulated me, told me to call him Hayden, signed the PhD papers, and reminded me to stay in touch. That was the last time I saw him. He is the person who has had a greater intellectual impact on me than anyone else in my life. His bright eyes, inviting smile, handsome look, and engaging demeanor will always remain with me.

On my drive back, I saw the kind of spectacular sunset one can only experience in California. And for a brief moment, I felt at one with the universe. Back in Little Rock, my plate was full again. There were the usual work deadlines and money problems. Sue, too, worked incessantly to keep up with her demanding medical training while keeping her part-time job as a medical assistant at the Morrilton clinic. But with her MD graduation coming up in early 1980, and with me having my PhD under my belt, plus the recent wedding, our lives took on a more predictable pattern.

We could finally envision an orderly future full of regular family life. This would benefit John in particular, as he suffered from our erratic lifestyle, though he had learned to show a stiff upper lip when daily life was like a roller-coaster. From what I could tell, he did well in school, better than the rest of the kids, and was good at sports, especially baseball. He had made close friends and seemed mostly happy, but I wasn't nearly as involved in his life as I should have been.

I knew he struggled with the idea that I might remain a regular feature in his life and probably had visions of escaping to live with his father at the beach in California. But Sue and I started planning a real "bourgeois" family, with more children, one or two more kids of our own. We tried to break it gently to John but were met with predictable resistance. He was only fourteen then, but we thought with time he would adjust to newly developing and, in many ways, much brighter circumstances for all of us.

To all the balls we were juggling came another one. In June 1979, Udo called us from Düsseldorf and wanted to know if he could come to live with us. His high school (Schloss-Gymnasium Benrath) had suspended him and three friends for spraying graffiti with political overtones on its beautiful outside walls. Our parents, ordinary blue-collar folks in their sixties who could not stand up to small academic minds with impressive titles, felt helpless and asked me for advice. I recommended that Udo come live with us. There was a lot of paperwork to handle, but eventually Udo got a student visa to attend the private Catholic high school not far from where we lived.

Our ramshackle house had a little storage room in the back with its own gas heater. We turned it into a "student room" the best we could. When Udo showed up, he was in good spirits and ready to start a new life. He had followed my own story from afar and figured he could do no worse than I had.

His first challenge was improving his English skills enough so that he could follow eleventh-grade instructions and successfully complete his homework. Challenge two was transportation. He was seventeen and, unlike in Germany, could obtain a driver's license in the US, but he also needed a car. For that, he had to work. But he had no work permit and no Social Security number. He found a taco place (Taco Bell) where he could work in the kitchen deep-frying tacos at 100-plus degrees, using my Social Security number. He walked to work and back that summer of 1979, over an hour each way. But it was a start.

The first car he bought was a Nissan, a real lemon. The engine broke down shortly after he bought it "as is" from a shady dealer. It had to be completely replaced. Eventually he got a different used car, a VW Bug, which worked fine.

Udo adjusted well, quickly made friends, and joined the school's soccer team. When the time came to graduate, he was several credits short and decided to do one more year at the nearby public Hall High School in Little Rock.

Sue's graduation was scheduled for May 1980, and we had to make some serious decisions. We would stay in Arkansas if I could find work there or move to wherever I was offered a teaching position. Sue would then apply for a medical residency in that area, hopefully in surgery. I had my PhD from one of the best universities and one of the leading authorities in modern European history. I was teaching part-time at the University of Arkansas at Little Rock, and soon there would be an opening in the field of European history, focusing on Germany. I had a good rapport with the students, and things looked very promising. So we started plans to extend the family, with the child to be born at the time of Sue's graduation.

Sue went off the Pill, and in August 1979, we started getting really busy, never missing a day to make sure. And it worked. The pregnancy didn't make things easier for Sue; quite the contrary. As the due date drew closer, I tried to help as much as possible. We joined a Lamaze class offered by Sue's gynecologist at the nearby Baptist Medical Center. The class was designed to prepare expecting mothers for safe delivery with maximum involvement by the father, who would be present at the birth. An amniocentesis had shown that our child was a boy, and we were eagerly looking forward to his arrival.

Sue's graduation took place shortly before the baby was born, and when she walked across the stage to receive her MD, the dean of the medical school shook her hand and said, "Congratulations to the both of you."

Curt was born some weeks later, on May 30, and I was present. For those observing the moment of birth, it is one of the most breathtaking a human can witness, while for the woman giving birth, it is sheer agony mixed with jubilant excitement. Everything went well, and Sue's relief at holding Curt in her arms was monumental. She was of course painfully aware that the delivery of Jason eleven years earlier had ushered in tremendous tragedy.

Seeing her healthy baby was certainly a crucial step in Sue's struggle to find peace in her soul. We called the baby Curt in honor of Sue's uncle and aunt, Sam and Connie Curt. My father's first name, Christian, became Curt's middle name. And from the beginning, Curt Christian Freyhofer enlivened his environment with loud and long stories that he needed to share with us no matter what. A few years later, his talents would rival the cartoon character Dennis the Menace.

TWENTY-SIX

Off to Germany and Back

In the year before Curt's birth, I did everything I could to land a job related to my field anywhere in the US. I applied for every open position in the country that was advertised in professional journals and regular newspapers. Of course, I was hoping to get the upcoming full-time position at the University of Arkansas at Little Rock, since I was already teaching there part-time. But I tried to cover all my bases. The job market for history instructors at the assistant professor level was very bleak. There were about ten PhDs for every job opening. Sue's prospects were much better. She could find a first-year residency at a teaching hospital almost anywhere in the nation. Therefore, she applied for positions at hospitals near universities where I had also applied for a teaching position.

We even did this for a few places in Germany, just in case. All of this kept us very busy, and because Sue had to work frantically during her last year of medical school, I did most of it between different painting jobs and lecturing at the university. Soon, the bad news started rolling in. All of my applications were rejected. Even the sure thing at my own university fell through. The only place that offered me a job was the Haus der Technik in Essen, West Germany.

It was an engineering school with a department for planning an energy museum for the Ruhr Valley region. The region was the industrial center of Germany, owing its dominance largely to the hard anthracite coal mined there. But lately Germany had become a progressive country in terms of energy research, preparing for a decrease in fossil fuel use and an increase in renewable energy. The planned museum would serve as a public information center dealing with such issues for the general public.

I had answered an ad looking for a social historian with a scientific background. In my phone interview, desperate to land any kind of job, I stretched the disciplinary reach of my field of expertise to "social and intellectual history" and stressed that my "secondary field" was the history of science, citing my dissertation on the philosopher-scientist Hans Driesch in support. They offered me the job, and I accepted, but not before clearing it with Sue.

We had often talked about the advantages of settling in Germany, particularly the generous support the welfare system would extend to Jason if he would join us in Germany. This was a major bonus for Sue, as we had always anticipated that much of our income in the US would eventually have to be used for Jason's continued care. At that time, he was still in foster care with the Lamers family, who in the meantime had moved from California to Oregon. But the agreement was that he would rejoin our family soon after Sue finished her medical education.

But there were also several things working against a move to Germany. At least in the beginning, Jason would be lost in an unfamiliar language environment. The same went for John. He had gone through this ordeal once before when we moved to Mexico. He was fourteen years old, entering ninth grade, and he knew no German. He would once again be torn from a familiar environment, leaving behind the routines of school life and friends. No one would wish this on their children. Still, Sue and I compared our own childhoods to John's. We figured he was a lucky boy, emerging from all his experiences stronger than his peers with the ability to become a successful professional speaking several languages. When this didn't sound convincing, we always said we had to do what was best for Jason in the long run, even if it didn't seem logical in the moment.

In Germany, Sue would have to enter residency training at a

German hospital without speaking German, provided that she could even find a spot. She has a knack for learning languages and told me somehow she would manage, so we filled out applications for a number of German hospitals. Eventually, Frankfurt University Hospital wrote her that she would be admitted as a resident (Assistenzärztin) to their surgery program, beginning in the fall of 1980. This was good news, but it had a flip side. Frankfurt and Essen were 150 miles apart. We would both have busy work schedules, with a fourteen-year-old boy going to school and a toddler to take care of. And how would we manage to take care of Jason? The fact that we had no place to stay or a car to get around in seemed a minor nuisance by comparison.

This, in short, was our situation in the summer of 1980. We were very undecided, discussing the pros and cons of going versus staying ad nauseam, and finally we decided to go. I had told Sue a few times when we were living in Mexico that, eventually, I would like to move back to Germany, and I'd asked if she would come along. The answer had always been yes.

Sue may have felt that I had gone to Mexico with her and it was her turn to go to Germany with me. A few weeks after Curt was born, I boarded a plane to Frankfurt, where we had decided to live. In Frankfurt, I got a used car and started searching for an apartment. I found one in a high-rise of Mörfelden-Walldorf, a suburb just outside the city. I somehow got some furniture together, which was not easy in Germany, so we wouldn't have to sleep on the floor. Soon, I was completely broke but able to earn some money by teaching night courses at several US bases (Mannheim, Darmstadt, Frankfurt) offered by the University of Maryland for GIs stationed overseas.

In the end, our plan looked like this: Sue would work regular hours at the Frankfurt hospital, getting there by train. John would attend the Walldorf middle school, several blocks from our apartment. I would work regular hours at the Haus der Technik in Essen. I would live in Düsseldorf with my parents, who had a two-bedroom apartment, and they would take care of Curt during the day until I would come home and take over.

On the weekends, Curt and I would join Sue and John in Mörfelden-Walldorf. John would have to spend most of his afternoons, the time between the end of school and Sue's arrival at home, by himself. We figured there would be school programs or other organized activities he could join but found they were sparse. Regardless, we felt we had little choice at the time and tried to console ourselves with the idea that all this was just a short transition to a more organized family life in the near future. In other words, I had to find work closer to Frankfurt, or Sue had to find something closer to Essen. We were confident that this would not take too long. However, the immediate problems for each of us were enormous. Without speaking a word of German, John had to sit in regular ninth-grade classes and try to make some sense of what was being taught. Fortunately, the school had dedicated teachers who tried to help him catch up with what he was missing, with much of the tutoring done in English. Sue's situation was similar.

From day one, she had to communicate with patients in German. She worked in the surgery department run by the all-powerful Professor Enke, who told her she would have to take German courses for immigrants, offered in the afternoons at a school next to the nearby train station, to improve her skills. There she met people from all over the world who, just like herself, struggled to communicate in very rudimentary German. After four weeks, Professor Enke told her she had taken enough German and was needed more at the hospital.

Communicating in a language one hardly knows is extremely tiring. In the evening, Sue had to take care of a similarly exhausted John. And I, who could have helped some, was nowhere in sight except on the weekends.

I, of course, had it much easier. I was a native speaker, and my parents took care of Curt until I came home from work. And my work was not strenuous. The planning staff for the new museum consisted of eight people. We were responsible for designing the museum's content, mainly displays about the different uses of energy throughout history and the prospects for the future.

My specific assignment was to study the social and economic aspects of these uses and develop ideas for how to represent this effectively in a museum. From the start, I felt that the museum's benefactors (government agencies and big coal-sponsored foundations) tried to paint a rosy picture of the fossil fuel industry. After all, we were in the middle of Europe's largest coal-producing region. But our group leader, Fritz Erbslöh, assured me that we were to study all uses of energy with equal focus, including wind and solar. We put together a few small exhibitions.

The first one dealt with using gas—past, present, and future. I wrote the texts for the displays and designed the presentation. The work was interesting. I traveled to other museums, archives, and libraries and talked to experts on energy research and media culture. I wrote exhibition guides and blurbs for the news. In my heart, I had always been an ideas person, wanting to teach intellectual history at some elite college in the US. But at that point, I could easily see myself morphing into a museum curator.

If only Sue could get a residency in a hospital in or close to Essen. I talked to Erbslöh about this. He was friends with the head of the Haus der Technik, who knew the head of the surgery department of the teaching hospital in Essen. He got the ball rolling. Meanwhile, Sue's German improved considerably, and she impressed her colleagues with her medical knowledge and skills. She even performed small surgeries. Professor Enke let her know that he would support her efforts to become a certified surgeon in Germany, an extreme honor given the fact that the specialty was very selective.

But things were not going too well for John. This did not come as a surprise. I met his school advisor several times and was told that despite John's brightness, he was unlikely to pass the exams for his German high school diploma, Abitur, because his German was not sufficient, and he did not have enough time to get to the required level. He had taken a number of tests, along with all the other students, and it was determined that he had a keen sense for the mathematical and practical things in life.

They placed him into an internship with an architectural company, where they suggested that John would do well as a draftsman or architect if he tried hard. John started to feel uncertain about a career in Germany and indicated that he would like to return to the States, where the high school diploma would be no problem and lots of colleges would be open to him. He also did not feel as though he had adjusted well to life in Walldorf. In the beginning, he tried to run with the German crowd, and for a while, that seemed to work. But he could not quite shake the feeling of being an outsider, a feeling that was confirmed when he met Stefan Luft, a classmate from Austria who had also recently moved to Walldorf. They became good friends, an apparent blessing for both, as they shared a growing rejection of the often petty-minded German mentality from which they planned to escape.

We discussed the general situation in Germany with John and the problems arising from not getting the Abitur. Returning to the US seemed to be the best solution for him, but for Sue and me, returning presented problems. So we considered a different option. John could live with Sue's Aunt Connie in Neodesha. I would try to get a job in the US as soon as possible. Sue would apply for a residency at the nearest teaching hospital if I got a job. As soon as Sue and I returned to the States, John would join us again. If I didn't get a job in the US, Sue and I, and of course Curt, would stay in Germany, probably for the rest of our lives. That option gradually became more concrete.

I had been offered a secure position in the administration of the Haus der Technik in Essen, and Sue had been offered a residency in surgery at a hospital nearby. So we were set, possibly for good. We were going to get a house at the Kettwiger See, a small, beautiful lake just south of Essen. But to be fair to John and to spare Jason possible culture shock when he would join us in Germany, I kept applying for every college teaching job in the States I heard about. The chances of landing one were still very slim. In my specialty, supply outstripped demand.

In the end, an old friend from UCLA, Gordon Patterson, came to the rescue. He eventually did get his PhD approved by Hayden White, and he had also moved to Germany, mainly to teach for the University of Maryland at various US military bases, and I had stayed in touch with him. He, too, had applied for several open positions in the US and was eventually hired to teach European history at Florida Institute of Technology (FIT), a private university in Melbourne, Florida.

The university was designed mainly to graduate hands-on engineers for a number of growing technical fields, like air transportation and space exploration. Gordon had started his position in the fall of 1979 and told me they were looking for someone who could teach the history of science and that I should apply. I did, tweaking my résumé a bit to focus on the sciences. I had an interview and was hired as an assistant professor to start teaching in the fall of 1982.

As good as the news was on the surface, it disrupted our family life dramatically yet again. In the summer of 1981, John had gone to

Kansas to live with the Curts in Neodesha, just as his mother had done twenty-two years earlier. As agreed, John would join us in Florida the following year. Sue would have to find a new residency close to Melbourne. When I went to Melbourne for my job interview, I visited a number of hospitals with residency programs in the Orlando area. I presented Sue's case to the relevant administrators. She wanted to continue her training in surgery and receive credit for her time in Germany.

People with important-looking faces told me this was an impossibility without giving me reasons why. But at the Orlando Regional Medical Center (ORMC), they told me they had a spot for a first-year internal medicine resident starting in the summer of 1983. It was a three-year program, but she would get no credit for her training in Germany. She had to start from scratch. They wanted her to commit right away. I called Sue, and she immediately signed up for the residency, sounding stressed but also relieved. We were all going to live together in the US again.

Now we had to manage our move back. The stuff we wanted to take fit into two small shipping containers. I flew to Florida in August, taking Curt with me. Once we arrived in Melbourne, I had to find a car and a place to stay before Sue followed. A trip to a used car dealer solved the car problem. Then I found a nice house for rent within walking distance of FIT and a five-minute drive from the beach. A day care center for Curt was close by.

Sue followed several weeks later, and John joined us from Kansas just before school started. There we were, a little dizzy from all the moving and apprehensive about the new uncertainties we had to deal with, but we were together.

Sue's internship started a year later. John had again been ripped out of a familiar environment and dropped into a strange situation, a new high school where he had to prove himself all over again. I had the easy job.

I started teaching classes at a beautiful campus, was given a nice office, and hooked up with my old friend Gordon, who made sure I was received favorably by my new colleagues right from the start.

In contrast, Sue had just given up the pursuit of her dream profession, being a surgeon, and had to wait an entire year to start a new residency in internal medicine, a field she had not previously considered. What was she going to do in the interim? She managed to find an assistant job at the Melbourne coroner's office. There she helped coroners and pathologists perform autopsies to determine the cause and nature of people's deaths. The more interesting parts of this type of work focused on finding incriminating material for legal cases. Sue sometimes told me about such cases and swore me to the utmost secrecy. I was glad to see that she had found meaningful work but was also aware that she was counting the days until she could get back to her medical training, albeit in a new field.

John had it the hardest. He was now an eleventh grader and did well in school. Being smart, good-looking, and friendly, he had no problems finding friends. But we noticed he missed the opportunities Neodesha High School had given him in sports. In Neodesha, he was a starter in all the sports he chose. In Melbourne, as a newcomer, he mainly sat on the bench, despite his excellent skills. And there was little we could do to console him.

Curt had it the easiest. He was only two years old and missed the full significance of our transatlantic ordeal. I usually picked him up from the day care center and could watch him coming down fast slides or climbing up pirate ships at nearby playgrounds, laughing all the time.

TWENTY-SEVEN

Florida

In many respects, Florida was a challenge for us. In Frankfurt, we often felt sun-deprived, with seemingly endless strings of overcast skies and long, drizzly days. In Florida, the sun seemed to scorch our faces, accompanied by hot and moist air that turned everyone sweaty and sluggish for much of the year. People were pent up in air-conditioned rooms and overcooled cars day and night. Mosquitoes and blackflies made life outside uncomfortable.

In addition, we had to adjust to a higher noise level in social settings and get used to a Floridian kind of "in-your-face" presence. For newcomers like us, things weren't just colorful and bright. They were flashy and glaring. People didn't just talk, they shouted, especially on television. They did not have conversations as much as yelling matches, seemingly designed to sell one thing or another. We experienced culture shock. We had lived in the States before. Sue grew up here. But in Europe, we had gotten used to a less noisy and slower pace of life, and we had to become reacquainted with the American pace again.

Americans who have never experienced more sedate societies usually don't understand what the talk of "noise pollution" is all about. And indeed, once you are back in it, you soon start wondering what the big deal is yourself. It doesn't take long to chime in, enjoy the vibrant colors that nature provides, and overlook the more glaring, commercially driven ones that people have added over the years.

Most people who move to Florida quickly adjust to the often lush, sometimes chaotic-looking landscapes, especially near the beach. Still, it is difficult to avoid a certain feeling of transience that seems to permeate everyday life. People settle here from all corners of the States and other countries, or they are children of people who came earlier and often admit missing roots. Of the roughly twenty people in my department at Florida Institute of Technology, only one was born in Florida.

One colleague I associated with closely was Nabil Matar, a Palestinian whose family had been driven off its land by Jewish settlers and who had come to the US to start a new life. There were Jews who had fled Nazi terror, Eastern Europeans who had fled Communist terror, and Latinos who had fled economic disaster, among many other transplants, though they were mostly Northerners who had escaped the cold or personal misfortune to try to start their lives over from scratch. FIT, a private university that attracted many international students, often from the Middle East, fit the bill. Most students wanted an engineering degree that guaranteed a well-paying job right after graduation.

With its lengthy stretches of beautiful beaches, Florida has long been a tourist state, ideally suited for honeymooners but also for retired folks who come to warm their weary limbs before kicking the bucket. Florida sells itself as the Sunshine State but colloquially is often called the state of "the newly wed and nearly dead." We learned to adjust but sensed that we would not stay for long.

Unsurprisingly, John was the first to point to some personal disadvantages of being in Florida. He was a high school junior at a completely new high school, trying to make new friends, excel in sports, and do well in college preparatory classes. He was good at math and had his eye on a possible technical career. We discussed college options, and he expressed a strong desire to attend the University of Kansas. He had just spent tenth grade in Neodesha and obtained all sorts of information about KU's academic programs, financial assistance, and campus life. KU was built very graciously with a land grant deed in the late nineteenth century and charged low tuition for state residents. John would lose his residency status unless he returned to Kansas and did his senior year in Neodesha. The Curts said they would like to have him back if it was okay with us. John seemed to have his mind made up, and therefore, we agreed that he would stay one year with us before heading back to Neodesha for his senior year.

Curt was still only two years old and was oblivious to our struggles. He seemed happy at the local nursery. Sue's internship at Orlando Regional Medical Center would start in the middle of 1983, right after John's departure. The distance between our residence in Melbourne and ORMC was over eighty miles, and it took way over an hour of driving. So we decided to move somewhere in between the two points.

St. Cloud was almost halfway, and we found a nice one-family house just a few blocks from Lake Tohopekaliga. Because of the hyper-inflation a few years earlier (in 1980, it had reached nearly 14 percent), banks were reluctant to lend money to people without a proven record of paying off credit. And my salary as assistant professor was not very impressive.

But when Sue produced her contract as a medical intern at ORMC, we were considered creditworthy after all but still had to accept 12.5 percent interest for our loan with the local bank. Still, we were glad to close on the deal and subsequently moved into the first house we ever owned, a three-bedroom place with a large veranda, which we closed in and encased with climbing rosebushes (Don Juans) on the outside. This room came to be my office. We had a large corner lot, and Sue filled it with many types of rosebushes, radiating brilliant colors in all directions and filling the air with exotic fragrances. People from the neighborhood strolling by would ask Sue for advice on their own efforts to grow roses. We had a few citrus trees, under which I loved to sit and read, often for hours.

Adjusting didn't take long, and soon we managed to do our daily chores along established routines. Sue had to get up really early and drive for almost an hour to ORMC to start her work as a medical intern. She usually came home exhausted after a ten-hour shift, often with material to study for the next day. I, too, had to drive almost an hour to FIT.

My work, too, was very demanding, mainly because I taught the history of science to science students who often had more specific knowledge in certain scientific fields than I did but who were less able to put their knowledge into historical perspective. That's where I came in. And to stay on top of the material, I had to always be on my intellectual toes. In general, I managed. I explained quantum physics and relativity to physics students, evolutionary biology to biology students, and the different uses of chemical energy to chemistry students. My focus was always on the emergence of scientific theories, the creative process of their construction, and their relations to theories in the humanities (including arts, literature, and philosophy).

Keeping up with the relevant publications on the topics occupied most of my time. Plus, I regularly attended conferences and presented papers, mostly at the annual meetings of the German Studies Association. My ambition of writing a scholarly work on the political role that ideologies have played in forming scientific theories remained just that, an ambition.

The nursery we had found was part of a small K-to-fourth-grade school (Rocking Horse Ranch) close to our house, where Curt spent most of his day. It was organized around Christian principles and was run according to strict disciplinary rules. Curt seemed pretty happy there, though much later we learned that he disliked the punishment codes, including paddling, but he was afraid to tell us. Usually, I took Curt to school before taking off for FIT and tried to pick him up again in the afternoon. He quickly made friends with some boys in the neighborhood, and they would play together whenever they had a chance, either at our place or theirs.

Later, either Sue or I would prepare dinner or we would go out to eat in one of the many restaurants just a few blocks from where we lived. Soon, we found a convenient way of rolling eating and entertainment into one happy event. Residents in our area could get an annual pass for the Disney World park, which was just thirty minutes from where we lived. It cost $120 for adults and was, I believe, half price for children.

The park had a section called EPCOT Center full of restaurants from countries around the world, serving authentic food from those countries. The food was generally better and less expensive than most commercial places outside the park. So, we all got annual tickets and drove a lot to eat at EPCOT. In fact, Curt and I made it a habit to drive there after school to eat and enjoy the rides and activities whenever we felt like it. Disney World became our second home. The many fireworks there have never ceased to amaze us.

Sue and I often went to the park for late dinner by ourselves. Curt stayed home with a babysitter. One of our favorite places was the Moroccan restaurant, which had the best lamb chops in all of Florida. There were also colorful performances by curvy belly dancers. On days when we just wanted to fill our own bellies with quick, good food without much entertainment or fancy service, we went to the huge Chinese pavilion, where we got the best Peking duck, smorgasbord style, in just a few minutes.

After a while, our lives had assumed a routine that allowed for times of comfort. Still, things were not always easy, and Sue especially struggled with the demands put on her by the rigorous workload of her internal medicine program. She could deal with the long working hours and the stress of too many patients, but she had some problems tolerating the antics of her direct supervisor, Barry Sieger, a wheeler-dealer type interested primarily in advancing his own reputation as an infectious disease expert in the wider medical community.

For instance, to show that none of his interns would fail the Internal Medicine Certification Examination, he would not permit interns to take the test when he had any doubts about their ability to pass. They were told of their fate just shortly before their test. Barry Sieger told a good friend of Sue's the bad news in this way. The intern, by all accounts an excellent physician, subsequently committed suicide. That raised certain anxieties in Sue that she could not shake off. She later told me if Sieger had treated her that way, she was prepared to kill him and pay the price of going to prison. At the time I knew of her conflicts but not of her plan to kill Sieger.

Shortly after we moved into our new house in St. Cloud, we were joined by Stefan Luft, John's Austrian friend from Frankfurt. He had been invited to come and stay with us whenever he liked. He would have liked to come with us when we left Frankfurt in the summer of 1982, but things were still unsettled for us all, and together with his parents, Manfred and Luise Luft, we decided to wait a year.

Of course, Stefan had hoped to spend time with his friend John, but John had just left for Kansas as Stefan showed up. Stefan decided to stay with us anyway. We felt he was glad to escape the tensions he probably faced at home and school. We registered him at St. Cloud High School in the graduating senior class without much of a problem.

Fortunately, his status as a "family member" was not challenged. However, Stefan soon ran into some problems at the school that threw things into turmoil. He got into a tussle with his American history teacher. As I recall, Stefan tried to correct him on some points regarding European affairs during the Cold War, which the teacher did not take lightly. In front of the class, the teacher remarked that if Stefan had anything positive to say about life in Eastern Europe, he might as well go back and live under Communism.

I wrote the teacher a letter explaining that speaking that way to the son of a political refugee from Communism (Stefan's father had fled East Germany in the 1960s) was highly insensitive. I requested a meeting. When the teacher replied that scheduling problems made it difficult for him to meet, I went to the principal of the school, who told me that he would look into the matter. Soon after, he called me back with all sorts of confusing information. Some had to do with the apparent oversight of enrolling Stefan as a "foreign" student, which the school had no authority to do. Also, he said, St. Cloud High School was overenrolled, but he had found a solution to Stefan's "problem."

The principal knew that I was an FIT professor and John had been a student at the nearby high school. When I enrolled Stefan at St. Cloud High School, I stressed that John had been an international student in Germany and that we would return the favor by having Stefan attend an American high school as an international student. This sounded logical but was not covered by the law. Stefan's American history teacher must have found out about it. The principal's solution was that Stefan could attend Melbourne High School, where the administration remembered John and, I gathered, also wanted to support FIT by helping its faculty. Surprisingly, at the end of his senior year, Stefan's high school credits would be transferred to St. Cloud High School, where he would receive his high school diploma.

As complicated as all of that was. I was glad that the principal could work something out, though I was reluctant to call it a "solution." For Stefan to get to Melbourne High School, he had to travel with me every day. We had to coordinate our schedules, which was not always easy. But we managed, and I got to know Stefan much better. After all, for him, I was some kind of old fart, someone of his father's generation whom he had ample reasons to resent. But we were helping him, and during our long drives to and from Melbourne, he opened up.

He started by wondering out loud why someone would listen to Brahms and Beethoven while driving long distances. I countered by wondering why anyone could listen to Ted Nugent or Judas Priest for more than five minutes and stay sane. After that, things improved considerably. Stefan became an integral part of our family and, in many ways, filled the painful hole that John had left behind. He soon had his own circle of friends and did many things with us as a family too. He did well in school and in May 1984 graduated with a high school diploma from St. Cloud High School.

I sensed Stefan's relief when he received the confirmation in the mail, and his parents called, excited to tell him that they would fly over to attend the graduation ceremony. It seemed like the whole thing was a surprise to them, and they were astonished when, after they arrived, Stefan told them that he would stay in the US to attend college. That, of course, would be a bureaucratic and financial challenge. But Stefan was confident he could manage, and we would continue to support him as best we could. His high school grades were good but not good enough for the top schools. And once admitted to any school, he would have to get a student visa. He applied at various places and decided to study business at Flagler College, a private school on a beautiful campus in picturesque St. Augustine by the sea. It wasn't cheap. But they worked out a financial aid package that required Stefan to get a job off campus to meet costs. I think he mainly worked in restaurants.

Soon someone else called and wondered whether she could stay with us for a while. Her name was Alexandra, and she was the seventeen-year-old daughter of Sue's cousin, Sammie Curt, from Neodesha. Sammie had apparently developed a strained relationship with her husband that ended in a messy divorce, leaving their daughter bruised emotionally. Alexandra was looking for a stable home that would help her develop the necessary discipline for starting a successful life. She must have heard about the happy story of Stefan and figured we could help her too. She agreed to live by our house rules, which were not overly strict, and with her mother's blessings she came to live with us in 1985. She had impressive educational goals but was ill-prepared to enter any kind of school. But we managed to get her enrolled in some vocational courses at the local Brevard Community College.

In the beginning, all seemed well. But after a few weeks, we got a call from the college asking how Alexandra was doing. She hardly attended classes and often called in sick while telling us everything was fine. She routinely ignored her curfew. A few times, she called us in the middle of the night because the car we had loaned her had run out of gas in the middle of nowhere, and we had to bail her out. Later, Sammie would call her daughter and explain the importance of discipline, then implore us to give Alexandra another chance. This went on for many months with no progress. In fact, things got worse. Eventually, Alexandra went back to Kansas, and we didn't hear from her for many years.

Sue's internship ended in the summer of 1986. She was a soon-to-be-certified specialist in internal medicine, preparing to enter the workforce. Some physicians with lucrative practices in Orlando were ready to retire and considered Sue a good candidate to take over for them. But I knew she had become an internist only because, aside from OB-GYN, internal medicine was the only specialty open to her when she left Frankfurt. She would have loved to work in surgery as she had in Germany. But, as she told me, in Florida, it's a men's club.

Then in 1986, ORMC opened up a training program for the new specialty of emergency medicine. Sue, much more of a hands-on fix-it type than one to observe and diagnose, inquired about joining the program. They told her that to become a licensed ER doctor, she would be required to do two more years of training instead of the usual three. She went for it. And it soon became apparent that she found the work of emergency medicine much more rewarding. It takes nerves of steel to treat people in dire distress, often fighting for their lives, where knowing the right thing to do in an instant, often instinctively, can make the difference between life and death. Sue had them.

Sue embraced the challenge and developed the skills to work calmly and efficiently in tense situations. Her whole demeanor showed that she had found her true vocation. There was one drawback. To the five years of residency she had already done (two in surgery and three in internal medicine), she had to add two more in emergency medicine before finally getting a specialty license. But Sue looked forward to working in her new field, and the journey, although long, was a rewarding one. We were holding it together financially. We made ends meet by Sue working in some doc-in-the-box outfit at various locations as time allowed and me working the extra summer semester.

We still found time for exploring sites around Florida, visiting family in Arkansas, and taking trips to Europe. We had many visitors, including some of my old buddies from Germany, who all wanted to see Disney World and seemed impervious to the sweltering summer heat. We also made some concrete steps to bring Jason back into our family life. Sue and Tony and Helen Lamers had agreed that Jason would join us as soon as Sue finished her medical training. That had been deferred from 1986 to 1988.

To get Jason used to our environment in Florida, we had him live with us for some weeks in the summer of 1986. He liked everything he saw right off the bat, particularly the lakefront area just a few blocks from our house. There was a sandy beach beneath lush palm trees and benches to sit on. We got him a tricycle so he could go there by himself. Within a couple of days, he developed his own back-and-forth kick to replace pedaling. He had difficulty moving in a straight line but didn't give up.

Curt spent a lot of time showing Jason around, understanding major adjustments lay ahead. They were brothers but they had never met. And Jason was a special-needs child. All in all, things were off to a good start, except for one thing: the weather. It quickly became apparent that Jason could not stand the heat or, worse, the humid air. Around midmorning, he started to sweat, developed problems breathing, and had to stay inside. We took him out during the early morning and late evening hours. But even then, he complained about the heat.

After he went back to the Lamers family several weeks later, we knew we had to change plans once again. With Jason in the house, we could not stay in Florida but had to move to a place that was more accommodating to his special condition. It should have a moderate climate with dry air. It could be cold but not humid. The most logical place was the upper Northeast: Vermont, New Hampshire, or Maine.

It's one of the nicest areas in the US tc live, but for me, it was a very difficult place to find employment.

I had a secure position at FIT in intellectual/scientific history, and given the job market at the time, I had little chance of finding a similar position teaching in a highly competitive area. Sue, on the other hand, had few problems finding employment anywhere. Most hospitals were looking for trained ER physicians. Their emergency rooms, until recently, had been staffed with physicians without the special training required to treat patients with severe trauma, such as from car crashes or gunshot wounds. Statistics showed that many lives were lost because correct care was not given efficiently or fast enough. Hence the creation of the new specialty of emergency care. In fact, the US was the leader in instituting it and has remained so ever since. In short, Sue would easily find a position at a hospital close to whatever teaching institution would hire me.

TWENTY-EIGHT

Moving Up North: Vermont and New Hampshire

Upon her graduation in May 1988, Sue was approached by many head-hunting firms that offered to place her wherever she wanted. She was prepared to go wherever I could find a job. I furiously applied to all sorts of colleges and universities in the Northeast but without success. Simultaneously, Sue would go to interviews in the Northeast and planned to accept a position in an area with many colleges and universities, such as Boston or New Haven. She interviewed at Porter Medical Center in Middlebury, Vermont, which had just enlarged its emergency room and was hiring its first ER doctor. The hiring committee told her that there were many connections between the hospital and Middlebury College.

In fact, Sue was told that the history department had long planned to add a position in the history of science and that, with my background, I would be an excellent candidate.

We took the chance and moved to Middlebury in the summer of 1988. We kept our house in St. Cloud as a possible residence for our retirement and rented it out to someone we knew well and who would take good care of it. Then we bought a new house in the country near Middlebury in the town of Bristol. It was surrounded by lots of land.

When we moved, we did everything ourselves, cramming all of our belongings into a huge U-Haul truck with a trailer and driving to Bristol in record time. Curt even brought his cat along. We set up the household in record time as well because Sue had to start working soon. I met the president of Middlebury College, John McCardell, and introduced myself. He assured me I could start teaching a course in the history of science as a visiting professor and things would progress from there.

Getting together with the head of the history department, John Spencer, was the next step, but it was still summer, and he wouldn't be back until the fall. We also had to get Jason back into the family. His foster father, Tony Lamers, brought him to us, and he and Jason had a very sad farewell. Aside from Sue, there was no one who had personally cared more for Jason than Tony. And as we came to find out, no one could ever fill the void Tony's absence left in Jason's life. Years afterward, tears would still stream down his face when he looked at a picture on the wall showing him and Tony together. He would still think of the Lamers as his real family for a long time. He proudly pronounced over and over a few Dutch words that Tony, a native of Holland, had taught him. We knew it would take a long time for Jason to transition and feel like a regular member of his new/old family.

Curt also had to make a big adjustment. He was suddenly being asked to live with a brother in constant need of help. We tried to do lots of things together. I became a Middlebury Special Olympics coach and once had Curt and Jason play on the same soccer team in "mixed" tournaments. Jason also participated in track and field, bowling, swimming, and cross-country skiing. I have done many things in life, but some of my proudest moments were those when I witnessed the joy of "my team" receiving a medal, including the gold, and the smiling faces on stage.

The Special Olympics group became Jason's emotional anchor, and it made him feel at home during the many sporting events as well as during private activities, many of which took place at our house. The local high school had a program for impaired children, designed to "mainstream" them, and Jason did rather well under the tutelage of one particular teacher, Mrs. Samler.

Curt also liked his new school, where he quickly made friends and excelled in soccer and baseball. He liked to show off on the field, often donning sunglasses. His coaches called him "Mr. Hollywood." And he finally got his dog, a beautiful black Labrador that he picked out himself at the local pound and named Bowzer. It looked like we were finally settling down into the kind of life we had planned for years. At least, we thought so.

I had a subtle awakening when I met John Spencer, the head of the history department. I later found out that he was a member of the Rockefeller family and a big deal in the Ford Foundation, among many other noteworthy things. He had a way of saying no without using negative language. His demeanor put others in their place without seeming to do so. When I learned that one of the Rockefellers taught Eastern philosophy at Middlebury, and it was he who got the Dalai Lama, one of his friends, to come to campus to break bread with the college community (at an event that I participated in), it dawned on me that I had little understanding of the kind of elitism that was still part of the fiber of much of New England education. It didn't matter that I had received my PhD at UCLA and from one of the leading intellectual scholars in the US, Hayden White. For Middlebury, I still was not part of a recognized network. White, son of a Tennessee sharecropping family and later professor at Berkeley and Stanford, had himself remained a maverick in an academic world whose elitist assumptions, he felt, were less sustained by merit than connections. I, too, would not fit well into that environment. I also had no publication record at the time. Merely hiring me, hoping I would publish something worthwhile down the road, was too risky for the college. Even I could see that. But what I found uncollegial and highly unprofessional was how this was communicated to me.

John McCardell welcomed me and let me know that he didn't doubt my ability to be part of the college, but he also left no doubt that the choice was up to the history faculty. I spoke to some of them, and everyone was very polite in a guarded way. But it became apparent that at least one history faculty member would block my hiring, no matter what. Her name was Marjorie Lamberti, and her specialty was modern German history, with a focus on the Holocaust. She never talked to me.

Later, at a conference of the German Studies Association, I approached her to say hello, and she lectured me loudly in front of colleagues, telling me I had no right to wear my Middlebury name tag because I had no "regular" teaching appointment at the college and was a mere "fellow." I knew then that I had to extend my job search to other colleges.

I applied at the University of Vermont in Burlington, about forty miles north of Middlebury, the only school within commuter range of our home. There was no full-time position available, but I could teach part-time undergraduate courses in the history of science and modern German history. Although this was unsettling to our family life again, we had to prepare for another move if I were to find a full-time position elsewhere in the Northeast. Eventually, I did. As it happened, world political events came to my aid.

Unexpectedly, the Berlin Wall fell on November 9, 1989. The wall had been the symbolic cornerstone of the Iron Curtain that had divided the socialist Eastern Bloc and the capitalist Western Bloc countries since the end of World War II. The wall ran through the middle of Berlin and separated families and friends for nearly thirty years. Suddenly, people across the world couldn't believe their eyes as they watched on television as people climbed the wall from both sides, falling into each other's arms as hapless border guards looked on. This event signaled the final crumbling of the border that had divided much of the world.

The Cold War between Eastern Bloc and Western Bloc came to an official end when the last president of the vanquished Soviet Union, Mikhail Gorbachev, took down the Soviet flag from atop the Kremlin during Christmas of 1991. It wasn't easy to keep up with the many events unfolding across Eastern Europe and beyond. The events surrounding the "fall of the wall" in particular seemed to generate many questions that baffled experts. Colleges and other places invited speakers to provide enlightenment and give context. Teachers and professors hastily searched for material that would put the barrage of daily news into some historical perspective. Some colleges even looked for new faculty to fill a growing void. That would prove fortuitous for me.

We also experienced another piece of luck at that time. Sue found a surgeon at Mass General, Dr. Montgomery, who agreed to close Jason's open trachea. A cut had been made through it and the vocal cords at his birth to allow doctors to insert a short tube through which Jason could breathe. The exchangeable tube was usually full of mucus and had to be cleaned often. It was a messy process that Jason hated. Plus, he had to close the hole in his windpipe with his hands to form barely audible words. Sue had approached various surgeons and pleaded for them to remove the tube and close the hole. They all thought the required surgery would be too risky.

Dr. Montgomery thought it was risky too, but it could be done in stages. He was one of the top surgeons in the US who performed such operations. He had been a field surgeon in Vietnam and had performed hundreds of tracheotomies under combat conditions. Later, as head of the surgery department at Mass General, he wrote the standard medical texts on the subject and developed ways to save and use airways without the need for tracheal tubes. He explained that Jason's windpipe had been badly damaged at birth and would be difficult to repair. He promised to try if we understood that this would be an experimental surgery and that we would not come after him if there were complications. Ultimately this was an agreement between two doctors who trusted each other.

It was also going to be an expensive operation. Dr. Montgomery's fees were low, but Mass General charged an arm and a leg. Sue's health insurance would pay a small portion of it, and the rest would have to come from us.

The operation was successful, and Jason's life changed dramatically for the better. No more coughing up spit and mucus all over the dinner table. An end to the constant need to clean the tube. And more understandable speech. Ever since the surgery, Dr. Montgomery has been Jason's biggest hero. Just mentioning his name will cause tears to spring to Jason's eyes. Sue and I, too, are forever indebted to him.

Sue still received calls from headhunters trying to recruit her. After it became obvious that Middlebury College wasn't going to offer me a regular position and that we had a lot of bills from Jason's operation, she switched to Rutland Regional Medical Center because the pay was considerably higher. When recruiters kept calling, she told them she would go anywhere where her husband could find employment. There was one recruiter from a Boston firm who took that very seriously. She called colleges close to places looking for ER doctors and asked them whether they had an opening in European history.

Among other places, the recruiter was trying to find an ER doctor for Lakes Region General Hospital in Laconia, New Hampshire. She called nearby Plymouth State College and was told they needed a historian who could explain the current turmoil in Europe unleashed by the fall of the Berlin Wall. An interview was arranged, and I was told by the head of the Department of Social Science, Bill Taylor, that I could start offering courses in German,'Eastern European history immediately, but as an adjunct, not as part of the tenure-track faculty.

I learned that some years before, the department had not filled its only position in modern European history, and at the time they could not offer courses dealing with the world-shaking events presented every night on the news. I was told the position was not in the budget yet, but it would be soon. I took that chance and agreed to teach the courses immediately, commuting from Middlebury to Plymouth, a 100-mile trip through the mountains, until we could transition a year later. At the time, Sue was working at Rutland Regional Medical Center but now accepted a position at Lakes Region General Hospital, not far from Plymouth. All in all, it was good news, but Sue couldn't warm up to it. She had accepted her position as an ER physician in Middlebury partly because everyone at the hospital had assured her that they would support my application at Middlebury College and that we could expect a good outcome. But that is not how things went.

Sue was the first and only ER doctor at the Middlebury hospital (Porter Medical Center) who went out of her way to bring standards of care to new professional levels. Additionally, she was asked to work closely with the Middlebury Fire Department on a volunteer basis, training them and supervising emergency procedures performed by its members. She worked hard to improve the firefighters' first aid skills, and they greatly appreciated her tireless engagement. When Sue eventually told them that she had to leave, it was a sad day for everyone, and Sue felt that the hospital, particularly the college, had let us down.

Meanwhile, we looked for a place to live in Plymouth and found one close to campus and next to the high school, a spacious two-story

ranch-style house with a bit of land around it. It was in need of renovation, and an architect friend of Sue's redesigned it, adding a fabulous fireplace. We moved in in 1992. We sold our house in Bristol at
a considerable loss. Inflated real estate prices, oil shortages resulting
from Iraq's invasion of Kuwait, and political uncertainties stemming
from global rearrangements at the end of the Cold War had led to a
stock market crash and tight money supply, causing real estate prices
to plummet in their wake. Still, as always, we managed.

Sue liked her new position. I had the full-time position I had always wanted. As sad as his departure from Bristol was, Curt quickly
made new friends and excelled in school, particularly in sports. Only
Jason paid a high price. Plymouth had no Special Olympics program.
I got in touch with the central New Hampshire Special Olympics office and was told that they couldn't find a coordinator for the area;
they asked whether I would like the job. It would be a time-consuming,
mostly volunteer position, and I would have to start a program from
scratch. I had to decline.

Instead, we tried to get Jason involved in some activities where he
could meet people in town. We signed him up for bongo drum sessions at the college, got him involved in church activities, and allowed
him to do odd jobs at the fire station. Nothing lasted. But our efforts to
find him fulfilling employment produced better results.

Until recent years, there were many programs providing different
kinds of workshops for people with impairments. Some shops merely
kept people busy for the sake of keeping them busy; they were often
run as nonprofit organizations. Others produced useful goods that
were sold at a profit. In some cases, impaired people worked under
deplorable labor conditions for the profit of the people running the
shops. Critics further argued that the workshops segregated people in
confined places away from public life. For the most part, though it was
not openly acknowledged, the workshops were a drain on taxpayers'
money. But this started to change in 1990, when Congress passed the
Americans with Disabilities Act (ADA). Among other things, it discouraged workshops for disabled people and required all employers to
provide conditions at the workplace that would allow disabled people
to pursue gainful employment like anyone else, to "mainstream" them.
As a result, the workshops were slowly phased out.

However, we learned that the town of Plymouth still had one of these shops running. It was managed by a cabinetmaker named Larry who was near retirement. He supervised four to five people with various kinds of disabilities. The shop produced wood items, mainly furniture pieces, often on demand. Larry agreed to take in Jason, who worked four to five hours daily. He taught Jason how to sand wooden surfaces to perfection.

Doing "real work" made him extremely proud, and he used his earnings to enlarge his CD collection, which was full of his favorite singers and bands.

Jason could walk to the woodshop and liked to hang out with the other workers there. But there was a hush-hush feeling about the whole operation because, with the newly passed ADA, the continued existence of the woodshop had become a legal liability. But it did employ people whose impairments made it almost impossible for them to find work in a commercial setting. If it weren't for Larry, they wouldn't be working or socializing with each other. And being together at the shop did not mean they felt discriminated against, as the ADA suggested— quite the contrary. They felt appreciated. It certainly boosted the image Jason had of himself. Without Larry's woodshop, Jason, like many others, would probably have been sitting at home, not doing much. Larry explained to me that, fortunately, his woodshop held its own financially and was no drain on the town. That's why they let him continue to operate, illegally, as it were.

We also found a place where Jason could work legally as a dishwasher: the Italian Farmhouse, a restaurant just one mile outside Plymouth. He worked there only one night a week, operating the high-pressure dishwashing machine. It wore him out. But he liked the restaurant atmosphere, sitting around a table with other restaurant workers when the job was done, feeling like a big shot. The restaurant owner, Alex Ray, ensured that Jason kept his weekly spot at the machine. Alex had opened a string of restaurants all over New Hampshire, each one with its own unique character. He cared personally for everyone who worked there. Jason definitely felt like he was part of the "Ray Family."

While Jason did well, Curt really blossomed in Plymouth. At school, he jumped into every kind of sport he could. He wanted to continue where he had left off in Bristol and signed up for baseball, wrestling, and soccer. When the football coach, Charles "Chuck" Lenahan, heard a kid on the soccer team had a mean kick, he told Curt that the football team needed a good kicker and that "real boys play football, not soccer." It convinced Curt, who quickly became the leading kicker and punter on the Bobcats team. He held several offensive starting positions and became crucial in securing many of the team's successes in the coming years, including a state championship.

In baseball, he played mainly as an outfielder, became a reliable high-average hitter, was known for stealing bases, and contributed greatly to the team's success, including a state championship. He was a very coachable team player but excelled mostly as an individual athlete, particularly in wrestling. He was strong and quick and had an unbending will to dominate his opponent. Seeing how he could turn a seemingly lost match around in the last few seconds was a delight. Jason, Sue, and I tried to see all of Curt's matches, though Sue's ER work often interfered. Sometimes she came following a brutal night shift and slept on the bleachers among the screaming spectators. I woke her up when it was Curt's turn to wrestle.

Things could get really tense during tournaments, with many teams from many schools attending. The wrestlers all knew each other and sized each other up during matches. During Curt's first year of wrestling, he encountered the projected winner of a district championship, a cocky kid from the prestigious Exeter High School. With an improbable escape, Curt beat him in the championship match in the last few seconds. Curt dominated in the 130-pound weight class and won many more tournaments.

In 1995, he again beat a supposedly unbeatable opponent to win the state championship. To celebrate, we went for a Big Mac at McDonald's, as we usually did. Life couldn't have been happier. But there were also some sad moments. Curt had problems holding his weight at 130 pounds. His natural weight was higher, especially during his senior year, but the team member who wrestled at the 135-pound class was his good friend, and he didn't want to challenge him. Also, "sucking weight," wrestling at a lower-than-natural weight by literally starving off pounds, was an ever-present temptation. For instance, Curt's coach Cleary once encouraged him to participate in the New England championship in the under-120-pound category with the high prospect of getting a medal. He had to lose over ten pounds in just a couple of weeks but thought it was worth it.

On the day of the tournament, Curt looked a bit skinny as he took off with the other team members. We couldn't be there from the start, and when we arrived, we found him in a depressed state. He had lost his initial match, after being pinned in the first minute. Things didn't improve much afterward, and he left ranking somewhere in the middle. It wasn't a good day for a guy who usually left tournaments with a medal. He gave up sucking weight, but not completely, as we found out later.

His greatest moment of high school sports glory, at least on the public scene, came on the football field. In 1998, his senior year, the Plymouth Regional High School team, the Bobcats, had an undefeated season, and Curt kicked the winning field goal against Conway for the state championship. He was featured as the Dunkin' Donuts Hometown Hero on the local evening news. As high school life goes, things don't get any better than that. His success on the Bobcats team would later help him become a walk-on kicker for the University of Kansas football team, the Jayhawks.

Like everyone who played football at Plymouth Regional High School, Curt benefited greatly from the superior coaching of Chuck Lenahan and his staff. Lenahan was the winningest high school football coach in New Hampshire history. He would receive the national high school coach of the year award twice and be inducted into the National High School Hall of Fame.

We tried to get Curt interested in playing an instrument. Sue had come from a musically talented family, though she never played any music herself. I have tried, intermittently, to teach myself some chords on the guitar but never got beyond playing "This Land Is Your Land" badly. We discussed it with Curt and convinced him to play the violin. Sue's grandfather was a legend in Arkansas and had once placed second in a national fiddle contest in Nashville. She tried to pass some of that tradition on to Curt. And Curt eagerly started violin lessons shortly after we arrived in Plymouth.

After a year of practicing, he played well and performed with other kids before small audiences at school. But his football friends thought it was an odd thing for a "real" boy trained to smash other boys into the

Curt in his legendary number 42 shirt. He kicked the state championship–winning field goal for the Plymouth Regional High School football team in 1998.

mud. They may have challenged his feelings of emerging manhood. At any rate, after a year, Curt told us he had had it with the violin. We told him he could only give up playing the violin if he chose to play another instrument instead. He grudgingly picked up the piano. So we bought a piano and hired a teacher. Again, he performed at school presentations after a year of training. But when the musical activities started interfering with sports, he dropped the piano and never picked it up again. Nor did he ever show any interest in playing music of any kind.

Given his talent, we always regretted it, but we did not put him under any pressure. He probably saw things differently. And during the subsequent years of adolescence, Curt tried to assert himself, pushing against what he perceived as parental overbearance. Sue and I did insist on observing conventional disciplinary rules. We also knew that Curt's situation differed from that of other kids his age. He had no sibling to talk to and play with, as Jason could not fill that hole. In many respects, Jason's special needs often took precedence over Curt's needs. Trying to calm stressed emotions with traditional discipline was not always helpful. We had to find more appropriate ways to help both of the boys mature.

Fortunately, Curt had many friends. Our large house was next to the high school and even closer to the football field. Many of Curt's teammates became regulars at our house. Sometimes we had spaghetti dinners for the whole team, and the house burst with testosterone and noisy laughter.

Sometimes, when friends would stay over, Curt seemed extremely happy. Sue and I thought it would be a good idea to have a boy Curt's age stay with us for a while, preferably someone from Germany. We thought that might encourage Curt to speak German again.

Plymouth Regional High School had a foreign exchange program. From a number of applicants, we chose Kai Radermacher, a tall sixteen-year-old boy from a small town in Germany called Hilgert, near Koblenz. Curt was especially intrigued by Kai's many athletic interests.

Kai, who was one year older than Curt, showed up in the summer of 1995. He liked Plymouth, the surrounding mountains, and the high school. He wanted to improve his English but gave in to our request to speak some German with Curt. The school counselor found Kai well

Curt's high school graduation in 1998. Sue, Curt, Jason, and I.

prepared for the challenges ahead and designed a program leading to his high school graduation by the end of his exchange year.

Kai surpassed all expectations. He became the number one player on the tennis team, received the Best Student Award for advanced mathematics, and achieved the highest grades in English composition, among other things. He quickly felt like a member of our family, and he liked to join us on our occasional trips, including those to Canada and Florida. He received his high school diploma and graduated with distinction in May 1996. Curt would follow him in 1998.

Kai and Curt weren't the only ones doing well. Jason continued his position in Larry's woodshop and kept his once-a-week dishwashing job at the Italian Farmhouse. Sue quit her job at the Lakes Region General Hospital and switched to the Speare Memorial Hospital, just two blocks from our house, so she would be closer to home and able to spend more time with Curt and Jason. Now everyone could walk to his or her place of work or schooling in a safe neighborhood. That doesn't happen very often.

I continued working on the book I had started at Middlebury College, *The Nuremberg Medical Trial*. It was a study of the American military tribunal's trial against Nazi medical doctors and administrators for performing gruesome and fatal medical experiments on concentration camp inmates during World War II.

During my UCLA days, I encountered reports of those experiments and the subsequent trial in my college readings. I was puzzled by attempts of the accused to justify their horrible acts not only on medical and legal but also ethical grounds. There had not been a single study dealing with this paradox, and by the time of this writing, there is still only one, the one I was writing. There is a plethora of texts that deal with the subject, but they all present historical accounts of what happened and do not broach the question of why the doctors thought they were right. Such questions are always precluded on the assumption that the acts committed were so evil that the only thing left to do was condemn them. No attempts were ever made to understand them. I tried to go beyond this approach, reasoning that if men of intelligence had justified their manifestly evil acts on ethical grounds, humankind could better understand how this kind of thing is possible and learn to prevent another similar catastrophe.

The standard work on the subject was still *Medizin ohne Menschlichkeit*, the study by Alexander Mitscherlich and Fred Mielke, two doctors who sat through the entire trial. It was published in 1947. It took more than forty years for someone, Robert Jay Lifton, to look at the atrocious acts from within the minds of the perpetrators themselves. His book *The Nazi Doctors* was published in 1988. Lifton was criticized by some, notably Bruno Bettelheim, as being too accommodating in trying to understand Nazi views. But Lifton, too, explained that this is the price to be paid for preventing Nazi views from ever flourishing again.

Regardless, Lifton had opened the door through which I wanted to walk. It was a difficult and time-consuming undertaking, especially on the research side. I worked on the book off and on and needed a sabbatical to finish it. Eventually, in 2004, it was published by Peter Lang Verlag with the title, *The Nuremberg Medical Trial: The Holocaust and the Origin of the Nuremberg Medical Code*.

TWENTY-NINE

John and Stephanie:
"Love and Marriage . . ."

During that time, John was studying architecture at the University of Kansas. We visited him a few times and found that he was doing well in everything he touched. But he did not pursue sports, as Curt would later do, and instead focused on his studies. He lived on a tight budget and had to work hard to make ends meet, especially during the summer. Among the many courses John took was statistics. He met a very attractive student with whom he studied for the course. Her name was Stephanie. Her father, Joe Reitz, was a professor at the Department of Economics. As the son of a German immigrant family, he mastered German quite well and naturally hoped his two sons and three daughters would also acquire some of the same skills.

Stephanie studied physical therapy and took German on the side. John knew rudimentary German from his days with us in Frankfurt, and he offered to help Stephanie with her lessons. From what we knew and what we observed from a distance, we could tell that this was the beginning of a fairy-tale love. We saw John and Stephanie off and on when we visited them and other folks in Kansas and Arkansas or when

John and Stephanie met at the University of Kansas.

they visited us. When they eventually told us they were getting married, it was no surprise.

Stephanie's family was very traditional and had Catholic roots. A wedding is no casual affair, as Sue and I discovered when we got married. John and Stephanie's wedding was meticulously organized for months by Stephanie's mother, Nancy. Nancy even designed and made Stephanie's wedding dress completely by herself.

The wedding took place in August 1992. The ceremony was held at KU's Catholic church, which was filled with family and friends. The reception took place at a theater in Lawrence with Larry Curt's band doing the entertainment, as they had at our own wedding in Little Rock fourteen years earlier. Some people in the hall joined the band on stage and sang along, including Stephanie's dad and Wayne, one of her brothers-in-law. I felt I had to follow them, and I accompanied Larry on the song he had dedicated to Sue and me when he performed at our wedding, "Silver Wings."

Fortunately for everyone present, I wasn't sober at that time. And as far as I could tell, neither was anyone else chiming in.

In the end, a beautiful wedding carriage drawn by a tall black horse drove up to the theater to take Stephanie and John to their hotel at the other end of Massachusetts Street. I have never attended such an elaborate wedding before or since. But it wasn't over. The next morning there was a brunch for all the family members, and Stephanie comes from a large family. Michael and his parents attended as well. Joe and I had to talk briefly about the significance of the event and the importance of family life. I promised that Sue and I would try to see everyone in Kansas as often as possible. And by and large, that's what we did.

The next day, John and Stephanie were off to the task of mastering life together. They rented a small but cozy house in Kansas City, got jobs, and made plans for their future together and the family they envisioned for themselves. For the most part, we could only watch from afar and always wished we were closer to help raise their three beautiful children, our grandchildren, Mason, Grace, and Justin. As much as we saw them through the years, it never seemed like it was enough. Sue planned a few memorable vacations with them, of which I will mention the one I consider to be the best.

Sue planned a trip for all of us to visit Colonial Williamsburg in Virginia. This early town has been preserved to show life in colonial America as authentically as possible, including the clothing worn. It is a kind of living history museum where the costumed townsfolk perform traditional tasks, from blacksmithing to weaving.

Sue made traditional outfits for all of us, and when we walked around Williamsburg, everyone watching us thought we were part of the show, even people who actually were. We did this for several days and enjoyed the confusion we created. My favorite part was when "Sir John" and "Madam Stephanie" put their three children into the pillory in the center of town. We found out later that Williamsburg, the colonial capital of early Virginia, also had a slave market, which was not re-created for the relaxation-seeking visitors. Still, this trip was a very enjoyable and memorable experience for us.

On our trip to Colonial Williamsburg, we dressed up like colonial residents and were mistaken for part of the official show. Sue and I are in the back beside John and Stephanie. Grace, Mason, and Justin are up front.

THIRTY

"Trust in the Lord with all thine heart; and lean not unto thine own understanding."

Back in Plymouth, Kai's year with us ended in June 1996. He had received his high school diploma with distinction and prepared to return home to his family in Hilgert. Curt had finished tenth grade and turned sixteen on May 30. A day later, he received his driver's license. He had gone through the high school's student driving program and had been taught to drive our Range Rover on safe streets around town by Sue and me. Curt handled the SUV well. When he drove the car by himself with us watching, to a wrestling tournament during the first days of June, we were amazed by his composure. I let him drive to Bristol over tricky mountain roads 100 miles away, and all went well. Then we let him drive around town by himself, mainly to visit friends, and it looked like we had little to worry about.

High school graduation was on June 6, and we all attended the ceremony to see Kai walk across the stage. He had grown some during the year with us, and I still remember him shaking hands and smiling happily down at everyone with a sadness in his eyes. He was sorry that he would have to leave us soon. Later that day, Curt asked me if he could have the car to pick up some friends to celebrate Kai's graduation on our boat at Newfound Lake. I said yes.

Curt and Kai left together to pick up three more friends. The last was Sarah Clapper, who lived in Campton on top of Ellsworth Hill just outside Plymouth. It was late afternoon. The sun was going down, and they were in a rush to get to the lake. Ellsworth Hill Road is a steep, winding mountain road. Curt was driving a large V8 SUV with almost 400 hp that handled well and can give the driver a false sense of security even when the car is traveling at high speeds. The speed limit was 35 mph, but Curt exceeded it considerably, apparently without noticing much. Five youngsters between the ages of fourteen and eighteen were in the car. At a tricky curve in the road, Curt lost control and hit a tree. The result was devastating.

Sue and I were winding down, lying on our bed watching the news, when we got a call from the local police saying there had been a tragic accident, and we should come to Ellsworth Hill Road immediately. We jumped into our Subaru and tried to stay calm. When we got to the site, we saw the Range Rover crumpled beyond recognition. Kai and another girl we knew lay in the middle of the road. They were conscious but did not move. A police officer motioned us to his car and showed us Curt and one of his friends sitting in the back, pale faced but apparently not badly hurt. Everyone was waiting for an ambulance.

We were told that an emergency helicopter had already taken Sarah Clapper to the nearby Dartmouth Hitchcock Medical Center. Soon, two ambulances arrived. They took Kai and the other girl to the ER of Speare Memorial Hospital in Plymouth, where Sue worked. Curt and his friend in the police car were taken there as well. The ER had to deal with four accident patients.

The hospital hallway was soon full of relatives, friends, medical staff, police, and the local district attorney, who observed everything. Of the four patients, three, including Curt, were eventually released without serious medical problems. But Kai had received substantial injuries. He had several broken ribs and a broken pelvic bone.

In fact, his whole pelvic area was torn, and his urinary tract had been ripped apart. Sue discussed Kai's X-rays with the surgeon, her close colleague. He suggested an immediate transfer to Dartmouth Hitchcock Medical Center for emergency surgery to reconnect the torn tract to prevent infertility and other lasting problems. We followed the ambulance that took Kai to Dartmouth, and our heads started spinning as we discussed bad outcomes for an hour. Kai was fully conscious as he was rushed into the examination room, giving us a sad smile.

A hospital grief counselor greeted us and steered us to the unit where Sarah Clapper was being treated. Although Sarah was referred to as a patient, we soon discovered that she was brain-dead and on artificial life support. She was only fourteen years old. We faced her parents and her sixteen-year-old brother and other relatives, who were nervously walking up and down the hallway in front of Sarah's room. The doctors would let in only one or two relatives at a time to say farewell to Sarah.

Sue and I approached Sarah's parents. Her mother, shaken by grief, did not want to talk to us. Her father, who looked helpless, wanted to know why we were there. We expressed our sorrow the best we could and asked permission to see their daughter for a few minutes. We received permission but were told to wait until the attending physicians said it was safe. Sitting on the hallway bench, we were approached by Sarah's brother, who wanted to know everything about us. Later, her father spoke to us as well. His voice was breaking, and he focused on Curt's role in the events that had led to this tragic moment.

Eventually, we were allowed into the room and saw Sarah on a ventilator, her eyes wide open but not focused. Sue approached her face-to-face and told her she was going to a better place. We could only stay for a few minutes, thanked her father, and returned to Kai's room. Nothing had been decided yet about his surgery, and we were told to return the following day.

Someone told us that Curt was at the home of his friend Adam Humphrey, who was not in the accident, so we drove there and talked with him and the Humphreys until the early morning, when we dozed off.

A few hours later, Sue and I drove back to Dartmouth to see how Kai and Sarah were doing. Sarah was still on life support, and we learned that her organs had been donated. Kai's doctors had gotten in touch with a urinary tract surgeon in Germany and suggested that Kai be transported there to get treatment as soon as possible. Postoperative care might be complicated and would be better given close to home. And the doctors expressed hope that the tract might heal back naturally. Kai's mother and his sister had arrived from Germany to see how they could help. Kai's father had problems traveling long distances because he had Parkinson's disease, and he waited for news at home in Hilgert. Kai's broken pelvis made it almost impossible for him to travel. But he felt he could do it with wheelchairs, crutches, walkers, and sitting pads. We contacted airlines about special seating arrangements.

In the meantime, Dartmouth took Sarah off life support, and her family arranged her funeral. The day before her burial at the Campton cemetery, Sarah would lay in state at the funeral parlor in a casket for the final viewing. Her family would be there, and we had to face them. Ultimately, I was the only one who went. Sarah's grandmother opened the door and showed me where to write my name on the condolence list. I sternly walked through a crowd of mourners and kneeled next to the casket, looking into Sarah's youthful fourteen-year-old face. I had seen that face the day before the accident, bright and smiling at our house. Now her eyes were shut. I heard her mother weeping loudly behind me. Those were the most difficult five minutes I have ever faced. I don't know how I was able to hold my composure, but I did.

After I got up, a lady approached me and told me that I was not welcome and that the Clapper family would never forgive Curt for what he had done. I left the parlor in a daze. Curt, Sue, and I had planned to attend Sarah's funeral service the next day, but the pastor of her church came by our house so that she could explain that the Clappers did not want to see us, but that we could stand in the entrance hall after all the other mourners had found their places. Following the service, we were to disappear quickly and not attend the burial. That is what we did. These were difficult times, and during the next few days, we spent a lot of time at Kai's bedside trying to get his spirits up. Then we drove him to Boston Logan airport in a large SUV.

With a lot of help, he managed to get into a wheelchair and then used crutches to get onto a blow-up mattress in the back of the car. Even the slightest motion hurt. But he had taken a lot of pain medicine.

His mother and sister were always doting on him, trying to hide their deep worry as best they could.

Getting him on the plane was not easy, and Kai displayed some heroic moves walking the gangway on crutches. But he made it all the way to Frankfurt. There he was immediately taken to the specialist for urinary tract trauma at University Hospital Mainz, who was already familiar with Kai's case and knew he was coming. The specialist decided against immediate surgery and ordered more observation.

Surgery would mean inserting a plastic tube to connect the separate pieces of Kai's urinary tract. Those tubes often led to complications later in life and could cause infertility. But if the surgery had to be performed, the sooner, the better. Now the doctors were waiting. In the end, that risk paid off. The tract healed by itself, as the doctors had hoped. There was no better news for Kai. Of course his bones had to heal and much else besides, but the doctor's assessment was that he would completely recover.

The other two friends involved in the accident had received no serious physical injuries but had to be treated for psychological trauma. Sarah Clapper had dramatically died in their midst. It could have been any of them.

The local district attorney charged Curt with negligent homicide. In a trial before the Grafton County District Court in Plymouth, he was charged with endangering the lives of his passengers by recklessly speeding down the mountain road. The judge found Curt guilty and gave him a probationary prison sentence. Because Curt was a juvenile, his records would be sealed and ultimately expunged, leaving him without a criminal record. Of course, what could not be expunged were the memories Curt would carry around with him for the rest of his life.

The same goes for me and Sue. We had let Curt drive our car without supervision when he obviously was not ready to do so himself. At his young age, Curt should have relied on such supervision for several months after receiving his driver's license. I should have been with him in that car when he drove to pick up his friends. Curt's accident was not an isolated incident. During 1996, there were quite a few fatal crashes caused by teenage drivers in New Hampshire and across America. The increase in such crashes was so alarming that some states introduced legislation to place more restrictions on teenage driving.

The media pointed out the dangers of letting "children" drive by themselves too early. Citizens formed community committees, TV stations hosted talk shows, and politicians urged legislative action, all designed to contain the increasing mayhem caused by youngsters on the road. Some New Hampshire legislators drafted a bill calling for sixteen-year-old drivers to be accompanied by a licensed adult at least twenty-five years of age and to have no more than one additional passenger in the car. I joined a citizens' committee in support of the bill. We attended a legislative hearing in Concord, and I went on record advocating for increasing the age for obtaining a driver's license to eighteen.

The judge presiding over Curt's trial had ordered Curt to talk to school classes about the dangers of irresponsible driving, using his own experience as an example. He gave several such talks, one at his own Plymouth Regional High School, which I attended. He was in tears as he told his peers about the tragic consequences of his careless actions.

Months later, the New Hampshire legislature passed a law restricting the driving of sixteen-year-olds. Curt attended Governor Jeanne Shaheen's signing ceremony and spoke to her for a while afterward.

The governor praised Curt for his engagement on behalf of a life-saving piece of legislation. New Hampshire was not the only state to pass such a law. And indeed, the number of accidents caused by young drivers dropped significantly following the spike of 1996, at least in some degree due to the new legislation.

We visited Kai and his family frequently in the years to come and were always glad to see him in a positive frame of mind, with no trace of the ordeal he went through with us. He later would receive a master's in administration and engineering, become a high-ranking executive in one of the largest ball-bearing manufacturing companies in the world, marry a beautiful and independent lady, and raise two wonderful daughters together.

THIRTY-ONE

Life Moves On:
Work and Illness

Despite the many ups and downs we experienced, our lives largely consisted of routines. Sue was deeply entrenched in her medical work and tried to keep up with the latest advances in her field. I constantly prepared for lectures and seminars and spent much time grading student papers. Curt tried to keep up with demanding coursework preparing him for college and, of course, sports. Jason had his jobs at Larry's woodshop and the Italian Farmhouse.

We all kept busy and shared much of the housework. But Sue, from the start, was set on a mission. With her previous training in surgery, internal medicine, and emergency medicine, she came to appreciate more and more the need for integrated concepts dealing with patients as a whole rather than carriers of isolated illnesses and injuries. She read up on the relevant literature and tried to use the holistic approach in her practice of medicine wherever possible.

Holistic medicine addresses the physical, mental, and social aspects of patients' problems as equal parts of an inseparable unit. It's a time-consuming approach, but the therapeutic results are remarkable.

Sue's eventual goal was to get her hospital to establish methods for offering holistic medicine as an option for patients. In the beginning, Lakes Region seemed very supportive. Sue acquired the skills to head such efforts by enrolling in a mind-body medicine program at the prestigious Benson-Henry Institute at Mass General in Boston. It was founded and directed by the leading scholar of mind-body medicine in the US, Professor Henry Benson of Harvard Medical School.

Sue concluded the program with distinction. For a number of years, she spent untold hours studying more of the new field between gruesome shifts in the ER in preparation for her anticipated role as leader of a mind-body division at the hospital. But Lakes Region never followed through on its earlier commitments. Recognizing the need for the field, it downgraded its earlier visions and merely added a homeopathic practitioner to its staff. This was one more reason for Sue to quit her Lakes Region job and switch to Speare Memorial in Plymouth. She focused on the special challenges of emergency medicine again but never lost her interest in and commitment to mind-body medicine.

I, too, worked a lot. I was hired as an associate professor in 1992 with consideration for tenure in three years. This meant I had to produce some quality academic work during that time, or I would be out again. My regular paper presentations at various conferences, mostly at the annual meetings of the German Studies Association, and occasional publications of these papers should have been sufficient. But I wanted to be sure, and so I kept working on my manuscript about the Nuremberg Medical Trial. I also wrote up several proposals for different types of research grants.

In 1994 I received a $25,000 grant from New Hampshire Humanities to organize a weeklong conference for twenty high school teachers on the effects of the downfall of the Iron Curtain on the lives of people in Eastern Europe. I had been in touch with various scholars of the former Soviet Bloc, and the grant gave me the resources to invite four of them to the conference. They came from Romania, Ukraine, Poland, and East Germany. All had lived under Communist regimes as supporters or critics, and they would engage New Hampshire teachers in conversations about meeting the challenges of surviving in a totalitarian system, the collapse of the system, and dealing with the aftermath.

The fall of the Berlin Wall a few years earlier was still fresh in everyone's minds. The conference was a great success and was discussed in the press. Video recordings became part of the university's permanent library holdings. I received much praise from the grant's administrators, and our university's president, Donald Wharton, indicated that I shouldn't worry about my future. And indeed, when I applied for tenure in 1995, it was granted as a matter of course.

The conference strengthened my interest in Eastern European affairs. At the invitation of one of the conference participants, I delivered a number of guest lectures at Copernicus University in Toruń, Poland. For several years, Babes-Bolyai University in Cluj, Romania, hired me as a visiting professor to teach summer courses in the history of philosophy. The professors there knew the work of my doctoral advisor, Hayden White, and were impressed by the fact that I had once taken a seminar with the much admired Jürgen Habermas. Several times they indicated they would offer me a full professorship if I were interested. But it wasn't in the cards.

Sue, who sometimes accompanied me on my Romanian adventures, and I were overwhelmed by the generous hospitality my colleagues and others showed us. I have never eaten so much as in Romania, though Sue managed to be more careful. Our hosts often viewed lengthy evening meals as an opportunity to see how long it would take them to drink me under the table. To my honor, they never managed. I was always one of the last ones standing.

Back in Plymouth, life was more conducive to serious work. I organized a couple more conferences, continued research on the Nuremberg Medical Trial, and pursued a few other projects. Some involved such things as fighting for the increase of our library budget to obtain more books dealing with current European affairs. Others focused on getting faculty interested in team teaching. I usually didn't get very far.

One of the greater challenges we faced at home had to do with Sue's health. Because of her erratic shift work in high-pressure environments, she often came home with pounding headaches and developed problems going to sleep. She took Tylenol and tried to relax by watching TV. When the headaches worsened, she had an MRI brain scan. It revealed a tumor next to the pituitary gland. It was small but apparently growing. The pituitary gland, also known as the master gland, is situated in the middle of the lower part of the brain and regulates most of the hormonal flow in the body.

Tumor growth usually distorts the regulatory function of the body and causes uncomfortable symptoms, ranging from loss of energy to nausea, anxiety, cold sweats, and more. Sue developed some of these symptoms and needed treatment. She consulted the best specialists in the field, notably Dr. Swearingen at Mass General. He observed Sue's tumor for a while and eventually suggested its surgical removal, which he would perform himself. Such a surgery, needless to say, is very complicated. The tumor, usually not more than one centimeter in diameter, must be cut away from the gland without damaging the gland itself. For this type of microsurgery, the equipment must enter the brain through the upper jaw.

Sue could follow all of Dr. Swearingen's explanations, but I was lost. He was a world authority on the subject and showed some pity for my ignorance. But we trusted him fully, and he performed the surgery in early 1996. By all indications, it was a success in that the tumor was gone, but Swearingen warned that such tumors tend to grow back and that he would have to watch Sue's brain closely. It took Sue less than a week to be back performing normal tasks around the house and another to resume work again. But the tumor did grow back, and the symptoms reoccurred slowly.

Two years later, Swearingen had to perform the operation again. And again, Swearingen warned Sue that the tumor might grow back and that a third operation would be too risky. Again, the tumor returned, but at a much slower rate. A few years later, in 2004, Swearingen suggested radiation treatment with one of the most sophisticated ways of delivering radiation around, using proton beams. Sue had to undergo a number of radiation sessions. Again, all went well, meaning almost all of the tumor cells were destroyed. Yet some of them did survive, and the tumor grew back very slowly, until it eventually stabilized.

In the wake of the treatments, Sue developed hypopituitarism, meaning her disturbed hormonal flow had a debilitating effect on her overall health and had to be treated with supplements the gland did not produce or properly regulate on its own. For her, it became a daily struggle, but she managed. With a lot of help from colleagues in her medical profession, especially endocrinologists, Sue constantly fine-tuned the doses of her many medications. I admire her for it and get irritated when I see people who should know better putting her under unnecessary stress that makes things worse. This would become more of a problem in the years to come.

Our days in Plymouth were characterized by many exciting events and, for the most part, fulfilling activities, leaving little time for brooding self-examination.

In 1998, Curt graduated from Plymouth Regional High School and was looking forward to attending college. Because he had been an outstanding player on the school's football team, a number of colleges tried to recruit him. He decided to enroll at the University of Kansas, mainly to be close to his brother John and sister-in-law Stephanie, who had both attended the university and lived near campus. Curt enrolled as a biology major with hopes of pursuing medical studies later and also managed to join the Jayhawks football team as a walk-on.

THIRTY-TWO

"I was a stranger, and ye took me in."

We were committed to helping people who were down on their luck. While he was still at home, Curt told us one day that he had made a new friend who had just moved to town from Boston with his father and younger brother and that they expected their mother to join them soon. The father was Black, and the mother was white. She had some roots in Plymouth, where the family wanted to settle. He would be the only Black person in this small, lily-white town, and we thought they could use some help. We invited them over and learned that the man had already found work as a welder but did not make enough money to support himself and his two sons. This was when Sue came to the rescue. She designed a plan to set this new family up to meet predictable challenges and to prevail.

The family would get a used trailer to be put on a piece of land and own the place outright. We would be their bank, meaning we would take out a loan to pay for the trailer and the land and deed them over to the family, who would pay us back in monthly installments so we could repay the lending bank. And so it went. Finding land and a trailer took longer than we thought. But eventually, the happy father and his two sons had a home they liked and were thankful for. They eagerly awaited the arrival of their wife and mother.

After weeks of waiting, she showed up. The first thing we heard was that she didn't like living in a trailer and rented an apartment at the edge of town, making the family move in with her. We ultimately learned that she had just been released from prison after serving time for check fraud. We were stuck with the trailer and the land. We started to look for another needy couple, which we found quickly. They were two young parents from the Plymouth area with three young children. They both had low-paying jobs but earned enough to make the monthly payments. It was their first home, and when we saw the happy faces of their three toddlers, we knew we had done the right thing.

But things went downhill quickly, and the father lost his job. The mother stopped working and sued her employer for bogus damages suffered at the jobsite. They stopped making their installment payments to us, so we had to pay off the mortgage, still in our name, to the bank with our own money. They told us that everything would be okay because she expected a big settlement from her former employer and because he would find work again soon. Meanwhile, they were trashing the trailer beyond recognition.

After months of waiting, she did indeed get her big settlement, which they were supposed to use to catch up on their payments to us. Instead, he used it to buy a new Harley and shook up the town with its noise. We tried to evict the couple using the legal system. The couple hired the sleaziest lawyer in town, who told us that he was going to prove that the couple held the legal title to the trailer. He said he would stretch the case out for years if he had to, unless we agreed on a settlement that they owned the trailer and the land, but they had to compensate us for our losses by paying us, when they were able, a ridiculously low amount of money. We took it on the chin. We were tired of fighting people we had just wanted to help. So we cut our losses. But there was a bit of consolation for us in the end.

The couple divorced, sold the place, and per court order, had to pay us the settlement amount. It wasn't much, but it was something. We had learned the hard way how difficult it is to help people who are unable and often unwilling to manage even the simplest affairs themselves. For the most part, chaotic childhood experiences and lack of education had been their lot. Often, they would even attack people who truly tried to help them, as we experienced. However, it did not deter us from helping others when we saw the need.

Shortly after we settled into our Plymouth house, we invited Linda Clodgo, a young woman from Bristol, to live with us in a large extra room with a separate entrance. Linda had a history of being abused and had low self-esteem. We had helped her already when we were living in Bristol and now invited her to live with us in Plymouth. Sue realized that Linda had great artistic talent and wanted to open a few doors for her. Linda took phenomenal photos and had the potential to become a successful photographer with some formal training.

Sue and Linda worked out a program that Linda would have to ad-here to while we supported her financially. It included taking nonde-gree courses in photographic art at Plymouth State. In the beginning, everything seemed to work out fine, but after a while, Linda got sloppy. She missed class, got high, and spent time with friends rather than at work. Sue gave her many second chances. But after about a year, she told Linda to pony up or get out. Linda left and went back to Bristol.

After that, we had the German exchange student Kai, who was a refreshing delight all around. When Kai left in June 1996, a Black high school student named Bernard came by and asked whether he could take Kai's room. He was from Philadelphia, where the wife of our local surgeon ("Mother Teresa" of Plymouth) went every year to work on the Catholic Church's inner-city soup kitchen. In 1995, she brought home two hardened boys from Philadelphia's low-income section doing court-ordered community service on that soup line. She would turn their life around in our small college town by opening her house to them and sending them to school for two years until graduation.

Things didn't go as planned, and "Mother Teresa" tried to pass the two troublemakers on to others. We had no idea how bad things were. Plymouth is a typical "hush-hush" New England town where you don't see trouble until it's standing in your kitchen. We took in Bernard. The other boy went to live with a missionary pastor in a nearby town. We really tried to help, but we failed miserably. We worked with the high school counselors on a school attendance plan. Bernard swore he would follow it. But we soon found out that he hardly attended classes or did any work.

Since we lived within sight of the school, we sometimes watched him enter the building, but as we were told, he would exit through the back door a few minutes later. Again, we tried to impress upon him how important education was. He agreed with everything we said but never heeded any of it. His room soon became such a mess that it was difficult to walk in it. Everything was on the floor, and he left it there until he needed something, and then he often couldn't find it. He asked us if he could have a pet. We told him it had to be a small one. One night we came home, and he showed us his pet, a giant tarantula in a dry aquarium. We told him he could never lift the glass top except to feed it. One day we came home and the tarantula had escaped. We never found it, but we were concerned because tarantulas can bite. We knew things had to come to an end and contacted the Division for Children, Youth and Families (DCYF), who placed him somewhere else.

Afterward the DCYF asked us if we could take in a troubled teenager who had been removed from her family because of abuse. She, too, went to Plymouth Regional High School and promised to follow all the rules imposed on her by the DCYF and by us. By then, Curt had left us for the University of Kansas, and we had enough space. So we agreed. She did just fine for a while. She was a beautiful blonde, but we learned that she was a cutter and had to be watched for razor blades. She proudly showed us her forearm scars from earlier days while assuring us that that phase of her life was over. We tried to help where we could, and she confided in Sue in particular.

One day when Sue was at work and I lay on the bed upstairs watching the evening news, exhausted after a long day, I heard a person frantically running up the stairs to my bedroom. I jumped up and collided with a policeman, who had beaten me to the door. We were both surprised, and he told me that the girl in our house had slit her wrists while sitting in the living room downstairs and had then called 911, saying she was bleeding to death. I had heard nothing, not even the approach of the police car, and was just one flight up. In the meantime, a second police officer had put bandages on the girl's wrists and taken her to the hospital three blocks away. Everything happened so fast that it made my head spin. When Sue came home later, I learned that she was not very surprised about the girl's behavior. After all, Sue was an ER doc who saw similar cases all the time.

The next day, we visited the girl in a locked unit at a large hospital in Manchester, where she was all smiles and pleasant as always. Later, someone from DCYF visited us at home and informed us that the girl would be placed in a treatment center somewhere. We felt relieved and guilty that we hadn't helped her more. We decided we had done our fair share of helping others. Still, when a local pastor called us to ask whether we could take in Peter, a fresh high school graduate from a nearby town who had been accepted at Plymouth State as a student, we said yes, but only for a year.

A local couple had adopted Peter through an agency in India when he was just a few years old. He was pleasant, intelligent, and eager to help around the house, something we really appreciated. He had stayed in touch with his biological family in India and, while living with us, had the chance to visit his mother and several siblings for the first time since his adoption. He was very nervous before he left, and he promised to tell us everything about the trip upon his return. He was hesitant to reveal anything about his background. Still, we eventually learned that he came from a very low-income family of the lowest Hindu caste and that his mother had been unable to feed him and had given him to a Christian adoption agency in her area. That's where a childless couple from New Hampshire saw him and adopted him.

When Peter came back from his trip, it seemed that he embraced his American identity more than he had before, although it was difficult to engage him much on this topic. He showed us pictures of him with his biological family in India, which made it obvious that, at least in a material sense, he was fortunate to be in the US. After a year with us, he got his own place in town, which he shared with a few other students. When I saw him later on campus, he looked studious and animatedly told me about his goals of making it into the business world. Sue and I figured that when you try to help ten people and one greatly benefits, it is all worth it.

THIRTY-THREE

Jason Becomes Independent, and Our Plans for Retirement

Our main concern through all the years of helping others continued to be Jason. Given his many challenges, he did remarkably well. His life followed a routine that kept him busy and content. He had his work routine. We took him to many of Curt's sporting events. We got him enrolled in evening bongo classes at the university. He liked to participate in the many get-togethers and parties we had at our house, often with the neighbors. And he especially liked the big hot tub we had behind the house. But he always told us that someday he would like to live on his own, although not too far from our house.

Our house was a large five-bedroom, too big for Sue and me to live in alone. We had long discussions about how to arrange our future. We ultimately figured that the best solution would be for Jason to get an apartment in a public housing project in Middlebury, which our friend Kathy Caswell pointed out to us. Sue and I would retire in a smaller house at nearby Lake Champlain.

The housing project, Middlebury Commons, was a newly built complex in a green area close to downtown. There were nice one-bedroom apartments for low-income Vermont residents who could live on their own. Somehow, we got Jason's residency requirement waived, and after Curt left for college in 1998, we put Jason on the long waiting list. We were told that it would probably be years before an apartment became available. That turned out to be correct. But eventually, Jason got a letter informing him that there was a vacancy for him at the Commons. He was full of joy and anticipation. We immediately drove to Middlebury, marveled at the nice apartment, signed the rental agreement, and started looking for things he needed.

Setting up Jason's household was complicated because we had to find things he could handle on his own, from devices for opening cans to aids for negotiating the shower. Plus, he had special wishes. For instance, he wanted to have a large bed with tall corner posts holding up a canopy. It took a while, but we got him one. Finding entertainment equipment and a telephone he could handle was a challenge too. But some of the toughest things for Jason to handle were door keys. He could stick the keys into the locks, but he couldn't turn them, no matter how hard he tried.

Sue spent hours teaching him, shedding many tears along the way as she realized the scope of Jason's persistent challenges. Eventually, weeks later, he managed to get into the house and his apartment using keys on his own. We had to check on him every few days, at least initially, to ensure he was all right. The drive from Plymouth to Middlebury was nearly three hours each way, negotiating windy roads through the Green Mountains. But it was all worth it. Jason felt quickly at home at Middlebury Commons. He met some friends he had known when we lived in the area between 1988 and 1992. I also reconnected him with the Special Olympics group, and soccer, bowling, and bocci became his favorite sports. Soon Sue and I started searching for a suitable home in the area for ourselves. We looked around Lake Champlain and found that houses with water access were considerably more expensive on the Vermont side. So we started looking on the New York side as well.

The Lake Champlain Bridge connects the two states where the landmasses are closest to each other, from Chimney Point, Vermont, to Crown Point, New York. We found a building lot in Crown Point about ten miles north of the bridge and right by the water. On a good

Jason and Sue in his Middlebury apartment.

day, one could get from there to Middlebury in a bit more than thirty minutes by car. The lot was part of an association of twenty-seven lots that had just been created. We bought the lot in 2004 and planned to build our dream house by the lake on it as soon as we could manage to sever our ties in Plymouth.

At the time, I was a sixty-six-year-old tenured professor at Plymouth State University, and I could have stayed on until I keeled over dead, as some of my colleagues surely did. But I had lost some of my drive for lighting up students' minds searching for "higher things" in life. Recently, my efforts to demonstrate Hegel's idea that systems of any kind, especially political systems, cannot sustain themselves forever because of built-in contradictions that eventually lead to conflict and collapse, fell on deaf ears. This message of the sixties rang hollow in the hinterlands of New Hampshire, where people were increasingly looking for knowledge that was useful in finding lucrative jobs rather than understanding complex political relations and improving social justice.

Over the years, my focus on developing critical skills, no matter the subject, found less and less acceptance. A book titled *How the West Was Won* raised more excitement than *The Decline of the West*. I figured I could retire and pursue my own interests more productively, doing research and writing more on my own time. However, I gave myself one more shot at opening students' eyes to the world as it really worked in contrast to what their high school teachers and standard textbooks had told them. I designed a new major centering around globalization. It required students to spend much of their time abroad. The major had different foci: economics, politics, and arts.

In the beginning, the university administration gave me the green light. I put together a faculty team interested in offering courses for this planned bachelor of arts. The difficult part was finding host universities in other countries that would participate in this program.

One of the faculty members, a professor of French and Spanish, focused on finding places in various countries around the world that offered related courses and that would accept our students. All this was a lot of work, and it took us over a year to put together a viable program. The two sticking points were logistics and money.

We had to demonstrate that the program would financially sustain itself through increased student enrollment and that the administrative costs would be low. Basically, I would run the program at no additional cost to the university, though some of the courses would have to be taught by adjunct faculty that we would need to hire. There were also logistical problems concerning the welfare of the students while studying abroad, especially regarding housing. These would add to the costs.

Surveys showed that our students were willing to pay these extra costs. But there were critical voices arguing that Plymouth State University should remain a university of "regional importance" and not develop programs with "global perspectives." We also already had an office that assisted students taking foreign language courses abroad, mainly for Spanish and French majors. That office would fall under the supervision of our new program, much to the dismay of the office's administrator. Still, the curriculum committee indicated that it would approve our program without reservation.

When I formally proposed the adoption of the new program for a vote, the dean of our university, a woman who so far had encouraged our efforts, showed up at the last minute and argued against the proposal because it might not attract new students the way we projected. Rather than let the curriculum committee defeat the proposal, I tabled it indefinitely. But because some of the arguments made were of a personal nature and had to do with "turf wars," I decided to throw in the towel and retire.

Sue also started thinking about retirement, or at least about an end to full-time work in the merciless grind of the ER. After Curt's accident, the administrators of Speare Memorial Hospital indicated that Sue's presence had become a bit of a liability, and she looked for work elsewhere. She was immediately hired by Memorial Hospital in North Conway. They welcomed her with open arms, and she found the working atmosphere very friendly. There was only one problem. The place was seventy miles away, and most of the drive was over the curvy Kancamagus Highway, crossing the White Mountains at high elevations. The drive took one and a half hours each way, often at night, even without traffic. "The Kanc," as it is locally known, became Sue's personal highway of fate. She'd had to drive to and from work for many years, often tired and under dangerous conditions. Occasionally she came home with stories of animals she hit; among them were a few deer. Sue sometimes drove way beyond the speed limit and had the tickets to show for it. But she was still a controlled driver who never had a serious accident, until she met the Kanc.

There was the scary episode of her car breaking down while going downhill on an extremely treacherous part of the Kanc. Eventually, a friendly driver came by, stopped, and helped her. But the biggest disaster happened when she hit a moose. It was getting dark when she was driving to work one winter evening in her Audi A6 hatchback. The road was slippery as she approached a downhill turn, when she was caught between a steep bluff on the right, a deep drop-off on the left, and a big moose facing her right in the middle. Another car was coming up the road in the opposite lane, so she couldn't swerve. She had no choice but to hit the moose head-on. It was fully grown, probably in excess of seven feet tall and weighing half a ton. Many such head-on collisions have fatal results. Often the car hits the moose in the legs, causing the moose to fall on top of the car and squash the driver.

Sue was lucky. She hit the moose full force, and it severely damaged the front and top of the car. But rather than burying the car, the moose fell backward, looking at the damaged car sitting upright in the road. The roof had caved in on the driver's side. Sue had crouched under the dashboard and held on to the steering wheel with one hand so the car wouldn't fly over the edge of the road and roll downhill or hit the steep rocks on the other side.

Cut up by flying pieces of windshield but without any broken bones, she managed to extricate herself. The driver of the oncoming car stopped and gave her first aid. Sue realized his car was full of children and was horrified about how close they had come to disaster. Meanwhile, the wounded moose kept staring at the car, unable to get up. Cell phones wouldn't work in the mountains, and when another car came by, the driver went on to Conway to send police up to the accident. It took a while, but eventually a police car came and secured the site. The officer shot the upright and still breathing moose in the head. It took six bullets before it finally died. By this point, a few more cars had assembled, and one young man asked Sue, who had the right to claim the moose, whether she would give him the moose to feed his family, which she did.

The officer noted the cuts on Sue's left hand and suggested calling an ambulance. Sue declined but asked the officer to call a tow truck and take her to the hospital. After all, she was late for her shift. At the ER, they stitched up her hand, and she switched from being a patient to being a doctor in less than twenty minutes. ER folks are special people. They never cease to amaze me.

Later that night, Sue called during a lull between two patients and, in the few minutes she could spare, gave me a quick rundown about what had happened. I had trouble going to sleep afterward and thought, "Another day at the office." The time had come to put our lives into a slower lane. But first, there was one more lane we had to rush down fast.

THIRTY-FOUR

From Grand Canyon to Crown Point

In August 2004, Sue was going to turn sixty, and for that occasion, we wanted to fulfill one of her life's dreams, zooming down the Colorado River through the Grand Canyon on a raft. The number of rafts allowed was strictly regulated. The demand for rafts was high, and there was a long waiting list. We were lucky to get two spots with a reputable company for the desired month of April. The group we were with went on two rafts, with ten people plus four scouts on each.

The trip began at Lees Ferry and followed the Colorado River through the Grand Canyon for 280 miles to Lake Mead. All the rafts were equipped with everything we needed for the seven-day adventure: tents, blankets, water, food, and other items, including grills for roasting meat.

The trip is physically demanding. Temperatures in the canyon can reach around 120 degrees, with extremely high humidity. Even doing nothing is exhausting. Sleeping at night is a sweaty affair. Putting up tents is a burden. We slept in the open for a couple of nights and marveled at the stunning sky with bright stars peeking through the steep rock formations.

Between dawn and dusk, we were either floating on the raft, shooting down turbulent rapids, or exploring the many natural wonders the Grand Canyon is known for. Just floating down the river generated wondrous feelings of timelessness, boundlessness, and being overwhelmed by the greatness of creation and the power of nature. At times I felt personally insignificant. For instance, as we floated by steep, almost mile-high rocky cliffs, one of the scouts explained to us the origin of the various visible sediments. Some were almost two billion years old. The scout pointed out strata formed during the period when cells, that is, life, emerged on Earth. We felt suspended in time and space, and only the blazing heat and suffocating humidity reminded us that we were human. And indeed, we also saw remnants of human life, some going back thousands of years, mostly caves cut into the rock and, more recently, drawings on the walls.

The scouts took us on many hiking tours, exploring natural caves, contributory brooks, waterfalls, and more. We usually divided up into three groups: the slow, intermediate, and fast ones. At sixty-six, I was the oldest participant. Sue was almost sixty and struggled with rheumatism. So we stuck to the intermediate group and were able to hold our own. But there was one excursion we both wanted to participate in that was designed only for the fast group: the climb up to Havasu Falls. The climb was high and steep and took many hours. The reward was great: the chance to stand under the world-famous waterfalls and swim in the blue-green natural pools. But only the fittest would make it up there. The slow and intermediate groups would also climb up the dangerous trail some distance but return when it got treacherous.

Sue and I volunteered for the top group, determined to go all the way. We were told it was a big risk but decided to go anyway. As expected, we fell behind, and the scout watching the rear told us not to go any farther and wait for the intermediate group to catch up with us. But Sue figured that at least I could make it and urged me to catch up with the top group again, which I did. I surprised myself, and before the last steep climb up straight and slippery rocks, the lead scout told our group that this was our last chance to bail out. We had all signed a waiver that said we would not hold the touring company responsible for any accidents. The risk was ours. No one bailed. It took another half hour of huffing and puffing, but we reached the goal. And what a sight it was! We had all seen pictures in brochures, and we knew it was an impressive sight. But nothing could beat the feeling of actually being there and absorbing raw nature with all five senses.

We showered under the warm falls and belly-paddled in the pristine pools for about an hour before our two scouts reminded us that we had to start descending to be in time for barbecue. In my memory, the descent was as tough as the ascent, partially because we tried to hurry down. I realize now that I had bit off more than I could chew, but I didn't let on that I was struggling. I managed to stay with the group without slowing everyone down. After about an hour, when we hit the trail again, we started to talk, mainly congratulating ourselves on the successful climb. Everyone but me was around thirty, and I found out they were all runners or bicyclists; one of them ran marathons. I was glad I hadn't known that earlier. It certainly would have discouraged me from joining them.

Farther down, I met Sue again. She had found a shady spot to rest while I climbed. Her hair was aglow in the evening sun. Her well-fitting clothes revealed her attractiveness. And her beautiful smile lit up the shady grove where she sat. I felt indescribably happy seeing her there waiting for me, and I have kept that happy moment in my heart ever since.

During the last two days of the trip, all twenty of us adventurers had gotten to know each other quite well. While slowly floating along the less turbulent part of the river, we managed to cut through the small talk and delve into more unfiltered personal aspects of our lives. In some cases, people unloaded their entire life stories.

There was the rich fish merchant who was shipping salmon by the ton from Alaska to California. He had worked his way up from nothing and looked like a guy who still couldn't believe that he'd gotten as far as he did.

There was the studious librarian who had prepared herself for the trip for a number of years and knew more about the flora and fauna of the canyon than all of the scouts together.

There was a successful Realtor who complained that "the government" hampered private initiatives of land developers who were bringing more tourist dollars to Arizona.

The most interesting stories centered on personal dilemmas, like divorces, barely surviving car crashes, or financial ruin. The stories Sue and I shared found interested listeners too. The Southern girl from a home with outhouses had gone to UCLA, got an MD, done a surgery internship in Germany, studied mind-body medicine at Mass General in Boston, and saved lives as an ER doc in New England. My story was similar. The poor German immigrant with an eighth-grade education had become a tenured professor. Four in the group were from the Hilton family, a man in his forties and three teenagers. They played their cards closer to their chests. About their headline-making cousin Paris, they apologetically stated that she was the loose cannon in the family.

When we drifted by the place where the Bright Angel Trail meets the river, we told the story about how, almost thirty years earlier, Sue, our son John, and I had hiked down from the top of the canyon and almost didn't make it back out. The group listened incredulously. The scouts told us that by now, climbers were urged to start their trip into the canyon long before dawn, dress appropriately, wear tough hiking boots, take plenty of food and water, and carry an emergency blanket and flashlight. None of that had been true for us.

On the last day, as we approached Lake Mead, the scouts encouraged us to share our impressions of the trip. Almost everybody mentioned having been overcome with a never-before-experienced sense of greatness and the beauty of nature. We all agreed that the encounter with the statuesque rocks endlessly reaching upward into the sky had reaffirmed our belief in transcendental forces ruling over everything, including us. For some people in the group, those forces were those expressed in the Bible. For others, it was a sense of something higher that surpassed words. But everyone agreed that they were now better equipped to put their own worries into proper perspective, and we were glad the trip had given us this opportunity. Most of us had something personal to add.

In my case, it was my satisfaction that I had climbed to Havasu Falls and back down again at my age. I felt especially good when the scouts pointed out that, to their knowledge, only one person older than me had done this before. He had been sixty-eight. When it came time for Sue to summarize her impressions, she started to explain how she had communicated with nature like she seldom had before, and she broke down in tears. The scouts assured her that her reaction was normal, and everyone else seemed watery-eyed as well. We all knew we had shared an experience together that no one would ever forget. We took the last pictures of each other and promised to stay in touch.

Back home, Sue and I quickly got busy planning our transition to our new home in Crown Point, New York. We had long discussions about the kind of house we were going to put on our building lot by the lake. Jason was happy to see that soon we would be living close to him. We contacted many building contractors but eventually decided to buy a ready-made Adirondack-type house that would be delivered in two halves on flatbeds and put together on-site. A Canadian company offered the kind we liked most, so we ordered it. We hired a contractor to build a large foundation that would accommodate extra rooms for offices and add sliding doors directly opening to a large terrace by the nearby lake.

Once the house was erected on the foundation, the contractor made many more changes and additions we had designed so that we could live in the dream house we had always imagined. The three-story house had large windows and plenty of French doors opening to wraparound porches and was full of light. We had a boat dock right in front of our house, which soon housed our *African Queen*, a pontoon boat, which we hauled over from Newfound Lake in Vermont. After all, this was going to be our retirement home.

Over twenty more building lots had recently been sold, and almost all were quickly filled with new construction, replacing existing summer cottages. A few of the cottages remained but were upgraded. The cottages and a couple of other buildings had been part of a large summer camp sold by its owner, Jack Daniels, along with the lots on which they were standing. Jack and his wife remained in one of the larger buildings. He had also created a homeowners' association, the LCHA (Lake Champlain Homeowners Association), which every lot owner had to join. This is where the trouble began.

At first, development of the parcels seemed to go smoothly, but

Grace and Mason jump off the African Queen.

after a while, Jack pulled out the association rule book and told the new owners what they were doing wrong. He became very petty about it. He wouldn't allow even small, inconsequential exceptions, and he seemed to enjoy playing the role of sheriff. After all, he had run the summer camp that way, and he would run the association the same way. The association had an elected board that picked the association president. But from the beginning, Jack had stacked the board.

He quickly made enemies with our friends and neighbors George and Kathy Caswell, who had also bought a parcel, over supposed rule violations regarding cutting bushes or planting flowers on common ground. George figured that things would be handled with more common sense if he were elected president. He ran for the position and got enough votes. But things got worse when Jack tried to show that George handled things too leniently and should be removed. To make matters worse, Jack made his religion an issue, claiming that as a Jew, he was discriminated against by the Christian members of the association, especially by the Caswells. Those claims had me worried.

As a German, I knew I had to be careful about what I said. I invited Jack for an earnest talk about my view on the matter and gave him a copy of my book, *The Nuremberg Medical Trial: The Holocaust and the Origin of the Nuremberg Medical Code.* I assumed it would put aside any questions about whether or not I held anti-Semitic views. It worked to some degree. But after a while, Jack began to treat me like an enemy too.

Soon the association split into two bitterly opposed groups, and the police were ultimately involved. Sue and I tried to keep out of the petty quarreling, but it was difficult. Sue especially suffered from it, as she tried to pursue her passion, gardening, without interference from Jack.

To keep ourselves afloat financially, Sue continued working full-time as a general practitioner at the nearby Ticonderoga Health Center. She needed quiet downtime after seeing sick patients all day long, and that was what her gardening was for.

I, on the other hand, had fully retired and tried to be of help around the house wherever I could, including cooking, something I had always done very badly. One reason we had moved to Crown Point was to visit Jason frequently and have him come visit us. After all, we still had the *African Queen*, which he remembered fondly from the days when we took him on rides at Newfound Lake in New Hampshire. We did this again at Lake Champlain, and he enjoyed it very much, though he did not want to go swimming. He particularly liked sitting by the bonfire on the shore with us when we, along with some of our friends, drank beer and sang songs the water carried for miles across the lake.

Some of us formed a choir, The Champ(l)ain Boys, specializing in tunes from the fifties. We had hootenannies, Hawaiian nights, Mexican dinners, Fourth of July blowouts with fireworks, potato gun shooting contests, and many more events. These were the good days of the association. Jack and his group never participated in any of these.

Jason was especially excited when other parts of the family visited and he could hang out with them. John, Stephanie, Mason, Grace, and Justin came for a week or more at least once a year. Every time they showed up, they seemed to have grown a few more inches, especially Justin. They took the *Queen* out, fished and swam, and further explored the lake with our kayaks. But what they all liked the most were the luscious breakfasts I made, with Justin playing the sous-chef.

My brother Udo and his family came up from Florida, but only once. Erwin in Germany said the trip was too far for him. And we saw

Erwin almost every year on our trips to Germany anyway. One of Sue's cousins, Jim Jones, showed up with his wife, Linda, a couple of times from Washington, DC. They only stayed a few days. Jim and I went fishing, and Sue and Linda talked. Jim and Linda were well-connected folks in DC. He was a runner-up Pulitzer laureate for biography, and his stepson-in-law, David Leonhardt, was a well-known op-ed writer for *The New York Times*.

Sue had invited all of her many cousins in Kansas and Arkansas to come by, but for them, upstate New York near the Canadian border was too far out of the way. But we were especially pleased when my best friend Günther Aufmwasser and his wife, Joanne, came to visit from Germany a couple of times and stayed a while. As always, we had the longest conversations about the shortcomings of the capitalist culture, whose end, for Günther, a former union official of IG Metall and Ver.di, couldn't come fast enough.

Our house was often full of neighbors as we rotated hosting barbecue dinners, especially with Glenn Vehr and Rhonda Idleman and George and Kathy Caswell. Jason participated often. We had to pick him up from Middlebury and take him back a day or two later, usually on weekends.

At one point, he asked us whether he could bring his girlfriend, Tori Spear. I knew Tori from the Special Olympics, where she played with Jason on the Middlebury soccer team I coached. Since we'd moved back to the Middlebury area, I joined Special Olympics again but was resigned mainly to coaching soccer. Tori had given me problems with her way of playing the game, keeping the ball too long and walking off the field when things didn't go her way. She was much more agile than stiff Jason, who often fell trying to kick the ball. She was also literate, if barely. She could read and write at a rudimentary level and handle a cell phone well. Her physical development had been stunted in several areas, but she was definitely higher functioning than Jason. She had a driver's license and drove her own car.

Since members of the soccer team spent a lot of time together, I did not catch on right away that Jason and Tori seemed almost inseparable. And in the beginning, it was an on-again, off-again relationship. She called the shots. We found that out quickly when she decided not to come with Jason to our usual outings because she didn't want to cross the bridge from Vermont to New York in her car. But Jason seemed not to mind her taking charge of their shared time. They both lived at the Middlebury Commons, saw each other routinely, and started to do many things together. When she seemed to boss Jason around too much, Sue started to get worried. We suggested counseling to the Commons' management, which had positive effects. Tori settled down, and the two ultimately got along quite well. However, we didn't see them much around the lake.

THIRTY-FIVE

The Burst of the Housing Bubble and Its Meaning for Curt

We finally had our dream retirement home, but Sue insisted she could not afford to retire right away. And she was right. We wanted to divide our retirement years between America and Europe. For many years, I had been scouting for affordable condos in or near my hometown of Düsseldorf. In 1994, I met an architect from Braunschweig at a conference dealing with East-West German relations. The conference was held at the World Fellowship Center in Conway, New Hampshire, not far from my university. The Center had a unique function. Hidden in a thick forest, scholars and others from East and West Germany could meet and discuss issues of common interest with more candor than they could back home.

The Center was founded during World War II and focused on getting people of opposing worldviews and political systems from around the world to come and, shielded from the media and public attention, discuss their differences and similarities. It was founded largely to protect free speech and had undergone many struggles to stay afloat. During the McCarthy era, it became a refuge for people accused of holding communist views. The Center had managed this, in part, by remaining low-key. I had not heard about its existence until I stumbled on it in the *German Studies Review*.

This is where I met Cornelia Thömmes, an architect who grew up in East Germany and later moved to West Germany, using the legal channels available. She had come to New Hampshire to talk about the ordeal she had been subjected to by the East German authorities during her transition from East to West Germany.

She made herself look like the ultimate victim. I was sitting next to her at the dinner table, and her exceptional gift of gab convinced me of her heroic fight against injustice inside the Stalinist GDR and of the scarred psyche she had been left with as a result. After the "fall of the wall," she had moved back to eastern Germany and was busy restoring buildings that were run down or had been abandoned under the GDR regime in Werder and the surrounding areas. When I told her of my search for a condo in Germany, she told me that she was the right person to help me, especially because buildings in the former GDR were to be had for "practically nothing."

When I told Sue about this encounter, she agreed that we should check it out. In the following years, we went to see Frau Thömmes and her husband, Wolfgang, several times in Werder, and they showed us various houses she was renovating, letting us know that the ability to purchase them inexpensively would soon end. Although she seemed very trustworthy, we didn't see any building at the time that particularly interested us as a second home.

Werder was a picturesque little town right by the massive River Havel, known mainly for growing fruits and producing fruit wines and juices for the nearby markets, mainly Berlin. During fruit-tree blossom season, Berliners flock to Werder in great numbers to bathe in the Blütenmeer (sea of blossoms) and get drunk.

The historic core of Werder was an ancient fishing island, accessible only by a small bridge. This was where Frau Thömmes did most of her renovating. She looked for unoccupied homes, got a few people together interested in living or investing there, and had them finance the whole renovation, including purchasing the house and paying her fees for the project. She incorporated all parties into a GbR (Gesellschaft bürgerlichen Rechts, a business partnership whose members share personal liability), where members held shares according to their financial contributions. She made herself a member, usually holding 10 percent of the shares, for having set up the deal, a kind of finder's fee. An investor friend of hers, Wolfgang Pittke, worked out the financial side of the project, for which he usually received 5 percent of the shares. Still, these projects were lucrative for everyone who participated.

The ruins to be bought were either sold for low prices by their former owners (who usually resided somewhere in the West and often had little interest in renovating or restoring them) or by governmental agencies that had obtained the properties in a number of ways during the GDR days. The new government encouraged such restorations with generous building grants (Fördermittel) and tax incentives.

When Frau Thömmes showed us a ruin on the island's Mühlenstrasse, with four apartments and two stores close to the riverfront, she told us it was the last restoration project she was going to do. We realized we'd better take advantage of it, so we went for it.

She explained that the project was going to finance itself. The 500,000-euro project would be financed with a 100,000-euro government building grant, a 300,000-euro low-interest bank loan, and a 100,000-euro contribution from the four shareholders. Thömmes had a 10 percent share and Pittke a 5 percent; I had a 25 percent; and an old school friend of Thömmes, Frank Castorf, had a 60 percent share. Castorf, I learned, was the director (Intendant) of the famous Berliner Volksbühne, a theater once run by Bertolt Brecht. The GbR had semiannual meetings, and I tried to attend as many as I could. Castorf never showed up. Thömmes had made herself the chair of the GbR and hired herself as the project architect.

She started getting busy right away, around the year 2000. At the first meeting, she announced that we were short on cash and that we all needed to contribute according to our shareholdings. I requested to see the documentation, and she said it would be forthcoming. But it wasn't, and I was in the States. The same thing happened at the next meeting, and I got suspicious. Sue, who had sat in on the meeting, was sure something fraudulent was going on. When I found that Thömmes had spent large amounts of the GbR's money without the required consent of its members, I hired a lawyer. Thömmes eventually admitted to spending money without consent, but she insisted it was necessary to continue with the work on the project. I contacted Castorf, and we met over a beer to discuss our options.

Castorf was not a numbers man; he lived and breathed theater. He handed off everything that had anything to do with money to his tax advisor. But Castorf let me know that Thömmes had always been greedy (habgierig) and could not be trusted. Things only got worse. Thömmes eventually spent several hundred thousand euros over budget without showing receipts. At this point, Castorf hired a lawyer to hold Thömmes accountable. I watched the developments mainly from the US and often had problems understanding the legal arguments of the correspondence between everyone involved. No matter how hard I tried to understand the legal system of reunited Germany, I felt I was always one or two steps behind.

To make matters worse, Thömmes and Pittke had withdrawn from the GbR at the earliest possible moment, that is, ten years after its creation, and left all its liabilities in the hands of Castorf and me. Plus, the agency that gave us the 100,000-euro building grant (Fördermittel) wrote that Thömmes never finished the Mühlenstrasse project and we, Castorf and I, had to return the money. It looked like things couldn't get any worse. But they did.

Thömmes claimed that she had spent more than 100,000 euros of her own money on the Mühlenstrasse project that she had never been reimbursed for. Even if that was the case, she never got, as required by the GbR contract, the consent of the members to go over budget. Castorf and I had no idea what was going on, and my frequent requests to Thömmes to show us balance sheets were never answered. To top things off, Thömmes further claimed that the GbR had never paid her the full architectural fees for her work and that she was still owed around 80,000 euros.

Thömmes found some shady lawyer who sued Castorf and me for almost 200,000 euros (60,000 from me, 140,000 from Castorf). At this time, my own contribution to the Mühlenstrasse projects had reached almost 100,000 euros. In short, Thömmes had spent in excess of 700,000 euros to renovate a house that at the time had a market value of, at most, 500,000 euros, of which, if Castorf and I were to sell it, almost 200,000 euros would go to Thömmes and 100,000 euros to the agency that had given us the building grant and now wanted it back because Thömmes didn't finish the project. The whole thing was a nightmare.

Our last hope was the German justice system. No matter how Thömmes presented her case, two crucial facts made it impossible for her to prevail in any court of law worth its salt. She had not received permission from the GbR to go over budget, as was required. And, more crucially, she had produced no evidence that she actually spent the money. I was very much encouraged by our lawyer's confidence that Thömmes had no legal ground to stand on.

The trial took place before the regional court (Landgericht) in Potsdam in 2008. Present was our lawyer and me (Castorf could not attend), Thömmes and her lawyer, and Sue as an observer. The judge had two jurors (Beisitzer) at his side.

Thömmes's lawyer presented the case for her plaintiff. She wanted the money she was owed. Our lawyer explained that there was no evidence the money had been spent. The judge then stated that Thömmes had presented photocopies of receipts to the head of the building renovation office of the City of Werder and that the originals had been lost. For him, this was enough evidence to rule in favor of Thömmes.

I expected our lawyer to laugh out loud and demand to see the originals, and if they could not be found, then demand that they be reproduced by the companies that had submitted them. But he did not object. Suddenly I felt defeated. I had expected justice to work. But what I witnessed instead looked more like a charade of justice. I realized that everyone in the room, except Sue and me, was a product of the East German system, where the word "evidence" had a different meaning. The "fall of the wall" happened nearly two decades back, but many features of the corrupt justice system were still alive. I felt especially bad because Thömmes, at times, could not help grinning, and Sue had to see her glee. Sue sat apart from me, and I could see her from the side as she watched Thömmes. Sue's instinct had been right from the beginning. Thömmes was a con woman, and we had been had.

Although Sue understood little of what transpired during the court proceedings, her body language was clear. And the judge looked guilty. It was crushing for Sue to see Thömmes taking off with the money Sue had earned by putting in extra night shifts so we could have a home in Germany. All we were left with were huge debts: close to 200,000 euros owed to Thömmes and 100,00 euros owed to the building grant office.

To cut my losses and get this nightmare over with, I offered for Castorf to become the sole owner of the Mühlenstrasse property, and he in return would pay off all of our debts. He accepted. The loss would not be as devastating for him as it would be for me. He could deduct it from his earnings when paying income taxes and perhaps break even. Since my earnings were made in the US, I did not have that option.

But before all of this came to pass, we did spend some time in a small bachelor apartment at the Mühlenstrasse premises, between 2002 and 2006. We explored Werder, Potsdam, Berlin, and much of the Brandenburg area and had decided that this was a place where we could spend much more time. Berlin's cultural offerings alone made moving there worthwhile.

In 2003, Curt decided to come to Werder and live in the bachelor apartment for a while. He had just received his BA in biology from the University of Kansas and figured it was a good idea to explore Germany for a while and learn more German before deciding on his next step. We had always told him that biology was a good field to study for getting into medical school. And he had always shown a real interest in things "being alive." But his real passion was still sports.

At KU, Curt had managed to be part of the Jayhawks football team as a walk-on kicker and punter. In high school, he also played running back and receiver. But at five-foot-eight, he stood little chance competing with scholarship players a foot taller and built like refrigerators. Even as a kicker and punter, he played as a backup and mostly warmed the bench. Still, he traveled with the team to such hallowed places as Notre Dame and Duke. Trying to keep up with the physically demanding program, he neglected some of his academic work, at least in the beginning. His biology major became increasingly demanding too. Plus, he took up German again.

He graduated in May 2003, and we all came to watch him walk the historic path down from the campanile to the football field with the other graduates. John, Stephanie, and many other members of the family had all taken that same walk, sharing the excitement of entering the "real world" with an uncharted future. Sue had also been a student at KU but missed that walk because she switched to UCLA.

After his graduation, Curt wanted to live for a year in Germany. He got much encouragement from Sue and me. After all, Curt spent his first couple of years there when we lived in Frankfurt and even knew some baby German at the time. Also, he would be getting in touch with part of the family legacy. To make the transition into German society as profitable as possible for him, we figured he could live for a few months with our friends, the Keschkes, in Cölln, a small town outside Bautzen in the state of Saxony.

The Keschkes even arranged for Curt to work with a roofing company during his stay. Since Curt is a German citizen, he was automatically registered with the national social service system, including national health insurance. After his stay with the Keschkes, he would move to Werder, stay in the bachelor apartment, and enroll at Humboldt University in Berlin. He started taking classes in biology but had to struggle with the bureaucratic maze left over from the East German days. The university reforms after the "fall of the wall" had not been easy to implement.

But Curt managed, all the while improving his German. However, his real interest remained getting back into sports. Potsdam had an American-style football team, the Potsdam Royals, that did quite well in the regional league. Curt introduced himself and was immediately made a running back and wide receiver. Soon, he became an assistant coach and helped improve the team's standing in the league. He wrote us that things were generally going well for him and that he would like to stay longer in Germany, perhaps even start a career there.

He had a BA in biology and spoke halting German. That narrowed down his options. He went to the German employment office, where they told him they couldn't do much for him. He found some odd jobs in construction around Werder. He tried to keep up with his student work at Humboldt, but after a year, he had difficulty handling academic German and did not re-enroll. His student services lapsed, including health insurance. He could not get any help from any German government office because he had repeatedly been told that he had not yet paid anything into the system.

But help of a different sort came from another side. Curt had met an attractive woman from Werder named Ulrike Günther, and things worked out well for both of them. She opened his eyes to the intricacies of life in Werder and the larger world. He introduced her to various American customs, such as hamburger grill parties and getting your head banged at a Potsdam Royals football game. He helped her with her English and she helped him with his German. More importantly, as a leading employee at a German debt collection agency, she showed him the ropes regarding how to fight and prevail over German bureaucrats. After a while, Curt and Ulrike became inseparable.

Curt had arrived in Werder in 2003 and saw many changes in the city in the two years he lived there. The old fishing village that had been run down under the Communist regime was continuing to slowly reawaken. Capitalism had moved in, for better or worse, and stirred things up. Large government grants were made available to preserve its natural beauty and restore its quaint-looking buildings. I showed how some of that money was mishandled in the Thömmes case.

In 2005, we were still on speaking terms with Frau Thömmes, and Curt was living in the small bachelor apartment of the Mühlenstrasse house. He had his eye on several houses on the island himself, but they usually sold before he could move. There was one house he particularly liked at Am Markt 22. It was just around the corner from where he lived. It was a two-apartment house in the center of town with a third apartment in a separate building in the back. The apartments were relatively large by German standards, more than 1,200 square feet, plus there was the possibility of adding a small shop up front. But the house had been abandoned for years and had to be completely rebuilt on the inside. The back house was in even worse shape.

Curt sent us all the information about the place, and we agreed to finance the rebuilding, if he could get it at a reasonable price. He went to Thömmes and asked whether she wanted to be the architect. She agreed and presented a financial plan, according to which she would finish the front house for 200,000 euros. Sue and I would take out a loan for 120,000 euros and cover the rest with 40,000 euros in government subsidies and 40,000 euros of our own funds. At this point, the house was owned by the City of Werder and auctioned off at the Amtsgericht Potsdam in December 2005. The starting bid was 16,000 euros, and I told Curt he could go as high as 80,000. He went to the auction and got the place for 45,000 euros. As an owner, I had to deal with the German bureaucracy and do it from the States, with Curt helping as much as possible on-site.

Thömmes had a good idea about how to reconfigure the two apartments. One was on the first floor and the other on the second. She would switch everything, converting the apartments into side-by-side town houses, with each side having its own entrance. She would also turn the attics into regular rooms, enlarging the available living area of each apartment to 1,400 square feet.

She also suggested turning the original entrance with its large stairway area into a small shop of roughly 350 square feet that could be rented out separately. That required the entrance to be moved to the back of the house and accessed from the courtyard that separated the front house from the back house. The back house would stay untouched for the time being and be revisited at a later date. A small movie theater called Fortuna that seated about 100 people had been built on part of the courtyard long ago, and it had to be torn down. That whole building had to be gutted, meaning a lot of muscle was needed right away. This is where Curt jumped in.

He ordered huge construction material dumpsters, got appropriate tools, and started to take down walls. Soon he had a friend helping him full-time, and neighbors would hear their sledgehammers from early in the morning to late at night. His ongoing search to find suitable employment with his BA in biology took second place to the renovation. In fact, he thought about going to graduate school and getting an advanced degree in a more marketable field. We discussed this with him on the phone several times, and an MBA came to mind. After all, the world economy had gone global like never before, and more and more companies everywhere had adopted American business methods.

Many US companies in Europe and worldwide were looking for young, digitally versed recent graduates fluent in English. All this made sense to Curt, who decided to return to KU and enroll in a two-year MBA program. It was early 2006, and he was accepted to start that program in the fall of that year. He worked frantically with his friend finishing the gutting job before taking off. There was, of course, the question of leaving Ulrike behind. But they felt their love had grown such that a temporary separation would not affect their lasting commitment to each other. Also, Curt would be back during the long semester breaks, and she could visit him on her company vacations. From all we could gather during that time, the MBA program was very demanding and interesting. His focus on international management allowed Curt to take a study trip to Beijing and Shanghai.

At that time, Sue and I were preoccupied with moving from Plymouth, New Hampshire, to Crown Point, New York, which presented us with many problems. In addition, I also had to keep track of the building activities on our new house in Werder. We had told Thömmes we were planning on moving in at the end of 2008, to which she had agreed. But we learned from Ulrike that after Curt's departure, nothing was happening. Thömmes had hired Muschert Bau to do the construction work and most of the other contractors (plumbers, electricians, and the like) she had worked with before to do the rest. They were waiting for her orders.

She eventually called me to tell me that she could finish only one apartment by the end of 2008, that we could move in then, and she would finish the second apartment and the little shop in 2009. Sue and I talked it over and reluctantly agreed. Pretty soon, the bills from the contractors came in by fax, and I paid them as I got them via bank transfer. At first, everything seemed fine. But after a while, I noticed that she was going over budget. In fact, at the rate she was going, the house would cost at least twice as much as her original budget. When I complained, we agreed to raise the ceiling from 200,000 euros to 250,000 euros. From a distance, I had little control over the situation, and Curt wasn't there to watch things for me.

When Thömmes spent 200,000 euros and had not even finished the one apartment she was working on, I canceled our contract and flew to Germany to see for myself. When I saw the house, I noticed that she had painted it in a very different color than I had picked without informing me. There were a few other odd things. At the worksite, I ran into Sigi Muschert, the owner of Muschert Bau. We had corresponded before, and he was aware of the dismal situation surrounding the house's renovation, including my firing of Thömmes. He offered to finish renovating the house without Thömmes and get ahold of a different architect, Frank Jendrzejczyk, to navigate the project through the eventual inspection process.

Given my frame of mind at the time, Muschert and Jendrzejczyk were a godsend. Work continued in a more predictable way and with refreshing financial transparency. Muschert finished the first apartment, and we were able to rent it out in January 2008.

Curt graduated with an MBA in May, and Ulrike, John, Stephanie, Sue, and I all went to his KU graduation, which was followed by a big party. This was Ulrike's introduction to Curt's side of the family, which generated many questions regarding life in Germany compared to that in the US. In the end, everyone went to bed happy. Curt and Ulrike planned on heading back to Germany, but before that, they came to see us in Crown Point.

When he arrived back in Werder, Curt moved in with Ulrike at her apartment on Am Finkenberg. Finishing the house on Am Markt would take a least another half a year. Ulrike resumed her work at the collection agency in Potsdam, and Curt was going to look for a job befitting his new MBA.

He probably had an inkling that he would encounter some problems, but the fast-changing realities in the business world at the time must have hit him like a ton of bricks. In 2008, the American housing market collapsed, pushing the rest of the economy into a tailspin. Relaxed credit policies had greatly increased demand for housing over the past several years. Prices rose disproportionately to the market value of real estate. New housing in desirable areas attracted new buyers. Such houses could be acquired and then sold again for a good profit as prices kept rising. People in the financial sector jumped in, selling risky mortgage securities for high profits. To make them look less risky, they combined them with more solid securities and sold them together as packages. Securities agencies gave those packages high ratings, meaning they were declared secure for long-term profits.

Major banks and investment institutions were loaded with them. And then it happened. More and more borrowers couldn't make their mortgage payments. Lending institutions foreclosed, starting a selling frenzy. Real estate prices dropped dramatically, and holders of mortgage securities saw the value of their securities nose-dive. Many large banks and investment institutions could not meet their liabilities and went under. Stock markets tanked, and the world plunged into financial disarray. What followed has been called the Great Recession, and it affected all parts of the globalized economy, including Germany. Many German banks had bought the now almost worthless mortgage security (subprime) packages. To save the system from collapse, governments infused huge amounts of cash into bailout programs. The newly elected president Barack Obama in the States acted swiftly. So did the Merkel government in Berlin. But they could not prevent a decrease in GDP and the vast increase in unemployment.

Certainly, companies were not going to hire fresh-from-the-university MBAs. Instead they would try to hang on to those they already had. To make things worse, Curt could not be hired as a low-level office worker either. His MBA made him dismally overqualified. He managed to get a short internship with Deutsche Bahn. But for the moment, there still was a lot of work to be done on the house, and he had to go on filling out job applications. Jobs requiring a recent American MBA were probably nonexistent in Germany at that time. The public employment office (Arbeitsamt) was of no help either. At best, they referred German graduates with a BWL (Betriebswirtschaftslehre) degree (the equivalent of an MBA) to German companies.

The fact that Curt had no native German language skills certainly added to the problem. Applying for a job in the US would have been very disruptive for Ulrike. So at that point in his life, things were very uncertain. If I understood him correctly, at one point Curt even contemplated becoming a full-time football coach for either the Potsdam Royals or the Berlin Rebels, two teams he had played for himself. He played baseball for the Potsdam Porcupines and had become their coach. But the team could not make it a paid position. He took on various odd jobs to pay his bills. The earlier optimism he had felt that an American MBA was the door into the big business world, even in Germany, had vanished. Sue and I were not always tuned in to his affairs because life in Crown Point kept us more focused on our own affairs than we had anticipated.

Sue was still working full-time. In addition, she had to fulfill stringent requirements for her ER doc recertification that was due in 2010, including taking advanced courses in the latest developments in her field. Most of the work she could do online. I helped her obtain material, such as medical articles in occasionally obscure journals. She had to read them all and answer specific questions about the content, usually finding correct diagnoses and treatments. The deadline for sending everything in approached as she worked at a very busy ER in Elmira in upstate New York. She worked there off and on when her full-time job at Ticonderoga allowed it, often on weekends, and I drove her the 300-mile distance.

It was rough driving to Elmira during winter, and we would stay at the Holiday Inn. The librarian at the hospital had helped Sue get especially hard-to-find articles and had them sent to the library as email attachments, which Sue read at the hotel when she was not at the ER. Time was running short, but she managed to turn in all her answers on the computer minutes before the midnight deadline. Without the help of the librarian, that would have been difficult.

We were also busy organizing our new house. It was right by the lake, and Sue had planned a magnificent garden that kept her occupied for many hours during the short growing season available in what could be a bitterly cold region.

She had high berms piled up to flank one side of our lot, extending all the way to the edge of the shoreline and protecting our terrace from nosy neighbors. The berms were adorned with large flowery bushes whose radiant blossoms brightened up the whole association in April. We had a large garage built next to our house, and Sue surrounded much of it with flat trellises made of vertical poles and horizontal wires to grow decorative fruit trees. She also found a large maple tree at a nursery in Vermont and placed it in front of our house.

Hanging geraniums adorned three sides of the house and cascaded down from all the windows. Sue stocked the flower boxes with all of the perennial geraniums she'd grown in a hot room she had built in the garage.

We separated the other side of our lot with a long line of fir trees. Sue put flower beds almost everywhere around our house. The icing on the cake was several gooseberry bushes she had imported from Canada. I told her those were my favorite fruits and reminded me of my (mostly troubled) childhood. The bushes produced so many of the luscious berries that we had to give most of them away. Although they have often been cited as native plants, they have never been popular in the US. After tasting them, everyone wondered why not.

THIRTY-SIX

Real Estate Problems in Crown Point: Our House Burns Down

The last plant we put in was a blue spruce. We had bought it with live roots in a bucket for Christmas 2009. It was a magnificent tree and, as always, was adorned with real candles that lit up our living room on Christmas Eve. We planted it in our garden right after New Year's. On the evening of that day, we went to sleep as always, discussing all of the projects we were contemplating for the coming year.

In the middle of the night, I had to get up to go to the bathroom. I smelled something unusual, turned on the lights, and saw that smoke had filled our room under the ceiling. I woke up Sue, and we immediately realized there was a fire somewhere in the house. I ran down to the first floor to check the fireplace. We always kept a fire smoldering low at night in the encased fireplace to help keep the house warm. But it all looked normal, so I stormed up the stairs again, where I saw the smoke thickening. We knew we had to get out of the house, but first, we called the fire department. Sue told me the phone was dead just as the lights went out. Cell phones didn't work in our area. Sue threw her fur coat on over her pajamas, grabbed her car keys, and yelled that she would drive to town to find a phone. I frantically started to collect the essential things we needed: passports, wallets, money, and keys.

Smoke was filling the upper part of the house quickly, and I had to grope around in the dark, holding my breath for as long as I could. Coughing badly, I managed to fetch some clothes before storming outside. There I saw smoke emerge from the northern side of the house from the area beneath the roof overhang. I circled the house but couldn't make out any fire. Then Sue came back, telling me that neighbors at a nearby house had let her make the emergency call and that the fire trucks would arrive soon. She was still in her pajamas and slippers under her fur coat, but we knew it was too dangerous to go back into the house for more suitable clothes. We sat in the car and waited for the fire trucks. The first two arrived a few minutes later and were soon joined by a third. The nearest fire hydrant was more than 1,000 feet away and had low water pressure.

By the time the hoses began squirting water on the house, some of the upper windows and parts of the roof had caught fire. Firefighters entered the burning house with extinguishers, and soon the whole site was in pandemonium. Sue and I watched the scene through the windshield of our Mercedes and felt like spectators in a nightmarish dream. It was bitter cold, and the snow-covered landscape, glistening under a moonlit sky, made the whole scene even more surreal.

A few hours before, we had been sleeping cozily in our warm bed, and now we were watching our belongings go up in flames with freezing butts. After a life of unbelievable ups and downs, this house was supposed to comfort our weary bones in our retirement. We had seen everything before, but not this. Now we could add this experience to our long list of you'll-never-believe-what-happened-to-us events.

Eventually, the EMTs arrived to check our physical and mental conditions, served us coffee, and reserved a room for us at the Super 8 motel in Ticonderoga.

After about four hours of fighting the flames, a fire inspector informed us that our house was a total loss. Some of the structure was still in place, but it wasn't worth saving. The firefighters had removed a few things of obvious personal value to us, mainly pictures, though some were badly damaged or completely ruined. Then the site was secured as a do-not-enter area, and Sue and I retired to the Super 8 motel as the day dawned. Before dropping into bed, Sue called the hospital to let them know an urgent matter would prevent her from coming in for work that day. We tried to sleep for a couple of hours, but it was in vain.

I forget the exact sequence of events that followed, but insurance people visited us, friends brought us food, and Sue's coworkers, someone from the fire department, someone from the Red Cross, someone from a local church, and others filled up our small hotel room. We were eager to see our burned-out home because we were curious if anything could still be saved. We disregarded the DO NOT ENTER sign outside the house the fire department had posted and took stock of what was salvageable.

Almost everything on the second floor, which had two large bedrooms and two bathrooms, had burned completely. The first floor, with the entrance hall, kitchen, large living room, and bath, had suffered severe water damage from the hoses. However, some of the furniture could be cleaned up and used again in the future.

The basement contained two offices, a mini-apartment with a bath, and a utility room. Nothing had burned down there, but everything had suffered water damage. Or, more accurately, the water itself had not done as much damage as the ice that built up quickly in the freezing weather. Our filing cabinets were blocks of ice. Many of Sue's irreplaceable medical files from the hospital were clumped together in icy chunks. Our folders with original documents (birth certificates, diplomas, promotion letters, and other paperwork) seemed hopelessly lost. We took many of the most important files with us to the hotel room and, after many days of thawing them out over hotel radiators, managed to save some of them. We lost many of our books, and those that could be saved required lots of work separating pages one at a time.

Many personal items were gone forever. I especially regretted the loss of Sue's pictures from her fencing days at KU. A particular one with her coach, Mr. Giele, proudly standing beside her, will remain ingrained in my mind.

We were able to store everything that was salvageable in a large garage owned by the local discount grocery store, run by Marion Sullivan, who is Kathy Caswell's sister, and her husband, John. We later hired Larry Scott's construction crew to do all the manual work. They had built our large garage and were known in the area for their professional workmanship. They also let us know they would be happy to rebuild our house if that is what we decided to do.

Sue and I rented a small apartment on Ticonderoga's main street near Moses Ludington Hospital, where she now worked. Her colleagues had taken up a collection, and their generous contributions really surprised us. Some people had reached deep into their pockets. I still feel thankful for it today after all these years.

The town's fire inspector determined the fire to have started in the chimney. Our homeowners' insurance, Liberty Mutual, accepted our total loss claim in full, and we were able to start rebuilding pretty soon, just weeks after the fire. We received about $350,000 for the house, another $100,000 for furniture and other valuables, plus funds for our temporary accommodation.

We made changes to the house, mainly enlarging the rooms on the second floor by flattening the pitch of the roof and adding more deck space all around the house. Our main contractor, Larry Scott, got most of the material from a Lowe's store that had just opened up in Ticonderoga.

My main job consisted of ensuring that everything was running smoothly, that the contractors kept working, that the insurance paid the bills, and that cost overruns would not get out of hand. I continued to salvage what was salvageable from the damaged belongings we had stored at the discount grocery store. Our most prized possessions had perished. The handwoven Persian rugs that had been laid out in the house were all gone. I had obtained them over the years at a famous auction house in Düsseldorf and brought them back to the States one by one. A costly limited edition print by Salvador Dalí, *Maximum Speed of Raphael's Madonna*, Sue's fiftieth birthday gift for me, had burned. Her jewelry box was missing.

As we had poked the ashes looking for it, we realized how close we had come to turning into ashes ourselves. If I had not needed to use the bathroom in the middle of the night, we probably would have succumbed to the toxic fumes and been consumed by the flames. Thank God for my prostate problems! The things we lost could be replaced, while some could be repaired and put back in their original places.

One day when Sue wasn't working, we sat together before the computer and worked out the interior details of the rebuild house. We completely redid the kitchen including adding a brand-new, top-of-the-line, six-flame gas range. When the house was almost complete in late summer, I started my part of the job: painting everything on the inside and all the decks on the outside. It kept me busy for several weeks. Once the new furniture was in, the house looked like a little jewel box, the walls decorated with pictures and photos. Everything was complete before winter arrived. Still, 2010 had been a hell of a year for us. But when we looked back on the year, going into 2011, we realized it had made us stronger and brought us closer to each other. Sue was going on sixty-seven and I was going on seventy-three, and neither of us felt like slowing down—quite the contrary.

We were also keeping busy finishing the house in Werder. Curt was doing the practical work on-site, but I was the owner and had to deal with the piles of paperwork only German bureaucrats can dream up, from overly detailed building permits to impossible-to-meet financial conditions. I remember a needless quarrel with a neighbor (the event center and hotel Lendelhaus) about parking rights that dragged on for years and turned vicious; eventually, we involved lawyers.

Curt insisted that I got the short end of the stick, but it was the best I could do under the circumstances and from a distance. The Werder project kept us in touch with Curt much more than before, and we realized that he was not too happy with the Berlin employment market, which seemed to have no place for a recent American MBA graduate. In fact, MBA graduates were still being laid off at that point in time. Curt had to decide whether to wait it out or change careers. He had a BA in biology and knew that many schools in Europe and the US were clamoring for science teachers. He asked me whether I could help get him into the Plymouth State University teacher certification program, which took two years and ended with a master of education (MEd) in natural sciences (biology). I gave him encouragement and he took it from there. He had found an American high school in Berlin (JFK High School) that would allow him to do his required internship there. He and Ulrike had been living together for several years at this point. His enrollment at Plymouth State University would mean another lengthy separation. Would their love endure again? They were both confident that it would.

THIRTY-SEVEN

Curt and Ulrike Get Married, and Jason Visits Holland

On our next visit to Germany, in early 2011, Curt and Ulrike invited us and Ulrike's parents, Lilo and Peter, to an intimate engagement dinner at a cozy restaurant overlooking the Havel, where Curt, at a very tender moment, slipped an engagement ring on Ulrike's slender hand. Everyone held back tears and wished them all the luck and love the world could offer. The wedding date was set for May 23, 2012, Jason's birthday. Curt had promised Jason they'd celebrate the day together, and Jason was overjoyed when we told him on the phone that he, Sue, and I would all fly together to Germany for the occasion.

But there was a lot to do before then. Curt immediately increased his efforts to get the house ready for him and Ulrike to move in and to move out of her apartment on Am Finkenberg. When it happened, they were aware that there still was a major task ahead of them. The back house Sue and I eventually planned to occupy had to be renovated too. But that would be many years hence.

For the moment, they were preoccupied with setting up a household, planning marriage and kids, and getting Curt off to Plymouth

State University for his teaching license. Sue and I still had our noses to the grindstone too. She was still working full-time at Moses Ludington Hospital in Ticonderoga, plus doing a few extra ER shifts in surrounding hospitals to bolster our retirement portfolio. The Great Recession had nearly halved our savings, and although the markets were slowly recovering, we felt very insecure about our coming "golden years." We thought that in the long run, we would probably not be able to maintain our fancy house by the lake. We had hoped it would attract family members and friends to visit us and stay for a while. Some did, especially John, Stephanie, and the grandkids, who came every summer and made the most of the lake, the boat, the kayaks, the hiking trails in the beautiful mountains, and other attractions that Kansas doesn't have. Some others came as well. But with time, the numbers grew smaller. Even Jason, after a while, thought the forty-minute drive was too long, even though we picked him up and took him back home again. Tori never wanted to cross the bridge with her car, thinking she was entering wild territory.

Maintaining the place during the long snowy seasons increasingly tested our weary bones. And taxes on lake property started to skyrocket. It cost us about $8,000 annually at the time, but it was increasing rapidly. Our neighbors started talking about moving to Florida, and that made a lot of sense to us. Now we regretted that we had sold our house in St. Cloud some years ago. We considered getting a small condo down there for the winter months. Sue even argued that she could get a Florida medical license and work part-time in some low-volume hospitals. We knew Florida. We had lived near Orlando for six years and recently visited the Sarasota area on short trips. My best friend from Germany, Günther, and his American wife, Joanne, visited her mother in Florida every winter, and we met them there for annual reunions.

Sue and I overcame our initial aversion to moving back to the land of the "newly wed and nearly dead" and started looking for a small place near the beach. The Caswells, our neighbors in Crown Point, who also intended to acquire a winter place in the Sarasota area, eventually helped us find one near theirs in a mobile home park next to a golf course in Bradenton. Our other neighbors and good friends in Crown Point, Glenn Vehr and Rhonda Idleman, would join us as well. But in 2012, things were not as clear to us as they would become later.

Despite the labor and cost our house by the lake required, it was new, built to our specifications, and we enjoyed it a lot. We could see the full lake from our bed through large windows that faced the morning sun. We could step out onto the balcony and have breakfast next to the hanging geraniums in the shade of a large cottonwood tree. We usually heard birds chirp and, if we were lucky, could see a bald eagle perched on a branch, waiting to pounce on some fish for his own breakfast.

During wintertime, the eagle would sit for hours and wait for some ice anglers to throw a fish they didn't like onto the ice, then he'd sweep down and grab it.

On lush summer nights, we would marvel at the change of light in the sky, the whispering trees surrounding our house, and the smooth water with its playful color arrangements. We usually had a drink, and as the sky darkened, I tried to impress Sue by tracing the different signs of the zodiac while smoking a cigar. I could always find the Big Dipper and took it from there. Sometimes my imagination got the better of me. I would serenade her with a few of my favorite old songs. I could be heard miles down the lake singing "Heimat deine Sterne" and "Capri Fischer." We both knew at the time that these were some of the happiest hours of our lives.

On Christmas of 2011, we told Jason that we would finally make good on a promise we had talked about for years; we would take him to visit the family of his beloved foster father, Tony Lamers, who lived in Holland. Tony had died years prior. No one had meant more to Jason than Tony. After Jason joined us following Sue's completion of her medical training, we stayed in touch with the Lamerses, and Jason visited them on occasion. Tony's death devastated Jason, and he always wanted to see Tony's family in Holland, where Tony had grown up.

We found Tony's sister's address in the small town of Mill in Holland, near Venlo, and wrote her a long letter in English, explaining the whole situation, including Jason's desire to visit her. One of her sons, Theodore, wrote back in perfect English that they would welcome us anytime. So we planned our visit to Tony's family for the week before Curt and Ulrike's wedding.

I was still coaching the Addison County Special Olympics soccer team in Middlebury and saw Jason often at the time. I had to take him off the team because he fell a lot. I put him in the special skills group, where he passed and dribbled the ball without confronting opposing players. I usually took Jason and Tori to McDonald's after practice, and Jason always brought up his coming trip to be with Curt at his wedding and to see Tony's family in Holland. Finally, the day came when Jason, Sue, and I left on a plane from Boston to Berlin.

It was a nonstop, eight-hour flight, and Jason handled it remarkably well. We had prepared him for the culture shock, but the only thing he commented on was that people in Berlin didn't speak English. He was overjoyed to see Curt and Ulrike again, though shortly after a warm welcome at their house in Werder, Jason fell asleep on the couch.

Over the next few days, we showed him around the neighborhood. What impressed him the most were the castles of Sanssouci and Neues Palais. When we described the famous owner, he drily commented, "Frederick the Great must have had good taste."

After that came the exciting part. Sue and I drove Jason to Nelly, Tony's sister in Mill, by way of my hometown, Düsseldorf. In Düsseldorf, we picked up Joanne, the wife of my friend Günther, who wanted to come along. The four of us—Jason, Sue, Joanne, and I— arrived in Mill midmorning. Nelly's family was overjoyed and had prepared for our coming. She and her husband lived in a very nice single-family home in a quiet, stately neighborhood right across from a large town park near the center of this small city. This house would have been the pride of any middle-class residential neighborhood in the US, which made me wonder: Why did people from here leave for the US? The answer was, of course, that when Tony was a little boy, much of Europe was ravaged by war, and people flocked to the "promised land" any way they could. I did too.

Nelly was waiting for us with many more members of her family, about a dozen in all. Her son Theodore, a teacher with an excellent command of English, made the introductions. Nelly looked much like her brother Tony, and Jason was in tears being close to her on and off for much of the day. Everyone listened attentively as Jason tried to explain how much Tony had meant to him and how glad he was to be able to sit among members of Tony's family. He had the feeling Tony was sitting among them as well.

After a sumptuous meal with authentic Dutch food, we all drove to the house where Tony had grown up. The people who lived there showed Jason around, and everyone told stories of long ago related to Tony's childhood. Jason was repeatedly overcome with emotion.

Then we went to see the logging mill where Tony and many of the young people in Mill had worked long hours during the 1950s while barely getting by.

The last place of note Nelly's family wanted to show us was a set of trenches where Dutch troops, according to local folklore, at the outset of World War II, had held back German invaders long enough to allow Dutch supply trains to get through and ensure Allied victory. This was the Dutch Alamo story. No word that in this part of Holland, the Dutch cooperation with the Nazis had been particularly strong. As always, when confronted with such situations, I kept smiling and nodding. We were there to brighten up an important memory of Jason's life.

After another round of Dutch herring and Heineken beer at Nelly's house, we said goodbye. Jason left with mixed feelings. He was glad that he'd met Nelly and her family and seen the place where Tony grew up. But he was sad because he would have liked to stay longer. We told him we would come back someday but that it was time to move on to Berlin and attend Curt's wedding. We had taken many pictures of this trip to Mill, and Jason later hung up some of them in his apartment in Vermont, where he often glanced at them with tears in his eyes.

Several days later, on May 23, 2012, our focus shifted to Curt and Ulrike's wedding. It was also Jason's birthday. The number of guests was relatively small, but the wedding was conducted in a traditional festive manner. Everyone was dressed formally, particularly Ulrike. She wore a beautiful white satin dress with lots of lace accentuating her slim figure. Curt wore a classic dark suit that made him look sharp.

The civil ceremony was held at the historic town hall of Werder, which was built in Renaissance style and was adorned with bright flowers on windowsills. The wedding song Curt played at the end of the short ceremony was Willie Nelson's rendition of "Always on My Mind."

Sobs could be heard, particularly from Lilo and Peter. After Curt and Ulrike exited the building under the traditional rain of rice and flower petals, it was time for the photographer. Landmarks that could serve as backdrops were within a few yards of the town hall: the old

Curt and Ulrike met in Werder.

windmill (Bockwindmühle) and the tall Heilig-Geist-Kirche. After that, everyone attended the feast at the Lendelhaus restaurant, where a whole room had been reserved for the occasion.

The Lendelhaus, also a Renaissance-style building and former home of the local landlords, was just a few blocks from the old town hall and was located next to Curt and Ulrike's house. Only a small parking lot separates the two. The meal was delicious.

There was music, so the traditional dances were performed (bride with the groom, groom with mother-in-law, the bride with father-in-law, etc.). Toasts and speeches focused on a successful future, lifelong love, happy kids, and other appropriate topics. My little talk covered the familiar advice Lady Astor supposedly had given to a journalist when asked what made for a lasting marriage. Her answer: "Consider murder, but never divorce." I think I got a couple of laughs out of that one. But I was only halfway kidding. When the party was over, Curt and Ulrike walked just a few steps into their house.

THIRTY-EIGHT

Becoming a US Citizen
(What Took You So Long?)

In 2010, I was still the owner of our Werder house. Sue was not on the ownership papers because her US citizenship would have complicated everything, especially with the loan applications. I was a German citizen, and as cumbersome as the workings of German bureaucracy can be, things followed a predictable routine.

In the US, I held a green card, which was as good as being a citizen, except green card holders could not vote for or hold elected office. That never bothered me. If I had become a US citizen, under US and German law, I would have had to give up my German citizenship. This would have made living in Germany quite difficult. For instance, in 1980 we moved from Arkansas to Frankfurt, and I could work in Germany like any citizen. Sue could work in Germany because she was my spouse. Without my citizenship, neither of us would have been able to live and work in Germany except on a restricted work visa. Therefore, I had no incentive to change citizenship.

But things changed after the terrorist attacks of September 11, 2001, which killed almost 3,000 people. One immediate consequence of this act was a law Congress passed a few weeks later, the Patriot Act, which was aimed at clamping down on terrorist activities. Government agencies were given new powers to monitor and apprehend people whose behavior indicated they might be engaged in or supporting terrorist activities, either directly or indirectly. The law came down hard on noncitizens, who lost certain rights, like the right not to be detained unlawfully.

The mere suspicion that someone might be involved in terrorist activities, even unwittingly, was sufficient grounds for arrest. A "suspect" could be held indefinitely, and no one, not even a citizen spouse, had a right to get information about the arrested person, not even confirmation that the person had been arrested or detained. Under the Patriot Act, such a fate could happen to me.

At first, this did not disturb me much because I was a university professor, had no criminal record, and was not politically active. But Sue was worried. Too often had she witnessed my irritation with petty border control agents who made wrong assumptions about what we carried in our bags. Sue pointed out that these agents now had the power to declare me, a green card holder, a terrorist suspect on spurious grounds and detain me without specific charges.

Plus, Sue had no right to information regarding my whereabouts. One incident in particular made us both think seriously about this situation. On one of our trips back from Europe, we had a short layover in Amsterdam. I bought some bananas to eat on the plane. When we got to Liberty Airport in Newark, I still had three of them in my carry-on but had forgotten about them. I did not check the box on the customs declaration indicating that we were importing agricultural goods. When a customs official asked us to open our bags, he found my three rotten bananas. He pointed to the customs form and told me I had falsified a federal document by withholding information on the bananas.

Things got bad fast when I couldn't suppress my urge to laugh. They got worse when I suggested that I would be happy to eat the three bananas right there and solve the problem. When he told me I had to pay a $300 fine, $100 for each banana, I couldn't hold back the laughter for a second time. Sue desperately tried to make me understand the seriousness of the situation. But we didn't have $300. I called for the supervisor. It took a long time for her to show up. But she, too, insisted

I had to pay a fine, though she lowered it to $175. When I laughed again, Sue said that she was going to take over the negotiation and motioned for me to move farther down the hallway and wait for her. But she had no success. Her argument that we were just two tired elderly people (she was sixty-six, and I was seventy-two at the time) with only a few dollars in our pockets, eager to get home and sleep, did not pull any weight.

When Sue eventually agreed to pay the fine with her credit card, the agent told her they would only accept cash, which she did not have. They decided she could withdraw the cash with her credit card from an ATM in the terminal. But because the closest ATM was quite a distance away, the agents called two Homeland Security guards, who accompanied her to the machine. They were two young men, considerably taller than Sue, carrying semiautomatic rifles. With her arthritic gait and worried look, people watching the spectacle must have wondered what kind of crime this little old lady was accused of to deserve such harsh treatment.

Sue was a US citizen whose worst offense in life was receiving a speeding ticket. She had to endure this public humiliation merely because her husband, a green card holder, tried to enter the country with three unreported bananas. While all this was happening, we observed other people also carrying forbidden snacks. But they, apparently US citizens, were given the opportunity to dispose of them in trash cans obviously put there for that purpose. Watching helplessly how guards of the US Department of Homeland Security treated Sue like a dangerous terrorist suspect convinced me that the time had finally come to exchange my green card for a US passport. So that is what I did.

Since then, US and German laws had changed, allowing for dual citizenship under certain conditions. When I was making my application, American authorities wanted verification from German authorities that I could retain my German citizenship upon obtaining American citizenship. And the German authorities wanted evidence that I would continue to have vested interests in Germany as a US citizen. Owning property in Germany was sufficient evidence. As far as the US authorities were concerned, all I had to show was that I had not been convicted of a felony or engaged in unconstitutional activities.

At that point, I had lived in the US for fifty years and, as far as I knew, never appeared in any police files other than for speeding tickets. If any records had been made of my lefty activities at UCLA during the Vietnam War, the dust had probably settled on them. After I cleared up things with the German authorities, I applied for citizenship with US Citizenship and Immigration Services. I had to appear for one interview and received my Certificate of Naturalization four weeks later, on October 11, 2013, at a swearing-in ceremony with about 100 others in a large hall of the US immigration office in Albany, New York. Sue and the Caswells were there to witness it as I raised my right hand and swore to uphold and defend the Constitution of the United States.

The benefits of US citizenship soon became apparent during one of our short trips to Montreal. US/Canadian border checks had become routine again. When coming back from Canada one day, the border guard asked my citizenship, heard the word "US," and waved me right through. No more "green card treatment." And that's the way it has been from then on. I should have gotten my citizenship much earlier. It took three rotten bananas to set me straight.

THIRTY-NINE

The Great Saint Valentine Storm and Curt's Struggle with the Not-So-Great German Health Care and Education System

Sue was still working very hard. Now serving as the medical director of Moses Ludington Hospital in Ticonderoga, she tried to bring medical services into line, especially with critical and emergency care standards continually upgraded by medical research. She tried equally hard to improve the working conditions of the medical staff and increase their compensation. In this, she did not always have the unwavering support of the hospital administration. Its job was to stop the financial hemorrhaging most small hospitals in the US, especially in rural areas, were experiencing at the time. The administration made attempts to integrate Moses Ludington with the growing network of smaller hospitals and clinics run by the University of Vermont

Medical Center in Burlington. Sue went to seminars discussing the relevant issues. But she always suspected that any takeover of the small hospital by a larger organization, public or private, would invite downsizing and outsourcing of medical services, so she remained skeptical. To study respective developments at the hospital, she sometimes worked extra hours. We had to ensure the roads stayed clear of snow when she came home late or had to leave on an emergency call at short notice.

During wintertime, the road to our house had to be plowed constantly. The road was about 1,000 feet long, and driving on it could be messy even after plowing. This led to one dramatic moment on my birthday, February 14, 2014. Sue was at work when a heavy snowstorm quickly covered the entire Northeast region and hit New York particularly hard. It brought traffic to a standstill, and the governor of New York declared a state of emergency, which meant that all nonessential activities had to stop. People had to seek shelter and stay in place. No nonessential vehicles were allowed on the roads. Sue's hospital had activated emergency services. Some nursing staff stayed on to look after patients. Most went home. Sue stayed until it became almost impossible to make it through the snow. She called me and let me know that she was coming home no matter what because it was my birthday and she had prepared a meal.

I tried to stop her but was not successful. She told me she was going to follow the last ambulance leaving the hospital, transferring a critically ill patient to the Vermont Medical Center in Burlington. It would drive through Crown Point. I told her I would stand by the window and watch as she came in. Normally the drive took twenty minutes. But because the snowstorm raged on and outside visibility was very low, I gave it forty minutes. After fifty minutes, I called the hospital and was told that Sue had left about forty minutes before. So I waited by the window, watching the snow pile up even further. Our cell phones didn't work, so I couldn't do anything but wait.

I thought of searching for her in my Toyota pickup truck. She was driving her 4Matic 240 Mercedes, which had never let us down, no matter the weather. As I contemplated my options, my strained eyes caught something like weaving branches in the middle of the barren snowfield between our house and the road about 1,000 feet away. I squinted and saw that it was Sue, up to her waist in the snow. She was calling my name in the middle of the howling snowstorm.

I ran outside and stomped through the snow in her direction, screaming myself. When I got to her, I was torn between yelling at her about how stupid she'd acted, thinking she could make it through this snow alive, and embracing her. She was absolutely exhausted and unable to extricate herself from the hole she'd gotten stuck in. I helped her out, and it was a while until we both returned to the house.

At the house, she told me that the ambulance she wanted to follow had left before she was ready. She followed the ambulance's tracks and got to the entrance of our association. She left the tracks, and the snow on the road to our house was so high that the car got stuck. She could see our house and thought she could make it across the snow-field. Unfortunately, I didn't see her from the window, at least not at first. Later, she agreed that without my help, she wouldn't have made it to the house.

This was probably the most memorable birthday and Valentine's Day we had ever celebrated. Sue and I cuddled under the sheets in our snow-covered chalet, cut off from the rest of the world, listening to the crackle in the fireplace, and humming a happy birthday tune. Joan Baez's lyrics from her famous song "Diamonds and Rust" came to mind. And yes, we both could have died then and there. But we didn't, and the next morning we woke up to a nor'easter that continued to keep the region on edge. Later we learned that many people lost their homes, and some died in one of the worst storms to hit the nation in a long time. The state of emergency lasted several days.

Eventually, the storm died down and left behind a pristine-looking landscape. The lake was covered with an endless blanket of snow that wind gusts rearranged in ever-changing patterns. Icicles formed by the afternoon sun reflected the light in mysterious ways. We talked to people on the phone, confirming that we were okay. As odd as it sounds, these were a couple of happy days for us. Then Sue had to head back to the hospital and take care of people who had been less lucky.

On the day of the nor'easter, which we have come to refer to as the Great Saint Valentine Storm, I turned seventy-six. Sue would turn "only" seventy later that year. Thoughts of retiring in a warmer climate started to crop up again: Florida in winter, New York in summer. Jason could visit us in Florida and not be separated from us for too long.

One more event spurred on that idea. One evening in early 2014, Sue ended up driving home from work late and in a very angry mood. She was angry because the head of the human resources office had ignored suggestions she had made regarding improvements to the new contracts for medical staff. Sue wanted to confront the person, but she had left early. Trying to vent her frustration, Sue called a trusted co-worker on her cell phone. She concluded her talk by saying that if her input was not going to be more appreciated by the administration, she might as well run her car into a tree.

Eventually, the concerned coworker tried to call Sue back to see whether she had calmed down. But Sue, driving home, had entered a black hole as far as her Verizon phone coverage was concerned and could not be reached. So the coworker called me at home, letting me know that Sue sounded very depressed and that she had also called the state police to search for her on the highway, which they did. It did not take very long before everyone appeared at our house. First Sue, who tried to tell me about her bad day at work. But before she could finish, her coworker showed up. A few minutes later, a police officer followed.

We all sat down and focused on the reason we were there. Sue seemed close to a nervous breakdown. The stress at work had finally gotten to her. The confrontation with the head of the human resources office had been the last straw. She had tried to hold herself together the best she could, and she had given me the impression she had things under control. But it became obvious that she had reached the end of her rope. She needed immediate rest and treatment to help unravel her psychic tensions.

We suggested an immediate and thorough evaluation of her physical and mental health and admitted her to the Vermont Medical Center in Burlington. There Sue was told she had suffered a mental breakdown and that she should stay in the hospital until her condition stabilized. She underwent a number of tests, all verifying that years of work-related stress, coupled with an effort to control the stress with painkillers, had finally led to the breakdown. Her physicians told her to look for less stressful working conditions and possibly reduce her working hours or retire.

Sue was discharged after a week and brought her concerns to the CEO of Moses Ludington. She requested more agreeable working conditions for herself and the entire medical staff. When he would not commit, she gave him three months' notice and terminated her contract. That was in the middle of 2014. From then on, she worked ER shifts at Lake Placid Health Center and the nearby Adirondack Medical Center at Saranac Lake. She gave up all supervisory functions and reduced her working hours considerably. She liked working at Lake Placid a lot because it was a large training center for the US Winter Olympics teams, some of whose athletes she came to treat herself.

In 1980, Lake Placid became famous when the Winter Olympics were held there. No American who was alive at the time will ever forget the excitement when a bunch of mostly college kids beat the seasoned, number-one-ranked professional ice-hockey players from the Soviet Union in a come-from-behind heart pounder. Everyone watching screamed their lungs out when the team captain, Mike Eruzione, scored the winning goal. A year later, Hollywood made a blockbuster movie recapturing the excitement of that game, titled *Miracle on Ice*. As much as sports movies can move people emotionally, it ranks right up there with the classic of all time, *Das Wunder von Bern*, the story of Germany's unexpected come-from-behind 3–2 triumph over the then-world superpower in soccer, Hungary, in the 1954 World Cup final. It also led to a blockbuster movie in 2014 with the same title.

After the 1980 Winter Olympics, Lake Placid became a tourist attraction, still displaying the original flags of the participating nations, including the old flag of East Germany, which earned more medals than any other nation, including the Soviet Union. Today, tourists can shoot down the bobsled course and live to tell about it. Sports still dominate this small town of fewer than 2,000 residents, and its sports clinic features some of the best doctors in the US, especially orthopedic surgeons. Sue worked with some of them, which turned out to be lucky for Curt.

In Werder, Curt had played soccer for the club Viktoria and later Eintracht. During one game, he seriously hurt his right ankle and was taken by car to St. Josefs Krankenhaus in Potsdam. Curt had no insurance, and he didn't receive much attention. No X-rays were taken. He was told to take some pain pills and tough it out, which is what he did, even though he developed excruciating pain over the following months. Stepping on his heel caused sharp pain, so he had to stop moving and rest his foot. He could not see a doctor because he had no insurance.

As a German citizen, he should automatically have been registered in the public health care system (gesetzliche Krankenversicherung) cost-free. But he always got the same answer no matter what governmental office he approached with his request. It wasn't their job to do that, and they were not sure whose job it was. He was supposed to find out on his own. With his limited command of German, every government official could see he needed help to solve this puzzle. But no one offered any.

Eventually, he gave up, but he continued to play high-level sports and bit the bullet when his ankle developed severe pain. Curt has never been a complainer, and he didn't tell us about his problems.

But in 2013, when he enrolled at Plymouth State University to get a teacher's license and we saw him again, Sue noticed his cautious gait, and Curt finally told the story. Sue immediately had his foot x-rayed and detected a broken piece of ankle bone that was sitting unattached in surrounding tissue. It called for immediate surgical correction, and she called the orthopedic surgeon from the Olympic bobsled team. The surgeon explained that the neglect by German doctors had decreased Curt's chances of a successful recovery but that he was going to try anyway, mainly because Sue pleaded with him. He succeeded in reattaching the bone splinter without major complications.

Curt recovered fully and was overwhelmed when he explained to the surgeon how much it meant to him. Sports were central to Curt's life. He was once again able to use both of his feet. The very hefty medical bills were paid by Curt's student health insurance.

Sue continued working at Lake Placid and Saranac Lake for a few more years, and I often drove up to the clinics with her, exploring the region during the day and sleeping in the on-call rooms at night. When her twenty-four-hour shifts had not been too gruesome, we would visit one of our favorite restaurants, preferably one with a terrace, and overlook the beautiful Adirondack landscape. The Indian summers there will always have a special place in our memories.

While mentally preparing for "the golden years," perhaps in the sunsets of Florida, we received the exciting news that we would witness a sunrise in the family. Curt called us up early in 2013 to inform us that Ulrike was expecting. What a joy, though the news wasn't entirely unexpected. The due date was in early fall, and it was going to be a boy.

We got out our champagne bottles, invited our friends, and had an impromptu beach party by the lake in front of our house. In the days that followed, we tried to figure out everyone's schedule for the rest of the year. In the fall, Curt was supposed to start his two-year program at Plymouth State University to obtain his high school teacher certification in biology. He was trying to rearrange his schedule so he could delay his enrollment for a semester and stay in Germany for the baby's birth and Christmas before heading to Plymouth State University and starting the spring semester. Ulrike would go on maternity leave and keep the home fires burning. Curt would stay for part of the following summer and make up the courses he missed.

During the spring of 2015, he would be back in Germany permanently because JFK High School in Berlin was going to give him the opportunity to do his required student teaching there. And because the biology position would become vacant at that time, there was even the possibility of JFK hiring him on as a regular teacher. At first, everything worked according to the plan. But when Curt returned to Germany, the biology position had already been filled in the fall of 2014 by a teacher from the States. She only had a one-year contract, however, and Curt had gotten the nod from the head of the science department that the position was his when her year was up. But Curt's advisor, a chemistry teacher and good friend of the newly hired biology teacher, boycotted that plan.

In addition, after Curt completed his student teaching, his advisor would not give him the lowest required grade, a B, needed to obtain a teaching license. Instead, she gave him a C. His official evaluation given during the course had been a B+. His academic advisor at Plymouth State University went along with the C suggestion, meaning Curt got neither a teaching license nor the biology position. Curt, of course, filed a protest with the dean of the university and demanded to be given a fair grade. The dean overrode the unfair grade and gave Curt a B. However, the New Hampshire Department of Education, responsible for verifying that Curt completed his program and the awarding of the MEd, requested that he repeat student teaching again at Plymouth State University. He had little choice and did so during the fall of 2015 at Concord High School. This time the grading was fair, and he received an A for the course, was awarded the MEd, and received the New Hampshire license for teaching biology at the high school level.

There were several negative results from this. Curt graduated half a year later than planned, had to pay extra tuition, and was separated from Ulrike and their baby boy, Carl, for longer than was reasonable. JFK did not hire him, but Curt, Ulrike, and Carl wanted to stay in Germany, perhaps with Curt teaching in the German high school system. Curt, and Ulrike for that matter, had no idea how hard the Land Brandenburg bureaucracy would fight to ensure that his New Hampshire teaching license would not be recognized in its Land, at least not fully. He was allowed to teach as a Quereinsteiger (someone not fully qualified) without much security, first in Werder and later in Beelitz. He eventually found that the City of Berlin was less restrictive in keeping foreign-trained teachers out. In 2017, the Peter-Ustinov-Schule hired him as a regular full-time teacher of biology and sports with an open-ended contract. Curt's advantage was that the high school offered courses in both German and English, both of which he by now spoke fluently. Curt subsequently received excellent evaluations at all levels, and the school expressed hope that he might stay permanently.

FORTY

Jason and Tori Get Married

Another exciting event for the family was the announcement that Jason and Tori had decided to get married. Tori's mother had recently died. She had managed Tori's life in many areas where Tori needed help. Her aging father could not, being confined to a caregiving facility. The loss of her mother hit Tori hard. Tori had held small jobs in the Middlebury community, most recently as a bagger in the nearby Shaw's grocery store. During her mother's long illness, Tori had struggled to keep herself going.

Eventually, her doctor told her to stay home for a while. Tori could be quite erratic in her behavior, and at times, she could physically interfere in other people's affairs. She was also hard of hearing and spoke extremely loudly, which could be annoying. I had problems with her when she would not follow instructions on the Special Olympics soccer team I was coaching. But she always had a soft spot for Jason, probably because he would listen to her frequent harangues without any sign of irritation. I would take them out to fast-food places and other restaurants in the area and noticed that he would serve as an emotional anchor for her. She was higher functioning, semiliterate, and could drive a car. Soon they went out together on their own.

When Tori's mother died, Jason became her major source of emotional support. Tori had an aunt, Mary Jensen, living in Brandon, about twenty miles south of Middlebury. They saw each other infrequently, but she acted very much like Tori's guardian. Tori had some friends, mainly from the Special Olympics crowd. But she seemed to be drawn most closely to Jason. And then one day, when we were visiting both at the Middlebury Commons, they told us about their plans to get married. They explained that Mary Jensen would help with the arrangements. The wedding was set for August 1, 2015, almost a full year in the future. This was a big surprise to us, but we congratulated them.

On the way home, we discussed the pros and cons of the marriage. On the con side, we pointed to the financial disadvantage. Once married, Jason and Tori's combined governmental support would be reduced. They would have to give up one of their apartments and move in together without any compensation. Dealing with their special disabilities and withdrawing into their own spaces could be very therapeutic, and they would no longer be able to do that. On the pro side, they would be able to appear before others as a legally married couple, which would increase their self-worth. But on balance, we figured it wasn't worth it.

We thought they could live together as they were doing already and consider themselves a happy couple like many others. So the next time we saw them, we brought up these points. But Tori wanted to have a big wedding. We called up Mary, who convinced us that this was in the best interest of both of them. Eventually we agreed. To make sure they would handle their money wisely together, we offered our help by becoming Jason's guardian. They thought that was a very wise move too, and Sue and I together applied for guardianship, which the State of New Hampshire granted us promptly without problems. And Tori and Jason very excitedly started their wedding plans.

They would be busy with those plans for almost a year until the day they would get "promised," meaning they would have a wedding ceremony without getting legally married. Some would call it a "promise ceremony." The real engine in turning this into a true success story was Tori. She reserved the big social hall of the Middlebury American Legion, got a top DJ from Burlington, wrote dozens of invitations, and,

Jason and Tori in their favorite Middlebury restaurant: Rosie's.

most importantly, made sure she had the right wedding dress. When she was unsure about something, she would call her Aunt Mary.

Mary was especially helpful with planning the meals. Jason was excited because his two brothers would attend with their families, traveling long distances to share in this happy day. John would come from Kansas with Stephanie, Mason, Grace, and Justin, while Curt, Ulrike, and Carl would travel from Germany. It would be a rare occasion that all three brothers would be together.

The wedding turned out to be the colorful occasion Tori and Jason hoped it would be. The hall was packed with nearly fifty guests. The carefully choreographed sequence of events ran like clockwork, from the "I do" to the cake bash to the first dance to the bridal bouquet throw.

Everything worked so well in part because of the DJ's talent for playing the right music at the right time. In the end, he had everyone dancing to exhaustion on the dance floor. The only bittersweet note I remember was the ill health of Tori's father. He had been in an old folks' home for some years and could only move with difficulty and by using a walker. He insisted on dancing with Tori by spinning the walker around a couple of times. I talked to him and noticed that he was on his last legs. A couple of weeks later, he gave up the ghost. But he had seen his daughter getting "unter die Haube."

Tori and Jason looked like they had the time of their life. Sue and I were glad to sit down with everybody again, even for just a few days. We promised we would try to do this more often, even if it was mere wishful thinking. In the end, Tori and Jason took off as the couple they wanted to be, holding hands and beaming like newlyweds.

Being "promised" also meant that Jason and Tori together would be able to take care of more of their own affairs. That was particularly true for Jason, who could rely on Tori's constant support in daily activities. She had provided some support, but with the wedding ceremony, it had become a structured part of their daily routine. Tori had a car and could drive. She possessed rudimentary literacy skills. Sue and I would continue to closely manage many of Jason's other affairs from a distance, particularly his financial and medical matters and the often-aggravating struggles with government agencies about his benefits.

Our wedding gift for the new couple was a Caribbean cruise we took with them. Mary helped make sure they got on the plane to Tampa all right. The cruise was a highlight for the couple, and we saw them sitting together at musical performances, holding hands and drinking Coke in bliss. That week on the ship cruising through the Caribbean may have been the happiest week of their lives.

FORTY-ONE

Moving to Florida and Kansas City

After the trip to the Caribbean, Sue and I reflected on the times to come. Our original plans to move to Florida for the winters and stay in Crown Point for the summers took on a new life. The only reason we would stay in Crown Point during summer was to be close to Jason and Tori. During winter we could count on Susie Pigeon to help the two when need arose. Susie Pigeon was a social worker of the Vermont Agency of Human Services who had dedicated her life to looking after the less fortunate. She always kept tabs on Jason, and we were in constant contact with her. During the winter of 2014–15 we rented a home at a trailer park in Bradenton, where our friends the Caswells from Crown Point already spent their winters. But we learned quickly that unattended houses up north do not always survive the harsh winter days undamaged. Upon return in the spring, we had to deal with blown-off shingles, broken pipes, wall cracks, and other problems. In the winter of 2015–16, our garage burned down completely in our absence.

Sue had equipped the garage with a hothouse where she kept her hanging geraniums during the winter months. We paid someone to water them and keep the temperature steady with an electric heater. The thermostat must have broken at one point, and the running heater set the garage ablaze. We had stored most of our personal belongings in the storage loft of this large garage, of which little was left. Our skis were gone too.

Also, the upkeep of the place during the summer increasingly took its toll. Sue had an ambitious garden that required extensive care. There was always something to be fixed, cleaned, or painted. Plus, there were chores the association had to take care of. In the beginning, that had worked rather well with members cleaning up beaches, maintaining roads, landscaping, and completing other work. But as time went by, cooperation deteriorated. Some members of the association accused others of rule violations for the pettiest reasons. Two camps emerged; one, under the leadership of the original landowner, Jack Daniels, started to dominate all association activities, favoring their own interests.

Things quickly became personal and vindictive, involving police investigations and court cases. We figured we had to get out. George and Kathy Caswell helped us to find a piece of land in Golf Lakes, a homeowners' association in Bradenton, close to where they had already bought a place a couple of years earlier. Like many places in Florida, Golf Lakes was a retirement community for people fifty-five and over, with a "no kids, no pets" policy. It consisted of manufactured homes and lots of recreational facilities, including, of course, a big swimming pool.

We bought a new manufactured home that we designed ourselves with all possible upgrades and moved into it in early 2016. It was situated right across from a golf course and gave us a grand view. Sue landscaped the place beautifully with palm trees, tropical plants (bougainvillea), and all sorts of flowers. It had a nice porch where I sat daily, smoking a cigar while sipping whiskey and reading *The New York Times*. We were able to sell our house in Crown Point for a decent price and felt quite relieved when we left.

A year later, our immediate neighbors in Crown Point, Glenn Vehr and Rhonda Idleman, got a similar place right next to us. We were now six New York expatriates and did many things together, mainly hanging out in restaurants. Sue and I loved going to the beach and often had dinner in restaurants right by the sand, watching some of the most spectacular sunsets anywhere in the world. These were some of the happier moments we enjoyed together, and we agreed that things could only go downhill from there.

Still, we always looked forward to visits, especially from our family. John, Stephanie, and their kids came every March during school vacation. They spent the whole time at the beach and couldn't get enough sun. We were always sad to see them leave and realized how isolated we were in "the land of the newly wed and nearly dead."

Curt, Ulrike, and their kids were able to visit us once, in the spring of 2019, when their little girl Clara was just one year old. Carl was five. We managed to get Jason and Tori to visit us at the same time so the family could get to know each other a bit better.

We also looked forward to the visits of my best friend Günther and his wife, Joanne. They came from Germany to spend a few months each winter on Anna Maria Island, not far from where we lived. Günther was a retired union representative at the federal level, and we never ran out of topics to discuss. He was also an active chess player and regularly played at tournaments in various countries. When I had a good day, and he had a beer too many, I was able to beat him, but it was rare. I started a chess club at Golf Lakes and won many games there.

Our place at Golf Lakes was used a few times by our grandkids Mason and Justin and their friends when we were gone during the hot summer months or when we were visiting family or friends elsewhere. We would see John and Stephanie, for instance, my brother Udo and his family in Pensacola, my brother Erwin in Düsseldorf, our son Jason in Vermont, Sue's cousin Jim Jones in Washington, DC, or many other members of the family in Kansas, Arkansas, and Germany. We often stayed for days or weeks. But most of our time away we spent with Curt and Ulrike in our house in Werder.

In 2008, the house in Werder was almost done, and Curt and Ulrike moved in. The attic had been turned into a small apartment, and this is where Sue and I stayed. It was small but sufficient. The big plan was to continue renovating the back house, which would be just for the two of us and was where we would stay mainly during the summer months while escaping the excessive Florida heat. For the rest of the time,

Happy family: Curt, Carl, Ulrike. and Clara (in front).

during the rainy fall and cold winter in Germany, we would stay in the Sunshine State. But at one point, as we were sitting on our beautiful Florida porch, we realized we were traveling thousands of miles every year to see friends and family all over the globe. Even when we visited Udo and Diane in our own state of Florida, we had to travel a full day by car. We needed to slow down and decided to give up our place at Golf Lakes and stay half the year with Curt and Ulrike in Werder and the other half with John and Stephanie in Kansas. We would spend several weeks each year with Jason and otherwise let people visit us. We had a place in Germany and so we needed one in Kansas.

In 2020, John and Stephanie told us that after Justin's high school graduation in May 2021, they would be empty nesters and were planning to sell their house in Eudora and get one close to the Plaza Area in Kansas City. The cultural life in that part of town has attracted many well-to-do people over the years and has driven up housing costs. John told us he would help us find a place we could afford, one that he would take care of during our absence, while looking for a similar place for him and Stephanie nearby.

We all started looking at the real estate website Zillow and realized that the housing market was in an unsustainable climb. Most houses were overpriced and moved quickly. John and Stephanie suggested that we would do much better if we bought a larger house for the four of us together. We agreed, and eventually, John spotted a place just south of Loose Park, in the older part of town, filled with large trees, parks, and walkways, yet close to nice (but expensive) shops, cafés, restaurants, and entertainment sites. The city's largest art museum, the Nelson-Atkins Museum of Art, was five minutes away, and so was the campus of the University of Missouri.

We bought the place together in May 2021 and began to split our time between Kansas City and Werder. That has allowed us to see the entire family on both sides of the ocean and work as a kind of emissary between them. Seeing grandkids on both sides brings great joy to our hearts. And so far, as of four years later, this arrangement has worked well for everyone, including Jason and Tori, whom we will continue to visit at least once or twice a year.

Jason and Tori have worked out a program for us that includes visiting such memorable places as Bartlett Falls or Church Street in

Visiting Udo and his family in Florida. From left to right, surrounding Udo are Alena; Irvin; Alex; Udo's wife, Diane; and Callie.

Burlington and ends in one of their favorite restaurants like Rosie's or Mister Up's in Middlebury. We always look forward to our time together and feel a bit sad when we leave. Jason and Tori are well taken care of materially. They have two nice one-bedroom apartments on the same floor in a federally subsidized housing project, the Commons, with about fifty residents in a tree-lined area near the green center of Middlebury. The Commons is full of people like Jason and Tori, and there always seems to be something interesting to do. Yet they, too, miss the family. Every time we see them, they want to know what everybody is up to. We assure them that everyone is fine and that they are all thinking of them and that they will visit them someday when they are not so busy.

We do not feel too good when we leave again, but we call or text them almost every day, listen to their stories, and plan things to do together on our next visit. We will continue to manage Jason's affairs, and to some degree Tori's, from a distance. We will remain Jason's legal guardians for as long as we can and are confident that longer-term arrangements for his and Tori's welfare will be worked out by the family as a whole.

FORTY-TWO

Some Final Reflections: Jason and the Struggle of Life

As much as our moving lives and advancing ages have allowed us to do, we have always found ways to find maximum fulfillment in whatever we are doing. And for as long as we can, we will travel. But we no longer have an ambitious bucket list. Machu Picchu, the Galápagos Islands, a trans-Siberian rail trip, and other places and projects that have graced the top of the list for the longest time have been scratched. Comfortable cruises to warm places have taken their place. Our latest cruise on a Hurtigruten ship up the Norwegian coast to the Arctic Circle in January 2023 to see the northern lights already was a bit of a stretch, mainly because Sue's recent hip replacement left her with an unsteady gait. Our great dream of spending an entire week at the Hermitage in Saint Petersburg, Russia, had to be buried, mainly for political reasons.

Many years ago, we spent an entire week at the Prado in Madrid, admiring hundreds of the greatest paintings of early modern Europe, focusing on the works of Goya, Velázquez, Titian, Rubens, El Greco, and others. We also have seen other great paintings over the years in the eminent galleries of Europe (including the Louvre in Paris, Rijksmuseum in Amsterdam, and Leopold Museum in Vienna). But we had never made it to Saint Petersburg, except once on a cruise ship a few years ago, which included a two-hour group tour of the Hermitage, one of the largest art museums in the world. The impressive collection of artworks includes a great deal of loot from World War II. It houses the greatest collection of German Renaissance paintings outside Germany, and I hoped to get a glimpse of it. But our tour guide rushed us by scores of masterpieces and made sure we didn't linger in front of any because the tight schedule was designed to funnel as many visitors as possible through the museum in the shortest possible time. And no one was allowed to separate from the large group.

When I remained in front of one of my favorite paintings by Rembrandt, *The Return of the Prodigal Son*, for no longer than two minutes, I got a real dressing down by a uniformed official in Russian. Sue and I later decided to come back on our own and do what we had done in Madrid: stay in a hotel across from the museum and go there every day until we had seen everything. But since Putin attacked Ukraine and bombed and froze the people there to death, Russia is off our bucket list. We may go back to Venice instead, another one of our favorite cities, where we have spent much time over the years, or Rome or Vienna if the current inflation does not eat up our little nest egg too soon.

Coming to the end of our life's journey, I have tried to put the many individual events Sue and I experienced into a larger context. At first, the journey looks chaotic. But a closer look should reveal some coherent strands of development. For instance, you may have gathered that our story is one of trying to beat life's odds, especially when they were most heavily stacked against us. Another strand should show that love conquers all. Another is that it pays to "keep your eyes on the prize." You, the reader, may find many more such strands on your own. And while our story goes on, I feel I have to draw a concluding line here and finish by pointing to some open questions that this biography could not adequately address but should not ignore either.

They could perhaps be ignored if Jason would not be part of our story. But he is. His presence has reminded us again and again how limited our mental tools are when trying to understand the mystery and purpose of human existence. For instance, the struggles we have described here—what are they for, beyond mere survival? Why do some people have to struggle more than others? Why do bad things happen to good people and good things to bad people? More to the point, why do innocent children have to suffer the way they do? Particularly, why did Jason have to meet the fate he did?

In my studies I found that Western tradition, the tradition Sue and I grew up in, has produced two general answers, one based on reason and one based on faith. The first goes back to early Greek philosophers, notably Socrates. He argued that a realm of perfection exists that, if understood and emulated correctly, leads to a fulfilled life free of pain. Pain is a result of ignorance, of not knowing perfection and therefore committing errors in judgment. The key to overcoming ignorance lies in education, in a lifelong search for truth, beauty, and goodness. That requires intelligence, an innate ability to reason correctly. People possess intelligence to different degrees. Therefore, people with little intelligence will make more incorrect judgments than people with greater intelligence and consequently will suffer more. But how about people with so little intelligence that they cannot function, the mentally ill and physically afflicted? People like Jason? People who live in perpetual pain, mental fogginess, or sheer agony from having missed the right path in life as a result of forces beyond their control? Here Socrates offered euthanasia as a solution. He took the hemlock himself when he thought his work in educating the youth of Athens had run afoul of Athenian laws.

Yet despite such inescapable dilemmas, the Socratic tradition of searching for perfection, for creating the best possible society human reason is capable of, has dominated much of Western thought ever since. It has been associated with such thinkers as Aristotle and Plato and later Hume, Locke, Kant, and Hegel, among others.

The Founding Fathers of the American republic certainly saw themselves in this tradition. Accordingly, evil is not so much a force existing on its own but an absence of goodness, that is, an inability to make right decisions. Eastern philosophies share some of those thoughts, in that suffering, according to Taoism, can be removed through an array of exercises designed to gain wisdom. Similarly, in Buddhism, suffering is overcome by enlightenment gained through a set of rigorous physical and mental exercises. But the people who desire an end to suffering the most are often the least capable of performing these exercises.

Jason and millions like him have no real place of value in a society based solely on classic ideas of reason; in it he serves only as an object of pity and a target for welfare. But Western society is also based on faith. It is, in fact, rooted as much in faith as in reason. With this faith, people have the ability to intuit forms of existence beyond those provided by reason and material senses, forms that, in fact, are more basic than those given by reason and senses because faith underlies and sustains all of them. For instance, the existence of love in the Greco-Roman tradition is demonstrated in the union of Venus and Mars, where the generally understood concepts of beauty and strength merge to become one in the perfect union of harmony.

In the Judeo-Christian tradition, by contrast, the love that binds Adam and Eve is a mystery, something fully understood only by its creator. Any attempt to try to understand it will be punished, as Adam and Eve experienced when they ate from "the tree of knowledge," committing the "original sin." Knowledge acquired through reason diminishes mystery. In fact, it denies the power of the miracle, including the miracle of life, the greatest of them all. And, per the stories of the New Testament (for example, the Sermon on the Mount), the value of life is unfathomable and is shared by all human beings alike, no matter their condition or behavior. Hence, for Christians, Jason's value is the same as that of any other human being. There still is the question as to why he has to suffer and why he had to endure torturous misery as a helpless child. Why, in fact, should anyone suffer such a fate?

The answer suggested by reason points to little more than the accidental luck of the draw. Some people get lucky, and some don't. The answer suggested by faith, on the other hand, points to the purposeful will of a creator, who, according to the Judeo-Christian tradition, is an all-powerful and benign God. Suffering is not accidental but designed. But why would an all-powerful and benign God inflict pain and suffering on his own creation? Throughout the ages, the greatest minds have tried their best to explain this riddle. The Old Testament offers the story of Job, on whom God inflicted great pain to test his faith and then rewarded him manifold for not having denounced him. The message is clear: Obey God, no matter what, and don't ask questions.

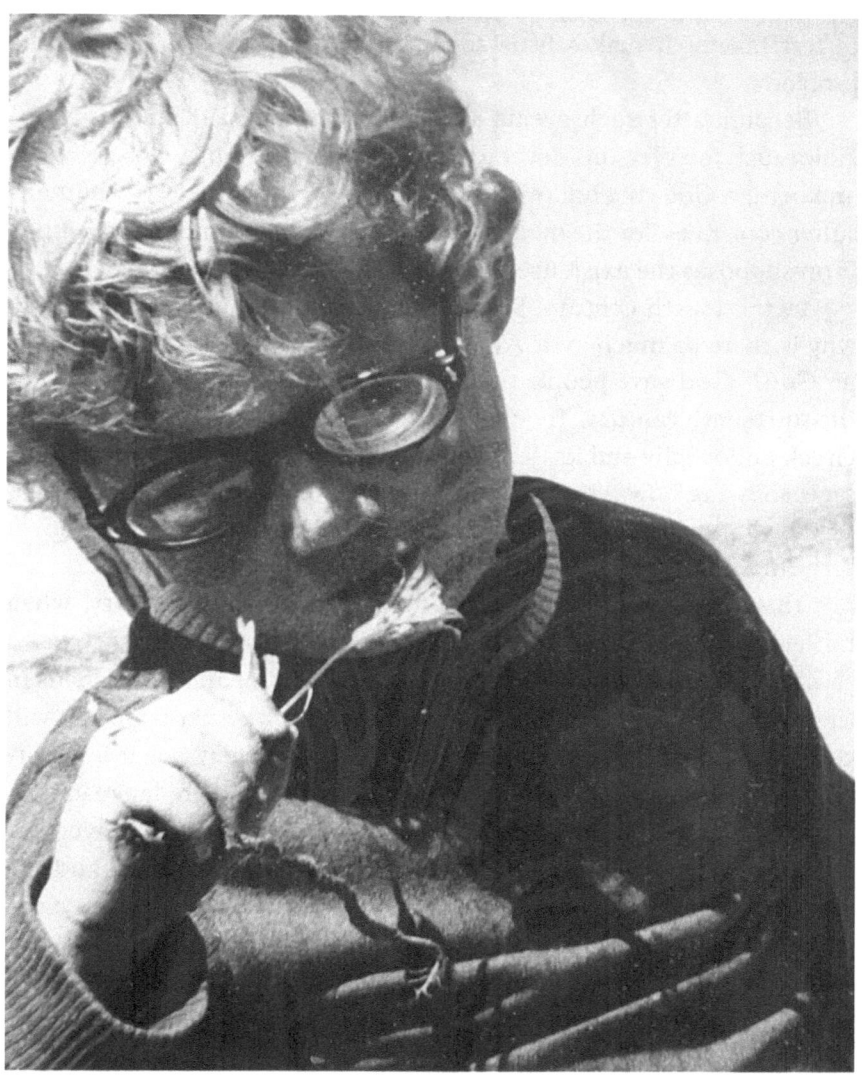

*And Jesus called a little child unto him, and set him in the midst of them,
and said, "Verily I say unto you, except ye be converted, and become
as little children, ye shall not enter into the kingdom of heaven."*

Two arguments can be made against this, both equally valid. First, someone like Jason is incapable of taking the test and, therefore, cannot pass or fail it. So why include him, or others like him, in the group of test takers? It makes little sense no matter how one looks at the problem.

Second, after such events as World Wars I and II, including the Holocaust, Job's lessons never to doubt the greatness of an all-powerful and benign God ring hollow. Still, while the debate about why humans suffer continues, for the most part, this debate has remained academic. It presupposes the existence of a dualistic world of good and evil.

In the fourth century, Saint Augustine asked, "If there is a God, why is there so much evil? And why is there so much good if there is no God?" God gave people the ability to choose between the two. In the thirteenth century, Thomas Aquinas even tried to integrate classic Greek philosophy and its denial of absolute evil with this biblical message, showing how Aristotle, too, would have chosen God's goodness by denying evil rather than trying to find it by reason had he known scripture.

That view remained doctrine until the sixteenth century, when Luther and Calvin started the debate all over again. Calvin stressed that God's infinite power includes the knowledge of all that happens in the world, past, present, and future. He knows whether someone will go to heaven or hell, no matter what the person may do. It is preordained by God. The consequences of this argument were far-reaching.

In short, God has already selected the people to go to heaven beforehand. Acting well to avoid hell will make no difference, and the same with suffering. No attempt to escape it will make any difference. Many Christians who adopted this view in Europe came to be disliked and looked for safety in the New World, like the Puritans in New England. Americans generally know this beacon-on-the-hill story, the place where God gathered all those he had selected to join him for all eternity. But eventually, Puritanism lost its spell over America as other Protestant factions, including the Lutherans, showed God as a benign being that affirmed individual free will. But the old question of why God would tolerate the suffering of children remained a mystery.

There were some philosophers, especially in England, who argued against the divine arbitrariness of predestination and proposed that

God had created a universe with laws that would allow it to run on its own without divine interference. This view, known as "deism," was associated with the ideas of Isaac Newton and later absorbed by such Enlightenment philosophers as Hobbes, Hume, and Kant. But it, too, was unable to explain the nature of human will sufficiently or provide acceptable explanations for why children have to suffer. But it did eventually give rise, with much prodding from Locke, to the idea that humans can indeed run their own affairs on the basis of laws enshrined in nature, laws that also confer inalienable rights to life and liberty. Jefferson and others turned these ideas into a legal framework for the newly constituted United States, which had much success. However, Jefferson was less successful in trying to wed these ideas of the Enlightenment period with the principal ideas of the Bible, particularly those of the New Testament. His *Jefferson Bible* is an attempt to combine reason with faith, using the words of Christ in an attempt to overcome the more mindless doctrines of America's Calvinist tradition. He had a vision of a future that is still under attack. Today few people have even heard of the *Jefferson Bible*.

Against the backdrop of centuries of debate about how to find certainty about anything given the conflict of reason and faith, Immanuel Kant came along and offered answers that changed the entire nature of the debate. He proposed that humans possess at birth (a priori) a finite set of "categories" of thought that allow them to make true statements about things they experience after birth (a posteriori). Kant argued against Hume's idea that humans are born with a "clean slate" (tabula rasa) and that everything they know, they have to learn through experience. Quite the contrary. For Kant, the categories (for example, substance, modality, and quantity) shape experience. Experience does not shape the categories. First, Kant introduced categories for making true statements and later for making right judgments. He spent his entire life refining his philosophy, and many subsequent thinkers spent their entire lives demonstrating its benefits and shortcomings. What almost everyone agrees with is that with Kant's categories, it is possible to make statements about certain areas of the world that are absolutely true. The rest of the world remains unknown but can be envisioned through understanding and faith, including the existence of God.

What makes Kant's philosophy so revolutionary is the fact that the key to making true statements (what is) and right statements (what should be) rests in knowing and using the a priori categories of the mind. Without them, statements tend to be false and wrong. As a result, the focus on making sense of the world shifts to the inside of the mind and away from the world outside it. Only knowing the inner world first opens the doors to understanding the outer world. So far, according to such thinkers as Locke and Hume, the world was all around and merely had to be explored by an open, albeit empty, mind. Now the world within had to be explored first, before the world around would make any sense at all. And the world within was one of pure reason, not faith. Faith still has its place in the human world but is beyond, and not the basis of, reason. Later philosophers, notably Hegel and Marx, wanted to expand Kant's inner world of reason to encompass more of the outer world, ultimately of everything (being) as well.

I mention all of this to give you a quick view into my own mind and its development over the years. Earlier, I mentioned that I had adopted Marxist ideas as a student at UCLA. As a student of Hayden White, and with his guidance, I traced Marx's ideas back to Hegel and many of Hegel's ideas back to Kant. Today I see myself following the post-Kantian tradition of trying to get a better grip on categories of mind humans use in coming to terms with the world they experience. Much of this kind of search of late has moved into linguistics and rhetoric, manifesting in such theories as those of Heidegger, Foucault, Derrida, and others. My dissertation dealt with Hans Driesch, a philosopher of vitalism who tried to complete Kant's fixed table of twelve categories with one more, namely uniqueness. It did not catch on. And while I have followed many of the ancient and modern philosophic debates about the best way to find truth and goodness, the question of why people, especially small children, have to suffer needlessly remains unanswered to me; it may well be unanswerable.

Biological evolutionists, like Darwin and Haeckel, can somewhat explain it. But their theory, in which only survival counts, is mindless. To many people, understanding their own physical survival and little beyond may be enough. But they cannot explain Beethoven's Fifth. So what's the use? Jason's daily struggle dealing with his debilitating conditions requires the existence and understanding of a higher order.

My two brothers, visiting me for my eighty-fifth birthday.
(Erwin in the middle, Udo on the right.)

He will remain at the center of our concern for his well-being. And indeed, his struggle to prevail in life has been an inspiration for everyone who has been in touch with him. For someone who was not expected to live for more than a few months after birth, he has done remarkably well and defied every doomsday diagnosis along the way. He is, in fact, a much more content and happier person than most people nowadays, thanks also to his partner, Tori. They share a story of personal despair and eventual triumph. And they have come out stronger because of it.

Humans may well be destined to pursue a life of searching for finite answers to salient questions without ever finding them. Rilke's conclusion, therefore, was to learn to love the question rather than the answer. Kant's three questions are these: What can we know? What shall we do? What may we hope for? In my case, I have tried to find my own answers to these questions the best I could over the years. I feel blessed to have had the opportunity to do so, to dedicate much of my life to this endeavor. The opportunities were given to me by the country I have adopted as my second home, the United States of America, not by the country of my birth, Germany. For this, I am grateful beyond words. But the country I have thus embraced—its people, culture, and democratic institutions—is also a country I have vehemently criticized at times when I felt I needed to, from the days of the Vietnam War to the Age of Trump.

Now, at age eighty-seven, I see myself more and more sitting in comfortable chairs on the terraces at our homes in Kansas City and Werder and drinking Scotch, smoking Cuban cigars, and reading *Der Spiegel* or *The New York Times*. Sue, now eighty-one, will join me with her old-fashioned and *The Washington Post*.

For as long as possible, we hope to remain witnesses to the stories of all the people we know who have been mentioned in this book. They are part of our personal memory, and they are the dearest to us: our sons John, Jason, and Curt and daughters-in-law Stephanie, Tori, and Ulrike. A special place in our hearts is reserved for our grandchildren: Mason, Grace, Justin, Carl, and Clara. We certainly hope their lives will be spared the tragedies we had to face. But those tragedies faded as Sue and I found joy and fulfillment later in life. Aside from our love for each other, the key to our happiness was mainly education and the ability to use it to our advantage and help people around us. Knowing and understanding the world and being of help to others is the greatest reward life can offer. Given the dismally ignorant environments Sue and I both came from, we sensed it all along and, as a result, did not always decide to go for the more lucrative options in life, even when we had the chance to do so. A mentally and materially healthy life has remained our goal. And we wish the same to all of you sharing our life journey through this book!

Auf Wiedersehen

About the Authors

HORST FREYHOFER was born in Düsseldorf, Germany. Eventually Horst immigrated to the US, where he received a PhD in intellectual history from UCLA under the tutelage of one of America's leading thinkers, Hayden White. Horst held various professorships in the US, including visiting professor at Middlebury College in Vermont. Before his retirement in 2006, he was a full professor at Plymouth State University in New Hampshire.

SUE FREYHOFER was born in Bauxite, Arkansas, and holds an MD from the University of Arkansas. Before retiring in 2013, she held the position of medical director at the Moses Ludington Hospital in Ticonderoga, New York.

Horst and Sue split their time between Kansas City and Berlin and are the proud parents of three sons.

www.ingramcontent.com/pod-product-compliance
Lightning Source LLC
Chambersburg PA
CBHW021700120626
46545CB00004B/1336

9 7 9 8 2 1 8 7 1 1 9 7 9